The River Cottage Fish Book

Hugh Fearnley-Whittingstall and Nick Fisher

Photography by Simon Wheeler

Additional photography
by Paul Quagliana and Marie Derôme

BLOOMSBURY
LONDON · BERLIN · NEW YORK

Hugh is a writer, broadcaster and food campaigner. He has been presenting the River Cottage programmes for Channel Four for almost a decade now, and this is the fifth River Cottage book he has written. Amazingly, there may be more of both. Hugh lives in Dorset with his wife Marie, three children and many animals, which they eat when they can't get fish. He shares a boat with his friend Nick.

Nick is a journalist, screenwriter and broadcaster. He presented two angling shows, *Screaming Reels* for Channel Four and *Dirty Tackle* for Radio Five Live; and he received a BAFTA award for *The Giblet Boys*, a series he created for ITV. In a wide-ranging career as a columnist he has been film critic for the *Sun* and agony uncle for *Just Seventeen*; nowadays he writes about fishing for the *Shooting Times*. Nick lives in Dorset with his wife Helen, four children, various livestock, a lake full of trout and several boats.

First published in Great Britain 2007

Text © 2007 by Hugh Fearnley-Whittingstall and Nick Fisher
Photography © 2007 by Simon Wheeler
Additional photography © 2007 by Paul Quagliana, Marie Derôme and other contributors (see page 605)

The moral right of the authors has been asserted

Bloomsbury Publishing Plc, 36 Soho Square, London W1D 3QY

A CIP catalogue record for this book is available from the British Library

ISBN 978 0 7475 8869 6

10 9 8 7 6 5 4 3

Project editor: Janet Illsley
Design: Lawrence Morton (www.lawrencemorton.com)
Photography: Simon Wheeler (decourcywheeler@gmail.com)

The text of this book is set in Century Schoolbook and Trade Gothic
Printed in Italy by Arti Grafiche Amilcare Pizzi f.p.a.

www.bloomsbury.com/rivercottage
www.rivercottage.net

For Oscar and his
godfather Charlie,
my two other favourite
fishing companions.
HF-W

For my favourite
fish eaters, Helen,
Rory, Rex, Patrick,
Kitty and Spike.
NF

Introduction

We both love fish. And that is the overriding reason we have written this book. As anglers, cooks and (very amateur) naturalists, we've got fish under our skin. It's very hard – and rather stressful – to imagine life without them.

Over the years we've found all kinds of ways to scratch our fish itch: goldfish in a bowl, visits to aquariums, goggling at Jacques Cousteau on the telly, learning first to snorkel and then to scuba dive. Such enthusiasms have come and gone, but two have always been a constant: catching fish and eating them.

Between us, we have caught and cooked many fish. We have, of course, also caught a fair few that we haven't cooked, and cooked countless others that we haven't caught. But we are happiest when these two pursuits collide and we get to consume a fish that we have personally pulled from the deep. For both of us, our passion for fish as quarry and food began at an early age.

Hugh's first fishing expedition occurred at the age of six, when his dad took him to a stream in Richmond Park, armed with a bamboo cane, a length of string, a bent pin and a slice of bread. They actually caught a fish! Back home with his *Observer's Book of Fishes*, Hugh identified the catch as a mackerel, noting that this was a fish that was meant to live in the sea.

Being omniscient, his dad naturally had a convincing explanation: 'Er, it must have decided to swim up from the sea – like a salmon…' That was more than good enough for the young Hugh. There was no reason to be suspicious. After all, he had lifted the fish from the stream with his own hands, and watched his father knock it several times on the head with his own eyes.

Hugh's mum fried the mackerel in butter and served it with a slice of lemon. It was the first fish Hugh had ever eaten that wasn't finger-shaped, coated in breadcrumbs and doused in ketchup – and he enjoyed it very much indeed.

It was ten years before the sorry truth came out. Seeing his teenage son swearing blind to some disbelieving friends that he had once caught a mackerel in a London park with a lump of Mother's Pride on a bent pin, Hugh's dad was moved to a guilty confession. He came clean about the trip to the fishmonger's; the sleight of hand that slipped the fish on to the hook as Hugh was sent behind a bush for a much-needed pee; the ritual despatch of a fish that had, in fact, already been dead for two days…

Hugh was a little disillusioned to discover the deceit but, being sixteen, soon found other things to strop about. In the end he is, of course, eternally grateful to his dad. Grateful to be hooked on fishing, and hooked on fish.

Nick grew up in inner-city Glasgow. Other than breaking his foot with a paving slab and being made to eat mud pies by his two bossy big sisters, he doesn't remember much about being five. But what he can remember in uncanny detail is sitting on the end of a rock pier in Millport one sunny summer afternoon, holding a Winfield toy rod and catching his first totally unaided fish.

It was a wrasse. A purply-blue, mottled, spiny-finned ballan wrasse, with buck teeth and huge, rubbery lips. The fight between big fish and tiny rod had been a long one; many dads crowded round, eager to 'help' Nick land the fish. But he never did let go of that rod. Instead he dragged the wrasse up the wall on to the pier and whacked it on the head with a gaff handle.

Sadly, Nick never got to eat his first fish. In the 1960s, any fish that had the temerity not to be born a cod or a haddock was deemed 'inedible'. On the way back to their caravan, Nick's dad told him to throw the fish on the beach 'for the seagulls'. As they walked away, the beautiful creature that had lived underwater with such style and exuberance lay dead, dull and greying, speckled with grit, waiting to be pulled apart by herring gulls.

Much as he loved fishing from the start, loved eating fish, and loved the tackle, the boats, the danger and the sheer manliness of it all, what Nick realised at that moment was that there are right ways to treat fish, and there are wrong ways.

For many years, both of us carried around a kind of fat store of joy, based on happy fishy memories. Anything to do with fish was always good. Any opportunity to go fishing was always gratefully taken. And just about any piece of fish offered on a plate was gratefully devoured.

Most of the time, fish still work that simple magic for us. But they have also muscled in on our work lives – meaning that, now and again, we find ourselves taking fish and fishing quite seriously. We've both written and broadcast about them – Nick extensively, Hugh more incidentally – and it was this shared professional interest that first brought us together. Hugh was an avid fan of Nick's Channel Four series, *Screaming Reels*, and decided to stalk Nick with a view to collaborating on some fishy telly. We met, we talked, we went fishing (Hugh caught nothing, Nick a small roach) and, as we became friends, we let the telly idea drop. We enjoyed being fishing buddies too much to let work get in the way.

We've known each other for well over a decade now, and are not remotely embarrassed to admit that we have spent most of our time together if not actually fishing, then cooking, eating or talking about fish. Many of our conversations have been simply the recollection of past fish and the anticipation of future ones – you can never take the boy out of the fisherman.

One long, fishy chat ended with a joint resolution: let's do a book together. A big one. One where we celebrate the nation's fish and trumpet those species that have been 'forgotten' and ignored; where we do our best to take the fear and mystery out of handling and preparing fish, and try to communicate the tremendous pleasure and satisfaction that a few fish skills can bring; one where we don't shirk the ecological and moral issues of fishing. And, of course, one where we share all our favourite ways of cooking all our favourite fish.

Roughly three years later, here is that book. We're proud to say that, though it's taken us more time and more words than we had perhaps originally imagined, we feel we haven't flinched from our self-imposed brief. Now that we've finished the writing, we can't wait to get back to the fishing.

Hugh and Nick, Dorset, September 2007

1. Understanding fish

The nitty-gritty of this book is the delightful activity of cooking and eating fish. And we think you'll derive even more pleasure from your fish and shellfish if you understand a little, or perhaps a lot, about the business of catching and preparing them.

Besides being delicious, fish are uniquely nutritious. So you would think the very least we could do, given their contribution to our well-being, would be to nurture them in return. At this we are failing spectacularly. The prognosis is gloomy on a number of fronts, as the destructive fishing practices of the past half-century have taken their toll. The fact that we can finally acknowledge just how bad things are does offer, paradoxically, a glimmer of hope. We haven't, thank goodness, passed the point of no return; we still have a stunning range of native fish and shellfish to celebrate. We would both argue that their future lies largely in the hands of the consumer – that's every single one of us who loves to eat fish.

The angler-cook will, of necessity, prepare much of his fish from scratch, and knowing how to wield a filleting knife is clearly essential. But even the landlubber fish enthusiast may once in a while enjoy taking a live crab home or gutting a mackerel at the sink. Our two chapters covering fish and shellfish skills will show you the way.

Fish as food

searched the globe for new microbes. But the land-based microbial sources needed to produce effective new antibiotics have been dwindling alarmingly fast. It's time to look elsewhere. In research co-funded by the University of California and the pharmaceutical industry in 2002, microbiologists studied sediment samples taken from deep beneath the Pacific Ocean, the Red Sea and the Gulf of California. Bottom muds from up to a kilometre deep were found to contain up to one billion micro-organisms per cubic centimetre. From these, scientists have so far identified and studied over 100 different strains. Over 80 per cent of these produced molecules that inhibit cancer cell growth, while 35 per cent revealed the ability to destroy pathogenic bacteria and fungi. 'Never before has this level of biological activity been observed within a single group of organisms,' announced research group leader William Fenical, of the Center for Marine Biotechnology and Biomedicine in San Diego.

We scarcely understand the complexity and potential of these submarine muds, or our own influence on them. Yet there is no question that, by our hand, the marine environment is changing. Extracting vast quantities of life from it creates vacuums and imbalances; and pouring synthetic chemicals and waste materials into it must have consequences at the microscopic level. The oceanographer Sallie Chisholm, of the Massachusetts Institute of Technology, is researching the combined effect of global warming and human pollution on the marine environment – specifically how oceanic microbes react to changing sea temperatures and levels of nutrients. Her research shows that the microbial community of the sea is in a constant state of flux. It is made up of collections of mobile genes that interact to create unique combinations, depending on which microbes meet when, and under what conditions of temperature and sunlight.

These combinations of old and new genes are carried around by the mind-boggling number of viruses known to exist in seawater. Some viruses are good news, excellent news in fact, because when they infect the right microbes they create a fundamental and vital reaction – the bloom of a primitive group of photosynthesising organisms called prochlorococcus. This is the world's most abundant plankton species – the very first link in the marine food chain.

However, this good news story could take a very dark turn as a result of our meddling. According to Chisholm, these planktons could hardly be more fundamental, as they 'form an important part of the food chain in the oceans, supply some of the oxygen we breathe, and even play a role in modulating climate'. In other words, they help keep our planet on an even keel. Breaking any link in the food chain is bad enough (just look at what happens to salmon, cod and sea bass when you remove sand eels – see page 503), but taking away the very *first* link, the one that joins sunlight to sea life, would be a colossal cock-up of unimaginable consequences. But you wouldn't put it past us, would you?

If pollution was the only problem in the sea, some cautious optimism about the future might be in order. We are perhaps beginning the long and challenging process of cleaning up global industry. But there's another problem with the marine ecology, also of our own making, that runs even deeper and seems even harder to solve. It is a grim irony that our fish-built, fish-loving brains have applied themselves so thoroughly to the business of removing fish from the sea. We are now so good at it that in the case of some valuable marine species the prospect of 'total success' – i.e. extracting and killing every last one of them – is all too real. Quite how and why we are doing this, and how you as a consumer can make a difference, is the subject of the next chapter.

Sourcing fish

Like most anglers, we tend to jump for joy every time we catch a fish. And, as far as the cooking goes, we can wax lyrical till the herrings come home about the pleasures of a self-caught mackerel or a just-landed red mullet, the sweetness of a live scallop served raw, or the smoky aroma of squid over charcoal. Yet we know, in our heart of hearts, that the Big Picture doesn't look good. Our seas are in crisis. There is really no other way of putting it. According to the UN's Food and Agriculture Organisation, a quarter of the world's fish stocks are already overfished, while another half are being extracted at 'maximum biological capacity' – which basically means there is no buffer left for them between survival and eradication. They are on the brink.

In our UK fishery alone, the once seemingly inexhaustible cod stocks are close to total collapse. The common skate is as good as gone. For monkfish and bass, victims of food fashion and restaurant hype, the future is in the balance. Meanwhile, we are pouring pollutants into the ocean, wiping out whole marine habitats with destructive fishing methods, and killing countless other creatures we don't even want to eat – dolphins, turtles, albatross, to name the few we actually care about – all in our ravenous quest for more fish. How have we got ourselves into this awful mess?

In the name of 'progress'

In the past, our capacity to impact on the fish population was limited by the relative simplicity of the methods we were able to use to catch them. But today, sophisticated new methods are challenging the very concept of limits. The advances made in commercial fishing over the last few decades have been nothing short of revolutionary.

After the Second World War, the British fishing fleet (like everyone else's) was in tatters. Ancient, steam-driven tubs were all we had left – and since many of these had been requisitioned for the war effort they were in a pretty sorry state. However, since the war had all but put a stop to serious offshore fishing, the fish stocks in the North Atlantic were in excellent shape. A brave new fleet of fishing vessels was built to target these marine riches – and it was able to tap into much of the state-of-the-art technology that the conflict had spawned. All manner of military engineering was taken up by the industry. Notably, there was the Royal Navy's new echo-sounding technology, which delivered detailed three-dimensional images of the seabed, and enabled fishermen to detect vast shoals beneath their very feet. By the 1990s, affordable GPS sat-nav systems allowed any old boat to equip itself with a satellite-powered plotter that could guide it to any spot on the globe and record the exact position of successful hauls.

And so, twentieth-century fishermen were able to hunt top-grade fish with unprecedented success. Engines got faster, fuel got cheaper (and subsidised), weather forecasting became increasingly accurate, and the fishing industry entered what seemed like a golden age. The new boats could not only travel further and fish for longer than ever before, they could also fish much deeper. Dragging their gear at depths of 1,000 metres and more, they were able to exploit a whole new world of deep-dwelling fish. The sheer volume of fish that the new vessels could catch and process must have seemed like a cause for celebration. But as technology surged forward, our understanding of its effect on the marine environment lagged behind, with fatal consequences.

The trawlers' extraordinary effectiveness gave rise to a concept hitherto undreamed of: overfishing. It is simple enough. Reduce a population below a certain level (known as its 'biological limit') and it will lose the ability to reproduce itself. Every different species has what would now be called a 'tipping point'. The dwindling shoals reach a critical lower limit at which the odds are suddenly stacked massively against them. Finding each other, breeding successfully and ensuring that a significant number of young survive becomes first hard, then impossible. Species such as cod have already reached this crisis point in many areas, and plenty more are being pushed towards it.

It's not just the number of fish we catch that has damaged the health of our oceans, it's also the way we catch them. Fish are part of a highly complex ecosystem that can be harmed – even destroyed – by insensitive fishing methods. The industry euphemism for this style of fishing is 'non-selective' – but what it means is 'indiscriminate'. In the pursuit of a valued food fish, the collateral damage to other species can be immense. The (distinctly un-euphemistic) industry phrase for these is 'trash fish' – because they are literally thrown away. But mammals and birds too find themselves in the way of many commercial techniques worldwide. Even those so-called 'dolphin-friendly', 100km-long tuna long-lines still manage to snare turtles, seabirds and sharks.

There is one fishing method that perhaps more than any other symbolises the way our appetite for fish has outstripped our common sense. Beam trawling is a technique used extensively in the North Atlantic fisheries to catch bottom-dwelling 'demersal' fish (see page 21), including some particularly valuable species such as sole and monkfish. A heavy iron beam, up to 10 metres long, carries heavy chains that are dragged along the bottom to flush out fish on and under the soft seabed and scare them up into the trawl net that follows behind. Hauling the chains across miles of sea floor can be extremely destructive, ploughing up a delicate habitat of weeds and soft corals, and scooping up all manner of bottom-dwelling sea creatures such as crabs, anemones and starfish. The catch is dumped on the deck for sorting, and anything up to three-quarters of it may be discarded – dead.

Greenpeace has long been calling for a total ban on beam trawling, which it sees as a threat to one of the planet's last great strongholds of biodiversity. Its website invites us to 'think of it as driving a huge bulldozer through an unexplored, lush and richly populated forest – and being left with a flat, featureless desert'. Public awareness of the issue is gathering momentum, and in 2006 Waitrose took a lead on behalf of the consumer when it decided to stop selling beam-trawled fish in its stores.

It's easy to demonise the fishermen who practise beam trawling. But we should perhaps remember that in the 1970s, when it was first developed, the technique was viewed as a state-of-the-art solution to the challenge of catching bottom-dwelling fish. It was applauded as an efficient and highly productive method, and beam trawlers, working their new machinery in challenging conditions, were the brave pioneers of the fishing fleet. Back then, no one was really aware of the conservation issues. Thirty years later, however, scientists are measuring the destruction that beam trawling has wreaked on the seabed, and the alarm bells are clanging. It must be gutting for today's beam trawlers to be cast as the 'bad guys', when their forerunners were the heroes of the industry. Nonetheless, even they are starting to accept that their methods must be refined if beam trawling is ever to play a part in a sustainable fishery.

If we continue to mismanage our fisheries, we could effectively empty the oceans. One 2006 study by an international team of scientists even predicted a marine doomsday scenario, citing the year 2048 as the end of the line for all commercial fishing, full stop. Led by Dr Boris Worm, assistant professor in marine conservation biology at Dalhousie University in Nova Scotia, the group concluded: 'Our analyses suggest that business as usual would foreshadow serious threats to global food security, coastal water quality, and ecosystem stability, affecting current and future populations.'

Their report emphasises that the decimation of fish populations is not only disastrous for the marine ecosystem but also devastating for the human race. Worldwide, over 20 million people are employed in fishing at sea, and a billion rely on fish as their primary source of protein. If we don't look after the astonishing resources that the ocean offers us, the consequences will be grim. Not just grim in the sense that we won't be able to eat rare tuna steaks or battered cod again: grim in that we'll be faced with environmental, social and economic collapse on a global scale.

This may sound like scaremongering, but the scary precedent happened right on the research team's own doorstep. The collapse of the Grand Banks cod fishery is a classic example of how greed, political ineptness, consistent dismissal of the scientific evidence and procrastination all caused the total collapse of a 400-year-old industry that had provided a living for fishermen and fish processors in countries all around the world (see page 426).

The dreaded CFP

So, surely there must be official mechanisms to prevent the seas from commercial abuse? Measures set in law to protect our oceans and the fish that swim in them? Well, yes, there are. The problem is, they don't work.

All members of the European Union are subject to the 1983 Common Fisheries Policy (CFP). This is an agreement that aims to protect stocks from overfishing by placing an internationally agreed limit on the numbers of certain species – those considered to be under most pressure – that can be caught each year. Besides these annual 'quotas', as they are known, there are rules about the kind of gear that can be used (such as the mesh size of nets), minimum landing sizes for certain species and the amount of time allowed at sea. These rules and regulations are enforced by a clipboard-wielding inspectorate that is empowered to scrutinise catches as they are landed, enter fish processing plants and even board fishing boats at sea.

Unfortunately, it is no exaggeration to say that just about every fisherman, marine scientist and conservation campaigner from the Shetlands to the Scillies *hates* the CFP. No one trusts it; very few people within the fishing industry or even the European Parliament fully understand it. Both trade and conservation bodies see it as an unmitigated mess that is signally failing to protect our fish or, indeed, our fishermen. It is also incredibly complex. We could completely lose you, and ourselves, in the myriad contradictions and questions it provokes, but rather than tie ourselves in knots of bureaucratic red tape, we'll just highlight a few of the failings of the CFP.

How the system is supposed to work is as follows. The CFP identifies the commercially valuable species available in the overall EU fishery and then sets 'total allowable catches' (TACs). For species under particular pressure, these 'totals' are then divided into individual national quotas – each nation, in effect, is told the maximum tonnage it is allowed to land. These figures are – in theory, anyway – recommended by the scientific advisers to the EU, in the form of a body called the International Council for the Exploration of the Sea (ICES). This independent panel assesses fish populations, estimates stock sizes and proposes a sustainable TAC. So far, so good. But the theory of quotas is very hard to implement alongside the stress of international politics and the pressure of global business. In order to smooth over tensions between member states, the European Commission is allowed to adjust the scientifically recommended quotas to take on board what are known as 'socio-economic concerns'. The revised numbers are then presented to the fisheries ministers of each member state, who, after making their own further adjustments (which are almost always upwards), will set the actual quotas for their fishermen.

Those member states with massive investment in commercial fishing, such as the Spanish, Portuguese and French, have a huge vested interest in keeping political control of the seas. 'This is where the system breaks down,' says Dr Tom Pickerell, fisheries policy officer for WWF, the global conservation organisation. 'The ministers are not accountable to anyone. They can ignore all the advice if they so choose. We've analysed the quotas for the last fifteen years and they are, on average, thirty per cent higher than the ICES has recommended. Ministers are heavily influenced by sustained lobbying from the fishing industries within member states.' These fishing lobbies are far too powerful, and the politicians who wish to appease them simply ride roughshod over the ICES's recommendations.

The scandal of 'high-grading'

A system of quotas for pressurised species sounds sensible, even vital. But quotas have serious drawbacks, which can backfire on the very species they set out to protect. Jim Portus, head of the South Western Fish Producer Organisation, gives his view: 'Quotas have encouraged the race to fish and have done nothing for fisheries conservation. I can think of no reasons for praising them.'

The quotas relate to the quantity of fish that can be landed (as opposed to caught), and one of their greatest flaws is that they encourage the practice known as 'high-grading' – which is industry-speak for throwing lower-value fish back into the sea in order to boost the cash value of one's quota. If a fisherman is only allowed to land a certain tonnage of a species, he will want to make sure that those he brings in are the most valuable specimens possible. That usually means the biggest ones, as well as those in pristine condition.

So, for example, say you are a fisherman with a quota for one tonne of cod – or, to make it easier to explain, say you are allowed to catch a hundred cod on a particular day. You haul your net and find you've hit a hot spot – you catch your entire quota in one haul. Great. But half the cod are on the small side, so you decide to trawl again to see if the cod are still beneath you. They are! So you pull on board another great net of fish, most of them much better than the first haul. What do you do? It's obvious: you chuck back the smaller fish from the first haul and replace them with the best of your second haul. Your catch is now made up of big, high-value fish. But what if you trawl just once more? You might get some even bigger fish… And so it goes on.

The CFP is in effect compelling fishermen to high-grade. Many skippers find this practice appalling, but there's no advantage in refusing to high-grade as they know that most of the other boats are doing it anyway; on the contrary, they'll only lose out. But by the time a trawler returns to port after a day's high-grading, which was carried out perfectly legally, it will have killed and discarded several times more fish than its intended share of the quota. 'The CFP brings out the worst of human nature,' says Jim Portus, 'because it provides a strong incentive to throw back into the sea any fish that would waste the precious quota.'

The farce of zoning

Another area of the CFP that is in a painfully bureaucratic mess is the system of zoning that determines which country is allowed to fish where. All European waters are governed by the CFP – even the waves lapping our toes on Chesil Beach are legislated by Brussels. Each member state has its very own 'exclusion zone', extending six nautical miles from its coast. In this six-mile zone, each nation is obliged to enforce the overall regulations set by the CFP, but it can also choose to add extra regulations, over and above those directed by Brussels. The six-mile exclusion zone was devised in order to stop vessels from other states fishing in these waters and to enable the protection of inshore waters with legislation that is sensitive to specific local needs.

Between six and twelve nautical miles out to sea there exists another zone, in which not just the local vessels are allowed to fish but other nations may have 'historic fishing rights'. Belgian boats, for instance, have a legal right to catch fish in the Thames Estuary; British fishermen work in Belgian waters too. Within the twelve-mile zone, the local state has the right to enforce extra legislation upon its own boats, but not those of the sanctioned foreign visitors. This can give rise to some ridiculous situations, in which local fishermen are not allowed to catch fish in their own waters but foreign boats can come in and help themselves.

A flagrant example occurred in the Southwest bass pair-trawling fishery in 2004. Pair trawling is a highly effective way of catching large shoals of fish in huge nets strung between two trawlers (a 'pair'). Recognising that pair trawling often results in a large bycatch of dolphins and porpoises, the UK fisheries minister of the time, Ben Bradshaw, banned the British fleet from pair trawling within the twelve-mile zone off the Southwest coast. He then asked the Commission to extend this ruling to all EU boats, some of which have historic rights in this twelve-mile zone. But, bowing to pressure from the powerful French fishing lobby, it was decided that the directive should remain voluntary. So now French and Spanish boats continue to pair trawl for bass in our waters while British boats may not. It is not hard to see how bitterness brews between nations.

'The law is so complicated in this area that no one really knows what's going on,' says WWF's Dr Tom Pickerell. 'We think countries should have full control in their own twelve-mile zone. Beyond twelve miles, blanket CFP rules should apply.' We agree. Increasing a nation's control of its waters from six to twelve nautical miles would pave the way for a much-needed simplification of the rules about who fishes where and when, using which methods. The benefits would be felt in *all* European inshore waters, because it would allow for genuinely constructive local zoning and fallowing policies, steered by the local fisheries themselves, that really could help build and protect stocks.

These examples illustrate what any fisherman will tell you: the CFP doesn't work because member states wield far too much individual power within it. Apply the right pressure in the right places, or use your lobbyists wisely, and you can wriggle out of any rules that don't suit your fleet. Not only are the CFP's benefits to European fish stocks questionable, it also fosters a counterproductive and often downright ugly culture at sea, and in ports and harbours around the Union.

The fact remains, however, that the CFP is here to stay, at least for the near future. Some argue that it's better than nothing. Dr Cat Dorey, oceans researcher for Greenpeace, says that while it clearly needs a radical overhaul, we shouldn't abandon the CFP altogether: 'If nothing else, it gives us the opportunity to hold some of the most irresponsible fishing nations to account. We can learn from other countries too. Iceland, for instance, has a lot of good policies. These include a "no discarding" law, where everything that's caught must be landed. It puts paid to high-grading, as well as giving fisheries scientists a much better idea of what is actually being caught out at sea.'

So, to make the best of a bad job, we need to apply our muscle within the CFP as hard as we possibly can – and, as you'll read below, some groups of fishermen and activists are already managing to take very positive steps in the right direction, in spite of the odds stacked against them by current fisheries policy.

Some good news

'What's all this got to do with me?' you might be thinking. 'I only *shop* for fish, I don't catch them!' But remember, change does not have to come from the top down. As our political leaders fail to make a positive difference or even reach basic agreements between themselves, non-government organisations and campaign groups such as WWF and Greenpeace have stepped into the 'action vacuum'. They, more than any government, are focusing the arguments and fostering a dialogue with the consumer – all those of us who shop for fish – in the knowledge that our power, constructively harnessed, really could make a difference.

It would be easy to conclude that the current situation is so hopeless that we might as well give up eating fish altogether – or gorge ourselves on what's left while we still can. But there's more than a glimmer of hope on the horizon: there is concrete evidence that public information and concerted consumer action can play a genuine role in halting the decline of threatened species and environments and helping them to thrive again.

Slowly but surely, it's becoming easier for consumers to choose fish from sustainable, well-managed stocks. Producers and retailers have realised that it's no good simply doing the right thing, they've got to shout about it too. So, the label on your fish may now give you valuable information about how and where it was caught. By choosing such certified products over anonymous fish of unspecified origins, you are voting for better, more sustainable practice at sea.

The MSC

At the forefront of this move for clear information is the Marine Stewardship Council (MSC). This international charity promotes the certification of sustainable fisheries around the world. The 'pass' or 'fail' for a given fishery is based on an independently assessed environmental standard that measures stock levels, the fishery's impact on the marine environment and its future management plan. Any certification is purely voluntary, applied for by the fishery or local council – fisheries pursue it because they believe it will help give them a future. Certified fisheries can proudly display the MSC eco-label and logo on their products, which immediately makes them more attractive to many retailers and their customers.

There are some inspiring examples of British fisheries that have been granted MSC certification, and they are reaping financial benefits as well as conservation brownie points. They include the South West Mackerel Handline Fishery, the Hastings Fleet Dover Sole Fishery, the Burry Inlet Cockle Fishery and the Loch Torridon Nephrops (Dublin Bay Prawn) Creel Fishery. As we write, many fisheries in the UK are currently undergoing the assessment process; visit msc.org for the latest details. And wherever you buy your fish, you should start looking out for the MSC label.

At the moment, the MSC's scheme pretty much stands alone in the breadth of its application and its ease of use. There are some other, more localised, labelling initiatives that we applaud too; the South West Handline Fishermen's Association, for instance, tags all its line-caught pollack and bass so that consumers can find out when and by whom it was caught. But there is scope for far more extensive and informative labelling of fish. We don't think it's overstating the case to say that it could deliver a monumental boost to fish conservation all around the world. The time is right to kick-start a virtuous circle: the more positive choices, with ecological upsides, that can be offered to the consumer, the better.

More friends of fish

The MSC is not the only non-government organisation blazing a trail for sustainable fishing. The Marine Conservation Society (MCS), for instance, is a UK charity dedicated to the conservation of our seas and seashores. Despite their teasingly similar acronyms, the two organisations have a different emphasis, the MSC being focused on promoting more sustainable practices within the industry, and the MCS on raising awareness of marine conservation issues.

The MCS campaigns on everything from clean beaches to endangered turtles, and its website, fishonline.org, is a fantastic resource for anyone worried about the provenance of the fish they eat. It gives clear information on the conservation status of over 150 fish and shellfish species and products, with helpful 'fish to eat' and 'fish to avoid' lists. The MCS has given us invaluable assistance in our research, and you'll see its sustainability scores alongside the different species we profile in the third part of this book.

As you'd expect, WWF, being the world's largest conservation organisation, is heavily involved in marine campaigning too. It tends to operate behind the scenes and its work includes engaging with supermarkets to improve fish sourcing and influencing governments on policy initiatives. It's been a crucial catalyst for the ground-breaking Invest in Fish South West initiative that we'll come to soon.

For a more 'direct action' approach, the Greenpeace campaigns against marine pollution and overfishing are beacons of well-organised, passionate defiance. Along with newer groups such as Bite-Back, which has a particular focus on shark conservation, they are leading the fight against overtly destructive fishing practices. You will find contact details for all these groups in the Directory (see page 592).

Proof that conservation measures can work comes courtesy of the beleaguered monkfish. Let's make one thing clear. We are *not* recommending that you rush out and start buying monkfish willy nilly – many stocks are still precarious – but we feel optimistic that the advice might change in the not too distant future. By the end of the 1990s, most monkfish stocks were near collapse. Now these extraordinary creatures seem to be making tentative steps towards recovery in a few areas (see page 493), owing to tough measures taken by some fisheries. These have included the decommissioning of fishing vessels, reduced quotas and the establishment of protected areas.

Another fish that has benefited from similar measures is haddock. Once in a state almost as parlous as that of cod, its North Sea stocks are currently better than they have been for twenty years (see page 434). Both haddock and monkfish have recently been removed from the MCS's 'fish to avoid' list (though in some fisheries monkfish still scores a worrying 5).

This is a direct result of successful conservation measures and consumer pressure. Dr Bryce Beukers-Stewart, fisheries policy officer for the MCS, says: 'Over the last two years the consumer's ability to influence the sustainability of seafood, and indeed the management of fisheries, has really come to the fore.' He cites the example of Icelandic cod, the quotas for which were recently cut by a third. The Icelandic fisheries minister publicly stated that the prime motivation behind this radical move was to maintain Iceland's reputation as a source of sustainable fish for the British export market. Bryce concludes: 'This is the holy grail of the sustainable seafood movement – collective individual actions are now influencing international fisheries' management measures, and ultimately helping sustain the long-term future of our fish stocks and marine environment.'

Fish farming: the problems

Fish farming might seem like the perfect answer to the problem of plummeting fish stocks – but too often it's not, because as it turns out, it creates more ecological problems than it solves. Creating fish life in a laboratory is no longer the challenge it once was: men in white coats are now able to simulate the complex spawning processes of sought-after species, including salmon, halibut, cod, sea bass, sea trout, bream and prawns. Even the mysteries of the eel's extraordinary migratory transmogrification have been unlocked from the depths of the Sargasso Sea (see page 528).

As three decades of intensive salmon farming have shown, captive fish can be raised for market in staggering quantities. Yet, ecologically speaking, the process is fraught with difficulties: the correct location of farms, the source of the farms' feed, the waste the fish excrete, the chemicals used for treating their diseases and the fish that escape into the wild – all these are problems that have dogged the fish farming industry ever since it began, and remain a huge source of anxiety.

The main business of farming fish is feeding them – and most, being piscivores, require a constant diet of other fish in order to grow big and fat themselves. The staple diet of captive fish is 'fish meal', and it is a huge irony that this is mostly made from wild fish: species such as blue whiting, Norwegian pout, capelin and sand eel (see page 503) that have little or no value for human consumption. These are hoovered from the waters in vast quantities, in a practice known as 'industrial fishing', then turned into fish meal pellets. Inevitably this deprives already threatened wild fish of a much-needed source of protein. And it is not very efficient either: according to WWF, it takes more than three tonnes of wild fish flesh, in pellet form, to create just one tonne of farmed salmon.

After the fundamental problem of where to source their food, comes (inevitably) the ugly issue of where to put their crap. There's an awful lot of it, and without sufficient tidal flow or water depth to flush out the effluent, a fish farm can quickly wreak havoc on the local marine environment. Some sea lochs, inlets and coastal bays have seen their biodiversity crash after years of being smothered by impenetrable layers of salmon excrement. These 'mulch out' the natural flora and fauna of the sea floor to create a marine desert. They can also spread toxins to surrounding sea life – scallop fisheries along the west coast of Scotland have been suspended over the summer months for several years in succession owing to dangerous toxic algal blooms, believed by many to have been caused by fish-farm waste.

The seabed can recover from such accumulations, and in good farms a system of fallowing is used, whereby fish cages are left empty for certain periods. Siting fish farms appropriately is critical too, and can go a long way to reducing the risks. But as with all intensive farming, the commercial pressures militate in favour of corner cutting and keeping things the way they are. There are still too many fish farms that need to clean up their act.

When you farm fish, you are at the mercy of the elements – storms and high seas will inevitably cause structural damage to cages, which will lead to fish escaping. Farmed salmon escape into the wild in astonishing numbers. In 2005, almost a million salmon were reported to have escaped from salmon farms on the west coast of Scotland. Breakouts on this scale mean that farmed salmon here may outnumber wild stocks by a factor of ten – or even, in locations close to the biggest escapes, a hundred or more.

On the run, these fugitives are free to mingle with their wild brethren. Some escapees will make it into local rivers, where they can interbreed with wild stocks. But the tame salmon dilute the wild strains, creating hybrids that are less well adapted to the challenges of the open sea. They are highly unlikely to return to the rivers and breed again (they lack that essential and mysterious homing instinct). So a wild female that mates with an escaped male is effectively wasting her eggs, and her genes, for that year at least.

Escaped farm fish will also transmit diseases and parasites to wild salmon – as indeed may fish that stay in their cages. Sea lice are blood-sucking parasites that exist at generally non-threatening levels among wild sea fish populations. They are attracted to large concentrations of captive salmon and powerful chemicals are needed to kill them (usually substances that are not permitted in any other form of food production). The fall-out from these lice-exterminating treatments inevitably affects the surrounding ecosystem, killing a whole spectrum of other invertebrate aquatic life, from shrimps to anemones – creatures that many other sea dwellers rely on as food. Yet if the lice aren't treated with something toxic, not only do the farmed fish become infested but local wild fish are likely to be attacked too.

Fish farming: the possibilities

Fish farming is by no means an ecologically doomed endeavour. It still has the potential to produce fish of marketable quality in a sustainable way, and thereby give our wild fish populations a chance to recover. While examples of poor fish farming practice are all too easy to find, many fish farmers are getting their act together.

We've looked in particular at the problems of salmon farming, but some other forms of fish farming are intrinsically less intensive and less damaging. Most shellfish farming is fairly benign. Mussels, scallops and oysters need remarkably little intervention to grow successfully, as they will feed on whatever is already in the water. The farming of these bivalves involves capturing them when they are young and relocating them to a good growing site. In the case of mussels, if you choose the right site, simply providing the structures on which they can thrive will do the trick. The seed mussels will arrive of their own accord, and even create a useful habitat and nursery for other species into the bargain (see page 569).

Some freshwater fish species have the potential to be farmed with less environmental impact than sea fish. Carp, for instance, offer an opportunity for enlightened aquaculture. It may be a fringe form of fish farming right now, but it has fantastic potential for the future. Being omnivorous, these fish do not require the fish-based pellet diet of farmed salmon; instead, they will happily graze on pond vegetation, algae, zooplankton and waterbugs. All of these can be encouraged to thrive in the carp's natural environment. Supplementary feeds, such as corn or compost worms, can be produced cheaply and sustainably on site. So, the farmer is farming the feed as well as the fish, which is a pretty holistic approach. Incidentally, organic trout farming (see page 519) is based on a similarly sustainably model, where the feed is mostly natural, or at least produced on site.

In the same way that meat and vegetables are increasingly produced on small-scale farms and sold through farmers' markets, we feel there is huge potential for organic freshwater 'microfisheries' to raise modest crops of high-quality fish. It could be done with trout, carp, perch or even crayfish (provided they could be contained – see page 546). These freshwater species were once a proud part of our fish culture – and they could be again. So how about a freshwater fish box scheme? If there was one down the road, we would sign up quicker than a pike can pounce.

Even the farming of salmon *can* be done well. Better siting of farms, regular fallowing of cages and minimising of chemical inputs are the goals of a new breed of conscientious salmon farmer. Regulating the origins of the feed source has to be next on the agenda. The Soil Association has recently granted organic status to a handful of salmon farms in Scotland, based on their lower inputs and stocking densities and the sourcing of sustainable feed. The feed comes from the fish processing industry, whose leftover skeletons and fish off-cuts are 'recycled' to create fish meal without killing wild fish. There is also at least one organic cod farm, in Shetland, that now sources its feed similarly.

So, the problems of fish farming can be solved. The know-how is there for modern aquaculturists to fulfil our demand for certain fish without wreaking havoc on the environment. If this is going to happen, then the consumer must want it to happen. And that means choosing the *right* farmed fish...

all the conservation bodies agree that it's in good shape (see page 475). But the best way to catch megrim – in fact pretty much the *only* way to catch megrim – is by beam trawling. You see? A nice simple piece of advice to the consumer – 'eat more megrim' – immediately becomes compromised because the only available method to catch a 'sustainable' species is an 'unsustainable' one.

Must we be permanently stuck on the horns of such conservation dilemmas? The aim of the IiFSW is to make sure we can wrestle ourselves free. The know-how exists to make beam trawling less damaging and more selective. Jim Portus of the South Western Fish Producer Organisation explains: 'Our fishermen are using emerging technology to minimise seabed impact. A fellow member of SWFPO recently won first prize in the Clean Fishing awards. His beam trawl design incorporated a 'release panel' in the floor of the net so that organisms such as crabs, starfish and sea urchins fall out – and it's now being mimicked across the Channel fleet of beam trawlers.' Other innovations, such as large rubber wheels that lift the beam poles off the seabed to minimise damage and increase fuel efficiency, are being trialled.

Even with such innovations, the seabed will need a rest from the effects of repeated beam trawling. So fallowing is key to these discussions, and the mutual agreement of marine protected areas – patches of sea where, for years at a time, beam trawling isn't allowed – is under negotiation. It seems that even the erstwhile 'baddies' can bring positive solutions to the table.

Consumers calling the shots

In all such negotiations, the role of retailers and consumers is key. A message that fishermen really need to hear is, 'Yes, we will buy your fish if you change the way you catch it. In fact, we will buy more of it.' The South West Handline Fishery offers a great example of how good practice can be rewarded. It's a small fishery that has always used the handline technique for catching mackerel. It's sustainable (like much line fishing) because mackerel are targeted so effectively that there is no unwanted bycatch, and no damage to the marine environment. This has always been the case, and now the fishery has introduced a strict quota limit and minimum landing size. It's won them a coveted MSC label and, perhaps more importantly, legions of customers who are prepared to pay top whack for these fish they can feel good about.

The fishery is extending its methods to the line fishing of pollack and sea bass. Individual fish are now being tagged and can be traced to their source at the point of sale in fishmongers, supermarkets and restaurants. This is the ultimate in fish traceability – and consequently in consumer confidence. It's the next best thing to catching your own fish. Of course, it would be great if we could all catch our own fish, but most of us rely on retailers and restaurants for the vast majority of the fish we eat. What initiatives such as tagged fish and MSC labels tell us, however, is that we are not at the mercy of these retailers and those who supply them. Quite the opposite – we can influence their behaviour through the choices we make.

However, it is still not always easy for a shopper to identify sustainably caught fish. In the absence of labels and tags (which are found on only a tiny percentage of retailed fish), what is the eco-conscious shopper to do? Ask questions, that's what. Where was it caught, and where landed? What sort of

fishing method was used? Is it male or female (and if the latter, might it be carrying eggs?) Is it farmed or wild? If farmed, then where, and what was it fed on? Is it organic, and if so, certified by whom?

You might not manage to complete the list of questions without exasperating your fishmonger – and you might want to vary the inquisition for each visit. But it's important to let your fishmonger know that he or she has at least one customer who cares deeply about the provenance of the fish.

Of course, in order to acquire the confidence to ask such questions, and indeed to make sense of the answers, you need to know a bit about fish in the first place. It will help if you understand what a bass pair trawler does (see page 32), for instance, or why a farmed prawn is best avoided (see page 542). If you know why inshore ling is a different environmental proposition from deepwater ling (see page 441), you can make a more informed decision. It's in the hope of answering these and other questions that this book runs to more than 600 pages!

Where to get your fish

Generally, buying fish close to source should ensure that you get the maximum amount of information about it. Straight off the boat is ideal, of course, and harbourside fishmongers or stalls are often good too. With luck, such small-scale businesses will stock fish bought directly from local inshore day boats. If they

Five rules for sustainable fish shopping

Once you've covered the freshness issue, you can start to apply your conscience to the best-looking fish on the slab. All the advice we've given on sustainability boils down to five very simple principles to keep in mind when you're out shopping:

1. **BONE UP ON FISH BEFORE YOU BUY** Find out how sustainable it is and which fisheries are the best managed. If you've set your heart on a particular recipe but discovered that the species in question should be avoided, then research a few substitutes (pollack for cod, lemon sole for Dover, bream for bass etc). Champion the more sustainable species; boycott those most under threat.

2. **NEVER BUY FISH BLIND** Question your fishmonger, or at least read the back of the packet, to make sure you know as much about it as you can. Try to find out where the fish came from, and what method was used to catch it. Favour fish and shellfish caught in the inshore fishery by local day boats.

3. **SUPPORT ECO-LABELLING SCHEMES** Buy their fish (see logos to look out for, opposite). This sends a powerful message to fisheries across the globe.

4. **DON'T BUY UNDERSIZED FISH** If fishmongers and fishermen know they can easily shift undersized fish (which may even be illegal) it 'lets them off the hook'. Delivering the message that undersized fish are unacceptable keeps the pressure on retailers to review their sources, and on fishermen to review their methods.

5. **AVOID BUYING FISH DURING THEIR SPAWNING SEASON** If this is hard to ascertain (different fish spawn at different times of year, and some spawn unpredictably), at least avoid 'berried' crustaceans, and try not to buy roe-carrying fish too often.

Fish to find, fish to avoid

Finally, in addition to the above 'rules', you might like to consider the following categories. Between them, they should help you to choose sustainable fish, and to enjoy some of the best seafood that our coastline has to offer.

The blacklist: ten fish to avoid
Make sure none of these fish ever passes your lips – at least for the foreseeable future – and you'll be doing a great deal to help protect our threatened species.
1 Whitebait (page 423)
2 Cod from the UK (page 426), unless MSC-certified or organically farmed
3 Hake (page 437)
4 Bluefin tuna (page 447)
5 Sharks and huss (page 452), all types except dogfish
6 Skate and rays (page 456), unless one of the three sustainable species
7 Wild halibut (page 463)
8 Sea bass (page 478), unless self-caught, line-caught and tagged, or organically farmed
9 Wild salmon (page 508)
10 Eel (page 528)

Ten most underrated sustainable seafish

These are the species we feel you can enjoy in good conscience. Fill your boots. Honestly, if we only ever ate fish from this list and nothing else, we reckon we'd be missing out on very little... provided we're allowed the Top Ten shellfish too.

1 Sprat (page 421)
2 Pollack (page 430)
3 Pouting (page 442)
4 Mackerel (page 444), ideally line-caught
5 Megrim and witch (page 475)
6 Scad or horse mackerel (page 481)
7 Black bream (page 483), especially from Cornwall, the Northwest and North Wales
8 Grey mullet (page 488)
9 Red gurnard (page 496)
10 Garfish (page 498)

Ten shellfish to seek out

In your quest for guilt-free seafood, never overlook the little guys in shells. Many are responsibly harvested from healthy stocks – or sustainably farmed.

1 Langoustines (page 546), creel-caught
2 Brown crab (page 551)
3 Blue velvet swimmer crab (page 555)
4 Spider crab (page 557)
5 Whelks (page 564)
6 Farmed mussels (page 567)
7 Dived scallops (page 574)
8 Cockles (page 578), especially MSC-certified from the Burry Inlet
9 Dived razor clams (page 582)
10 Squid (page 588), British, jig-caught

Aquaculture to feel good about

Fish farming can be bad news, but it can also offer a sustainable, high-welfare alternative to overfished wild stocks. We would happily eat the following, once in a while:

1 Organically farmed salmon
2 Organically farmed trout
3 Organically farmed cod
4 Farmed carp
5 Most farmed bivalves

Logos to look out for

When it comes to labelling schemes to identify sustainably caught or farmed fish, there's huge room for improvement. There are currently only three that we feel we can confidently endorse, but we are hoping for a labelling revolution.

1 Marine Stewardship Council eco-label for certified environmentally responsible fisheries (msc.org)
2 Soil Association organic certification for farmed fish (soilassociation.org)
3 Tagged line-caught mackerel, bass and pollack from the South West Handline Fishermen's Association (linecaught.org.uk)

Fish skills

All good ingredients are a pleasure to handle – and none more so than fish. Few amateur cooks ever get the chance to work with an entire pig, lamb or beef carcass. But taking a whole fish and dealing with it from start to finish is an act that will deepen your understanding of the animal that is going to feed you, and maybe even reconnect you with your hunter-gatherer past.

It is, of course, possible to bypass all the major elements of fish preparation by choosing either fillets or whole prepared fish that are, if you like, 'oven-ready'. One reason for doing so may be squeamishness – but a cook in a hurry may make the same choice. Few people have time to prepare all their fish from scratch. We don't. And sometimes it's pleasing to watch the fishmonger deftly gutting and descaling the fish you've chosen, performing in a few minutes a task that might take you twenty.

However, making time to do some fish prep yourself once in a while will keep you in tune with your fish and in touch with your inner fisherman (even if your outer one is still in the closet). So if you consider yourself fish phobic, we'd like to help you work through your anxieties until they evaporate, leaving you confident to deal with your fish in the future.

We know this kind of Damascene conversion can happen, because we have seen it many times. Since we've been running our Catch and Cook days at River Cottage HQ, we have fished, and cooked fish, with men and women who at the beginning of their time with us could hardly bear to touch a fish, dead or alive. By the end of the day we've had them pulling the guts out of mackerel and descaling pollack with gay abandon – happily working their way through the entire fish box and then asking for more. Learning a new skill that tears down an old barrier is one of life's great pleasures.

If you haven't handled much fish but now feel ready to confront your 'issues', may we suggest a good way to get you started: a mackerel fishing trip – the kind you can book for just an hour or two in harbour towns all around the British coast. A sympathetic skipper will provide the tackle you need, show you how to hold a live fish, unhook it, knock it on the head and, when you have recovered your composure (with a bit of luck your fish won't recover his), how to slit open its belly and remove its guts. By the time you've dealt with three of them, you'll feel like an old hand. If you enjoy the whole experience, you might consider graduating to a longer, half-day, reef or wrecking trip. With any luck you'll encounter a range of different species, and again, the best skippers will always be happy to show you the basics of on-board fish prep – not just gutting, but descaling and even filleting.

You can of course face your demons alone, at the kitchen sink, with a fish you've brought home from the fishmonger's. Read our instructions in this chapter, take a deep breath and go for it. On balance, though, we think it's good to have company when attempting breakthroughs of this kind. If you don't mind investing some time and a bit of cash in your future with fish, then we would wholeheartedly recommend a day at the Billingsgate Seafood Training School (seafoodtraining.org). You will be in the hands of serious (but good-humoured) experts, who will give you as thorough a grounding in the basic fish-prepping skills as you could wish for – and a damn fine lunch to boot. And of course it goes without saying that we'd love to see you for a River Cottage Catch and Cook day where, with a bit of luck, you will be dealing with fish you've caught yourself.

Killing fish

Let's start from first principles, in the hope that some of the fish you'll be working with will indeed be those you've caught yourself. When you've caught a fish, and decided you'd like to eat it, you should kill it without delay. This will not only minimise its suffering, it will maximise its eating qualities. Fish that thrash and gasp themselves to death on the deck or in the fish box may end up with bruised flesh.

The most effective way to kill a fish is by delivering a sharp crack across the head with a solid 'bosher', or 'priest'. You can buy these small truncheons, made from wood, plastic, metal or even the antler of a stag. Sometimes they incorporate a lead weight in the business end to give them, literally, more clout. But a well-chosen 'found object' will do just as well. Improvised priests we have encountered over the years include rolling pins, chopped-down broom handles, short lengths of steel pipe, suitably hefty bits of driftwood, small axe handles and even half a pool cue (the thicker end, of course).

It helps to hold the fish on a firm, flat surface – using a cloth, if necessary, so it doesn't slip from your hands – then crack it over the head, as if you're banging a nail in with a hammer. This should kill the fish instantly. One blow will usually be enough, but two, in rapid succession, is belt and braces. The fish may shiver or flap for a few moments – this is its nervous system playing out – but if it continues to do so for more than half a minute, another good whack may be in order. As you might imagine, the bigger the fish, the harder and more numerous the strikes required to despatch it (game-fishing boats in the tropics are often equipped with a baseball bat, to deliver the fatal blows to big fish such as dorado, wahoo, travally and tuna).

Many fishermen, particularly sea anglers, are blasé about the need to kill fish quickly once they have been caught. At the commercial end of the business, this is perhaps understandable. Fish are netted in such huge numbers that to despatch them individually would take hours – and by the time you'd dealt with a few hundred the rest would be dead anyway. But anglers don't have this excuse. They are catching fish one (or at most a few) at a time. The opportunity to give them a quick and merciful release should always be taken.

Sometimes, say in the frenzy of catching strings of mackerel in threes, fours and more, it's tempting to abandon this responsibility. On too many angling boats, it is the culture to fling the live fish in a box and let them expire in their own time. But just because this is the done thing, it doesn't mean you have to do it. You can easily kill a mackerel as you unhook it – by putting your thumb in its mouth, or gills, and pulling its head backwards to break its neck. This alternative method of despatch works for most fish under a pound.

Bleeding a fish

After you've whacked a fish and rendered it unconscious, its heart will still beat for a minute or two as the blood continues to circulate through its body. This gives you an opportunity to 'bleed' it. There are three good reasons to do this. First, it ensures the fish dies quickly. Secondly, it empties blood from the veins that weave through the fish's flesh. Bled fish have clean, translucent fillets, without vein tracks or dark patches of trapped blood, and both look and taste the better for it (this is particularly important if they are to be eaten raw as sushi and sashimi, or in a dish such as ceviche). The third reason for bleeding is to prolong shelf life. Blood attracts and nurtures bacteria much faster than flesh, so draining it off means the fish can be kept fresh for longer.

Ideally all fish, including freshwater species, should be bled. In Japan, most line-caught fish destined for the sushi markets are bled as a matter of course, in order to meet the consumers' high standards. If a fish hasn't been bled properly, its market value will be greatly reduced. In the UK, however, commercially caught fish aren't generally bled. It's simply not part of our fishing culture. But we are so convinced of the virtues of bleeding that we now do it with almost every fish we catch. By making sure a fish dies quickly and is bled thoroughly, we're not only paying our respects, we're guaranteeing it reaches the kitchen in the best possible condition – where a fitting send-off awaits...

You need to bleed a fish while its heart is still beating – so within a minute or less of that blow on the head. Cut its gills on both sides of the head with either a sharp blade or a pair of stout scissors. A major artery passes through the gills, whose job is to pass oxygen from the water. You should see the blood start to flow from the gills almost immediately. We like to bleed our fish in an empty box for ten minutes or so before rinsing them off and transferring them to the icebox. To achieve absolute optimum freshness, it's best to gut the fish before they go on ice (see page 57). But if you're too busy catching, the gutting can wait, just so long as your fish is kept cold.

Returning a live fish

If you decide you're not going to eat a fish you've just caught – it might be too small, it might be one of the less palatable, or less sustainable, species – then you should release it instead. (If it is deeply hooked or otherwise damaged, you should always kill it – and make a meal of it.) Handle a live fish that you are planning to return to the water carefully, ideally with a wet cloth or at least wet hands, to avoid rubbing off the mucus that protects its skin. Unhook the fish over the water if possible, or at least resting on a stable surface, because if you drop a fish you can damage its scales or even stun it, which greatly reduces its chances of survival.

Never carelessly fling a fish back into the sea. Treat it with respect. A fish returned in perfect condition has the potential to go forth and multiply, which is good for future fish stocks, future fish sport and future fish suppers.

Descaling

If you're keen to eat the skin of your fish (and we'd thoroughly recommend it), you may need to remove its scales. These vary in size and thickness from species to species. Mackerel have tiny, soft, inoffensive scales, most of which simply slip away as the fish is handled, rinsed and prepared. Any that remain seem to dissolve as the fish is cooked. So they don't need descaling. Bass and bream, by contrast, have coarse, fingernail-like scales, which are never pleasant to find in your mouth. If you want to make a virtue of the skin of these fish – by crisping it in your frying pan or oven – then you should definitely remove their scales.

Scales are arranged in overlapping rows, from head to tail, like the slates on a roof. The way to remove them is to scrape firmly 'uphill', from tail to head, in the opposite direction to the natural lie. The instruments that can do this effectively are many and varied, including tools especially designed for the job (see page 78). If you lack a patented descaler, you can use a blunt knife or the back of a sharp one, but you'll need to be careful.

Big bass and bream scales tend to flick and ping all over the place as you scrape; they can quickly decorate your kitchen, or boat deck, in a style that your partner, or skipper, may not appreciate. So it's a good idea to submerge such large-scaled fish in a bucket or sink while you scrape. Smaller scales, like those on trout, pollack and pouting, come off in a sort of scaly slime; you can descale them on a board and simply wipe the accumulated gunk away as you go.

Ideally you should descale your fish when it's whole. Descaling a fillet without bruising it is tricky; even descaling a gutted fish isn't as easy as one that has its belly intact. The fresher and wetter the fish, the easier it is to descale. If a fish has been in the fridge for a day or two, the mucus tends to dry, and can glue the scales together. (You can try re-wetting it, but it doesn't always work.)

Fish scales on your tongue are like toast crumbs in bed. They might not look like much, but they feel *huge*. So, before you bake or fry any fish or fillet with the skin on, always inspect it for rogue scales and eliminate any that you find.

When not to descale

It can be hard to remember which fish need descaling and which don't. Flatfish are particularly confusing – most do, but turbot and flounder don't; some, such as lemon sole, need descaling on the top skin, but not underneath. If you're not sure whether the fish you're about to cook has the kind of scales you need to remove, then test a small area around its tail – scraping towards the head, remember. If noticeable scales come away, you will need to remove them from all over the fish. If nothing much is dislodged, descaling won't be necessary.

Obviously you needn't worry about descaling a fish if you have no intention of eating its skin. In fact, if you plan to skin a fillet anyway (see page 73) it is easiest to do this with the scales on – their extra resistance will help prevent accidentally slicing through the skin. (On the other hand, if you descale and then skin a thick-skinned fish such as salmon or bass, you'll be ready to try our lovely recipe for Deep-fried fish skins on page 382.) Incidentally, any coarse-scaled fish that you're planning to fillet and skin – bass and bream in particular – should at least be descaled over the dorsal area, even if you leave the scales on over the flanks. Otherwise the heavy scales will deflect and divert the edge of the knife as you attempt the first cut.

Ready-cut fillets from a fish counter will not always have been descaled – you will need to check them before cooking. If they haven't, your best option is probably to skin them – it will be too fiddly to descale them, and you risk bruising the flesh. Fillets, cutlets and tranches that are to be added to fish soups or stews, skin on, should always be descaled, otherwise you'll end up with loose scales peppering the dish.

Here are some other occasions when we may decide not to descale a fish: if it's being barbecued, leaving the scales on will help protect its flesh from the searing heat of the coals. But it's a trade-off, as you won't be able to eat the skin. We always leave the scales on if we are baking a whole fish – usually a bass or bream – in a salt crust (see page 226), or a saltdough crust (see page 225).

The scales prevent too much salt leaching into the flesh, and again help keep the flesh tender and moist. Finally, if we know our pollack or pouting fillets are destined for the cold smoker, we'll usually leave the scales on, as we're exceedingly unlikely to want to eat the skin after the fish has been smoked.

SO THE GENERAL RULES ARE:

Keep the scales **ON** if you want to take the skin **OFF**.

Keep the scales **ON** if you intend to barbecue your fish or bake it in a salt crust. Take the scales **OFF** in all other circumstances, *especially* if you want to eat the fish skin.

Gutting fish

The belly of a fish contains not only its vital organs but also the food it has been eating, in a partially digested state. The spectrum of bacteria present here is diverse, far more so than in the fish's flesh. Even after death, the stomach continues to be active, its enzymes breaking down any food in the gut – a process that also generates heat, aiding and abetting decay. When a fish begins to go off, it is usually from the belly out. So it is good practice to gut a fish as soon as possible after it has been killed.

When we catch a fish, we usually remove its guts within an hour or two of its death – sometimes as soon as it has been bled. A lull in the fishing action is a good opportunity to get a bit of fish prep done. On boating trips, if the day's been busy or we've been a bit lazy, we might simply kill, bleed and wash our fish, then keep them on ice until the end of the day. Then, on the ride back into port, we'll get busy gutting, descaling and sometimes, with big pollack and the like, even filleting our fish. After a day or even half a day's fishing, when you finally get back home fatigue descends in an instant. To have your fish all ready for cooking will save time, effort and even injury.

If you prep fish on the boat or the beach, the guts can be thrown back into the sea, where they will be eaten by crabs, molluscs and dogfish, provided the seagulls don't get them first. But one thing we generally don't discard is the roes of our fish, as long as they are reasonably substantial. They can be fried up fresh or, from fish such as pollack and ling, salted and smoked. From certain species, including turbot and brill, the livers also make a nice little treat, fried and served on toast.

In many commercial fisheries it is standard practice to gut fish on board the boat on which they are landed, then pack them with plenty of ice in fish boxes, ready to be transported from the quay as soon as the boat arrives. But on certain types of boat the fish may be sorted and iced without being gutted first. This isn't necessarily *bad* practice. If a freshly killed fish goes straight on to ice, even with the guts in, the onset of decay will still be arrested. And provided the fish is kept at a temperature of around 0–2°C, it will remain in good condition for several days.

So when you see a fish on the fishmonger's slab that has not yet been gutted, it is not necessarily more likely to be off than a fish that has been gutted. But it should perhaps strike a note of mild caution. If the fishmonger tells you it's just come in that morning, and it has the sheen, firmness and brightness of eye to make that claim credible, then go for it. If it looks 'borderline', then its unguttedness is definitely a point against it.

Gutting round fish

The gutting process is pretty simple. All round fish, eels and dogfish have a clearly visible anal vent (yes, it's the fish's bumhole). This is where you should start your cut, ideally with a short, sharp knife. Lay the fish on a board (preferably covered with a few sheets of newspaper to prevent slipping), tail towards you, head pointing away.

Hold the fish with one hand – keep it lying flat on its side with the anal vent facing you – and the knife in the other. Insert the tip of the blade into the vent. Gently slice the blade through the belly flesh, moving from the vent along the belly of the fish in a straight line to its 'throat', to within a centimetre or so of where the gill slits meet. The cut doesn't need to be deep; just enough to split the belly flesh without slashing the innards.

The guts usually start to tumble out straight away, but you'll need to put your hand inside the belly to get them all out. There's no point in doing this gingerly. Everything that looks as if it could easily be pulled out, should be pulled out. Sometimes, particularly on larger fish, the gullet (the fleshy tube that leads from the throat to the stomach) is too strong and too firmly attached to come away with a simple tug. Don't force it or you may tear the fish. Use the knife to cut it out as close as possible to the back of the fish's mouth.

Inside the empty cavity of some fish (especially oily fish), you will find a deposit of black gooey stuff running along below the backbone, covered by a thin membrane. This blood-rich substance functions as the fish's kidney. Though it's perfectly benign, it's best removed, as it can accelerate spoilage and may taint the flavour of the fish. Simply slice the membrane with the tip of a knife and then scrape along the underside of the spine with your thumbnail or the handle of a spoon to remove the black gunk – perfectionists have been known to scrub it out with an old toothbrush. However you do it, working under a cold running tap will make it easier.

After a quick all-over rinse with cold water, dry both inside and outside the fish with a tea towel. Then your fish is ready to cook – or, if you're not ready to cook it, to be put back on ice, or in the fridge, or bagged for the freezer.

Once you gain confidence in handling fish, you can dispense with the board. Fish of less than a couple of kilos can easily be held belly up in one hand with a thumb in the gills to hold it steady. Then you can cut the belly from vent to throat with a knife held in the other hand, putting the knife down to free the same hand to remove the guts. Working like this you can gut a dozen mackerel, for example, in a matter of minutes.

Gutting flatfish

One of the reasons cooks love flatfish is that both flanks of flesh (upper and lower) sit on top of each other without much of a belly cavity in between. They're just pure meat – four nice fillets neatly separated by the fish's skeleton. The belly cavity of a flatfish doesn't run half the length of its body or more, as it does with a round fish. Instead it's in the 'throat' area, just below the head on one side. A quick prod with your fingers will determine where the soft innards stop and where the firm muscle flesh begins.

To gut a flatfish, stab it at the top of the soft belly area immediately below the pectoral fin and make one cut in a semicircle, following the outer contour of the gut cavity (as shown below). You only need to cut enough of a flap to get your fingers inside and pull out whatever comes away – it's usually quite a lot less than a round fish of similar size.

With most flatties, we like to leave the liver and any roe inside the cavity and cook them along with the fish, but if that doesn't bake your cake, you can remove and discard them, or give them to your cat or dog. As ever, a final rinse under a cold tap and a good wipe dry are in order.

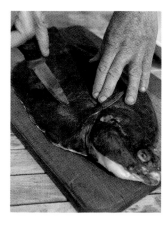  

out of the way it's easier to judge your first vital cut into the body. To minimise wastage, remove the head by cutting in a diagonal line from just behind the gill plate on the 'crown' of the fish (imagine where a fish king would wear his crown) to the tail side of the pectoral fin. If the fish is not too big, and your knife is a good, sharp one, you should be able to slice right through the fish flesh with a couple of sawing motions, right down through the spine, through the flesh and skin on the other side, until the blade reaches the chopping board. Then the head should come off with the 'bib front' of the fish – the fleshy bit at the head end of the belly to which the pectoral fins are attached. There's not much meat on this – except on really large fish – and the head, removed in this way, is ready for the stockpot.

If you're working on a big fish and the head end of the spine is too tough to cut through with a filleting knife, simply cut through the flesh, as above, until the edge of the knife is stopped by the spine. Then put down your filleting knife, pick up a hefty chopping knife or cleaver and place it in the cut so it rests on the spine, at a clean right angle to it. Now tap it firmly with a rolling pin to chop clean through the bone. Then pick up your filleting knife again and finish slicing through the flesh and skin on the other side of the spine.

With big (3kg-plus) white fish, particularly pollack, we'll often keep the head for roasting. When we know we are going to do this, we deliberately leave the head 'long' by cutting a few centimetres or so back towards the tail. This gives us some extra 'shoulder meat' for our lovely roast (see page 380).

FILLETING THE HEADLESS BODY There's a nice image to bear in mind when slicing fillets off the backbone of a fish. Imagine your two hands, held flat together as if in prayer, and a pair of combs, back to back, sandwiched between them. Each hand is a fillet, and the combs are the backbone. You need to slide your knife between the two hands – first one side of the combs, then the other. Start by laying your praying hands flat on a board. Your cuts will all be 'splitting' the hands, and so need to be made parallel to the board and, to minimise wastage, as close as possible to the combs.

Now, let's leave the hands-with-combs metaphor and resume business with our headless fish. With the tail pointing directly towards you, hold the knife parallel to the worktop and bring its edge to the point where the cut flesh of the head(less) end meets the skin, just above the backbone (it's the 'top corner' of your fish). Make your first cut with the edge of the blade, from the head(less) end along the entire back of the fish, passing just above the dorsal fin, in one long, controlled cut towards the tail. This first cut needn't be deep – one or two centimetres into the flesh is enough. It's really just a guide for your second (or third) cut, with which you should aim to locate, with the edge of your blade, those spiny bones that fan out from the central vertebrae towards the fish's dorsal fin (the teeth of your comb). At all times, aim for clean strokes of the knife, from head towards the tail, and avoid sawing the blade back and forth, which may tear the flesh and make it ragged.

Once you've located this line of bones, you're in the home strait, as you can allow them to guide your blade (as in picture four of the sequence), lifting the fillet as you release it from the bones. Some people like to angle their knives to use the tip more than the blade, to 'tick-tick-tick' along the bones as they go. Others are happy to go on cutting with the leading edge, drawing it lengthways through the fish.

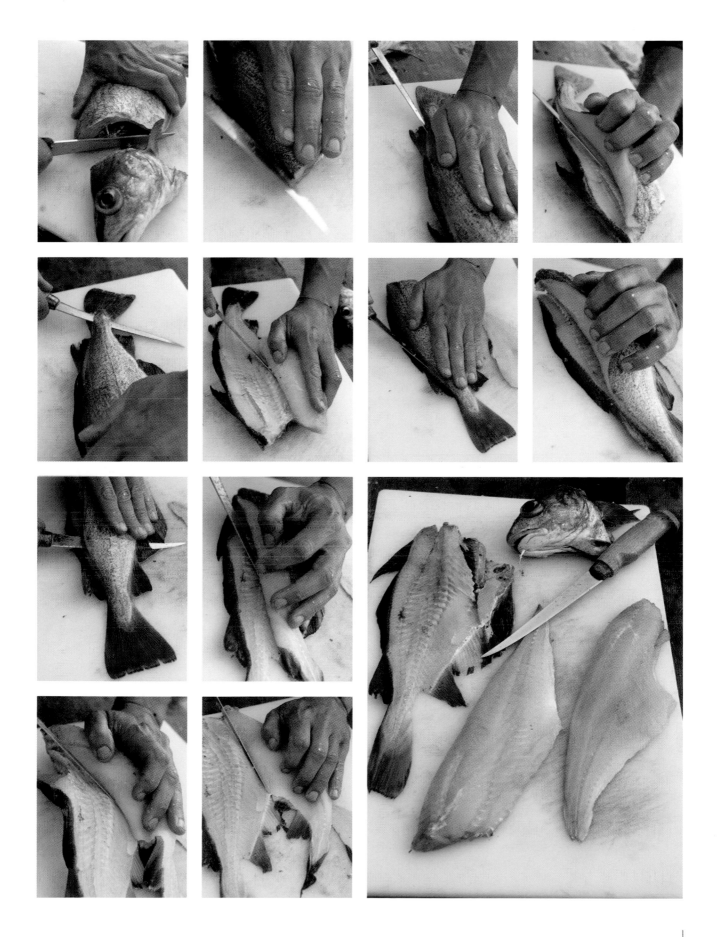

Either way, you should aim to slice tidily along the spiny bones (the teeth of the 'comb') until you get to the central bone (the back of the 'comb'). Here is where the 'ribs' that support the belly cavity start, arcing out around the belly of the fish. Leave them for a moment.

RELEASING THE TAIL FILLET You have just released the thick, dorsal part of the fillet. Now sort out the tail end. For this part of the fillet, it's almost as if you are reverting to bait-cutter style filleting (see pages 62–3) – but instead of starting right at the head, you are starting two-thirds of the way down the fish. Insert the point of the knife at a right angle to the backbone of the fish – just past the tail end of the belly cavity. Your aim is to push the point right through the flank sideways, impaling it, while passing as close as possible to the backbone, exiting somewhere around the anal vent.

The blade should end up resting across, and at a right angle to, the spine, with the meaty flank above the blade. Now cut towards the tail, scraping the blade along the spine inside the fish by tilting the leading edge down, and finishing when the blade cuts through the base (or 'wrist', as it is known) of the tail (see picture five).

THE FINAL CUTS INTO THE BELLY CAVITY The tail end of your first fillet is now free, along with everything above the central backbone. To finish off the head end around the belly cavity, essentially you have two choices.

The first option, which we tend to go for on larger fish, is to slice right through the ribs into the belly cavity so that the ribs and the flesh connecting them become part of the fillet rather than remaining on the carcass. It's better for big fish because it avoids wastage – there's really quite a lot of flesh around those ribs. To take this option, slice through the ribs all along the edge at which they join the backbone, aiming the blade directly into the top of the belly cavity. Once you've sliced through every rib, your first fillet – from head to tail – should be released. If you have not quite made a clean cut, or not quite reached the beginning of your tail cut, then there may be a point or two at which the fillet is still attached to the carcass. Just slice through any such points as cleanly as you can to release the fish.

The second choice – and the one we've shown in the picture sequence – is to guide your knife around the 'ribcage'/belly cavity instead of slicing through the bones. So, use the tip of your knife to make a series of delicate slashes guided by the ribs, releasing a few millimetres of the fillet with each cut (see picture six). When you reach the end of the ribs, simply slice away the fillet, cutting through the skin. The upside of this method is that you'll get very tidy and, with luck, completely boneless fillets. The downside is that there'll be some wastage on the carcass, but on smaller fish this isn't too much of an issue. The fillet's loss is the stockpot's gain.

THE SECOND FILLET – TAIL FIRST Your first cut on the second fillet should be the same as on the first fillet, except from tail to head instead of head to tail. So, as well as turning the fish over, rotate it 180° so that the head end is pointing towards you. Make your first cut from the tail end, along the back on the upper side of the dorsal fin, all the way to the headless shoulder. Again, a cautious centimetre or two is all that's required for the first couple of cuts, until you find those handy spine bones that can guide your knife down to the central backbone.

Detach the tail end of the fillet in much the same way as before – by skewering the knife through the fish, from back to belly, two-thirds of the way to the tail. Slice it off, keeping the knife scraping close to the bone.

Now lift as much of the fillet as you've already released to get access to those meddlesome ribs. What happens next depends on whether you've chosen to slice through, or work round, the ribcage. Either way, proceed as per the first fillet.

Finally, take a proud look at your two fillets. If their belly edges are a little ragged, give them a trim. Take a look at the remaining skeleton too: has it got anything still on it that's worth whittling off? A miniature fillet worthy of the pan or the sashimi plate?

Removing pin bones from fillets

A fillet of fish – whether it's one that you have prepared yourself or one the fishmonger has cut for you, and whether it is from a tiny little mackerel or a hulking great ling – may well contain pin bones, and you may well wish to deal with them (if the fillets are to be smoked, you can deal with them afterwards). These sharp little bones stick out sideways from the spine of the fish, so you'll find them buried in a line down the centre of the fillet, with blunt ends pointing towards you and sharp ends pointing down towards the fish skin. In big fish, pin bones can be matchstick-thick; in small ones they can be almost as fine as hairs. Either way, they are easy to remove.

To locate these tiny pin bones, run your fingertips lightly down the middle of the fish fillet from the head end to the tail end. You will feel the tips of the bones, and the movement of your fingers should pull them up towards the surface. Working methodically down the fillet, grasp the end of each bone with a pair of pin-bone pliers (see below) or stout tweezers, reserved for the purpose, and pull firmly upwards to remove it.

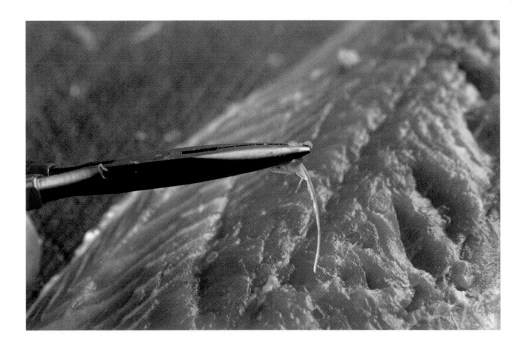

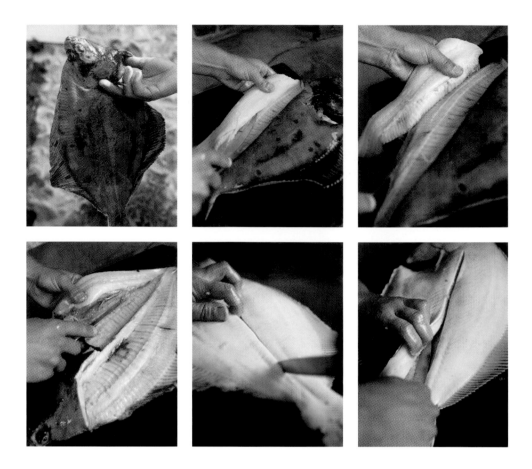

Filleting flatfish

Flatfish have two distinct sides. The upper side is camouflaged to resemble the seabed, while the lower side is virgin white. Traditionally, the white side was the 'posher' side, and some fishmongers would even charge extra for white-side fillets. We prefer the dark-side fillet, though, because it's thicker, and we're greedy.

You might imagine that flatfish are more difficult to fillet than round fish, but they're not. In fact, their generously wide skeletons will guide your filleting knife even more co-operatively. The key thing is that you are aiming not for two fillets but for four – one from each 'quarter' of the fish, or two from each side.

Take the upper, dark-side fillets off first. It's easier to tackle them because the fish will lie more naturally on its undercarriage. The fish should be gutted first if this hasn't already been done (see page 59) and, in the case of some species, descaled if you plan to cook and eat the skin (see the descale/tail test on page 56). The head can be removed before filleting if preferred, though if left on (as in this sequence) it remains conveniently attached to the skeleton for the stockpot.

THE MAIN CUTS Point the head away from you. Your first filleting cut should run from the middle just below the head, straight down through the middle of the fish to the centre of the tail. You should aim to cut all the way through the upper flesh to the bone, and with a bit of luck you'll be cutting right down the central backbone ridge of the skeleton. You're unlikely to miss it by more than a millimetre or two. From here, the spiky bones that will guide your knife radiate out to the edges of the fish.

Now you need to decide whether to take the left-hand quarter-fillet off first, or the right-hand one (left is easier for right-handers and vice versa). Slide the tip of your flexible filleting knife under the flesh on the side you've chosen, cutting sideways with the blade laying flat against the bones. Slice a couple of centimetres at a time, until you can peel back a portion of the fillet and so make it easier to work your blade deeper under the fillet, while skimming over those bones. Keep sliding the blade under the quarter-fillet from head to tail until it reaches the inside edge of the frill of fins that surrounds the fish, cutting until the point breaks through the skin.

Then peel the first quarter-fillet away from the seam along the fin, by gently tugging and cutting at the same time. Don't worry if some of the frill comes away too; fillets can always be tidied up later. Detach the other dark-side quarter-fillet in exactly the same way.

Now flip the fish over and repeat the technique on the other side, to give you two white-sided fillets. Sometimes you'll find a comet-trail-shaped lump of roe inside the gut cavity. This will usually stay attached to one of the white-side fillets; it makes a tasty little morsel when fried along with the fillet. You are now left with four fillets and a fish frame with the head attached for the stockpot.

Flatfish fillets prepared in this way do not usually have any pin bones.

Descalers

These come in a variety of shapes and sizes, including fish-shaped ones, which look terribly stylish, and plastic-handled utilitarian ones, which don't. Our favourite is a cheap and cheerful design that looks a bit like a doll-sized tennis racquet without strings. It has a plastic handle and a metal bow-shaped 'blade', with one jagged, almost saw-toothed, edge and one smooth one. Fish with small scales will need attention only from the smooth edge, while fish with big scales can be given a rough pass with the jagged edge, followed by a smooth pass with the flipside. If you expect to be descaling a lot of bass and bream, then (apart from the fact that we'd like to come fishing with you) we would particularly recommend one of these, as the long handle keeps your fingers clear of the fish and its wicked spines. They cost less than a fiver from tackle shops, so it's best to buy two: one for the kitchen, the other for taking out fishing.

For the thriftily minded, an effective scaler can easily be improvised, or made at home. A discarded scallop shell does the job pretty well. Even better is a small block of wood that you can hold in one hand, with a few tacks or short nails banged into it, the heads left a few millimetres proud of the wood. But our favourite homemade version by far – based on a 'design' popular in the tropics – is the beer-bottle-top descaler. Not only is it a very satisfactory bit of recycling but it also works brilliantly. How you make one should be self-explanatory from the picture on page 55.

Pin-bone pliers

Properly designed pin-bone pliers, sold through catering outlets, can easily cost the best part of £20, which really hurts – especially as an ordinary pair of thin-nosed pliers can be bought from a hardware shop for a fraction of that. The sensible option might appear to be to buy the cheap alternative. But workshop pliers don't do the job nearly so well, for one simple reason: the handles aren't sprung, like they are on proper pin-bone pliers.

Pin boning is a tactile affair that calls for a fair amount of dexterity (see page 67). You're using the fingertips of one hand to feel the fillet and locate the pin bones, while the other hand controls the pliers. With fishmonger's pliers, you simply release the pressure after pulling out the offending bone and they'll spring open, letting the plucked bone fall from their jaws; whereas workshop pliers don't spring open, so you need to use both hands to open them and drop each bone. This means you lose your place on the fillet and have to search again for the line of pin bones. With the wrong tool it's a job that can quickly turn sticky and frustrating – and correspondingly sweary.

Pin boning should be a rhythmic task: locate, grab, pull, release; locate, grab, pull, release… The more rhythm you can establish, the better you'll do the job and the more you'll enjoy doing it.

Some consolation for the price you'll have to pay is that real pin-bone pliers have other uses too; they're perfect when you're plucking poultry and game birds, to pinch out the last few stubborn feathers, and for removing tail and wing feather stumps. Made of stainless steel and dishwasher proof, pin-bone pliers are the perfect present for a fish-loving cook (hint, hint).

Chilling and storing

As soon as a fish is dead, the onset of decay will be a direct function of time and temperature. As fish are cold-blooded, and generally live in a cool environment, the spectrum of microbes and bacteria that naturally inhabit them are active at relatively low temperatures. But while a fish is alive, its organs and cells (the gills, liver, kidneys, blood etc) regulate their levels. Once it is dead, these functions rapidly fail. The bugs will have a field day. Those with the potential to multiply, by breaking down and feeding on the flesh of the fish, do particularly well. If the temperature of the fish rises, the microbial activity will also rise. And since these processes are themselves exothermic – they generate heat – the onset of decay in a warming fish is exponential. Oily fish are particularly susceptible. A newly caught mackerel or sardine left lying under a hot sun will be spoiled within a few hours.

Commercial fishermen have long understood the importance of getting fish as cold as possible as soon as possible. The quality, and hence the market price, of their catch depends on it. They know that if they can get the fish down close to 0°C within a couple of hours of catching, and keep it there, then fish that would be spoiled within a couple of days at a mere 6–7°C will last for well over a week. At the same time, they would rather not freeze it if they don't have to. Frozen fish will keep for weeks, even months, but freezing damages the cell structure of the flesh: the water in the cells expands, rupturing them. Later, when the fish is defrosted, its flesh will be wetter and softer – more sponge-like – than it was when fresh. When it is cooked, the taste should be unimpaired but the texture will often disappoint.

Crushed or flaked ice is the magical substance that keeps fish in prime condition, and trawlers the world over carry tonnes of the stuff in their holds. It works so well because it rapidly chills the fish to around 0°C, and holds it there steadily. It is far more effective and economical than giant on-board fridges ever could be. The 'wet' contact means the chilling happens rapidly and evenly, while the way in which the ice can be shovelled around gives the fishermen maximum control. And ice, unlike fridges, cannot break down; it can only melt. Deep in the hold, insulated several feet below the deck, this happens very slowly indeed. That's why, when commercial fishing boats carry their own refrigeration units, they are usually there to make fresh ice rather than to chill and store the catch.

Ice for anglers

Some anglers are rather lackadaisical in their approach to storing the fish they have just caught. They'll leave it on the deck of a boat, or lying on the beach, for several hours after catching it (maybe partially draped with a warm wet rag to 'protect' it from the full glare of the summer sun). Back home, as often as not, they will bung it straight in the freezer – ungutted, unchilled and generally unloved. Should they ever muster the energy to defrost and attempt to cook it, they are surely destined for disappointment. No wonder so many sea anglers leave the fruits of their day's fun on the boat with the charter skipper and pick up a portion of fish and chips on the way home.

In fairness to our anglers, however, they are definitely improving in this area. If you want to catch fish, and you want to eat what you catch, then the sooner

you get an 'ice habit', the better. All the best charter skippers now carry a large icebox on board their boats. But you should take your own icebox, too, pretty much whenever you go fishing. Continuity of the chill is vital to keep your fish in good nick. It's a shame if fish that have been carefully iced all day on the boat are then transferred into a couple of bin bags in the boot of a car, so that they warm up on the drive home.

A good, 'family-sized', plastic picnic cool box is therefore an essential bit of kit for the angler-cook. In a perfect world, you'd fill it one-third full with crushed ice or ice cubes. In this less than perfect world, those blue plastic ice packs that you put in the freezer are fine. Lots of little ones are better than a couple of big ones. Once in a while, you may catch a fish that is so big it won't fit in your cool box (5kg is, we reckon, the upper limit). Frankly, that's a problem to relish, isn't it? You may have to fillet such a fish, or behead it, or betail it, to enable cold storage. Of course, it won't look so impressive when you get it home. So, just in case, make sure you remember your camera as well as your icebox.

Superstitious anglers are convinced that such scout-like preparations will guarantee a lousy day's fishing. But if you take an icebox with you *every single time you go fishing*, you will soon break the jinx.

It's not just the angler-cook who should consider using ice to transport fish back home; sometimes the shopper should, too. If you're going to be buying fish, and you know that it's likely to take an hour or three to get that fish home, then you should take a cold box, or insulated cool bag, plus ice pack, with you to the fishmonger's (or even the supermarket, if that's where you buy your fish).

Fish in the fridge

When you get your fish home, you're obviously going to put it in the fridge. Where else is there? The only drawback is that at somewhere between 5 and 10°C, most domestic fridges aren't cold enough to keep fish at its best. This is not really an issue if you are planning to consume the fish on the same day you have caught/bought it. But if you want to keep it for more than 24 hours, fridge temperature matters. Were you able to store your just-caught pollack at less than 2°C, it would keep for at least five days.

So it's worth getting to know your fridge a bit. You may be organised enough to remember to put it on maximum chill when you're 'expecting' some fish (we're not). Or you may discover that, even on its regular setting, it has a cold spot. (The Fearnley fridge, for example, has been noted for its annoying habit of lightly freezing salad leaves that were pushed too close to the back, on the middle shelf. Clearly the temperature there is close to zero...)

The best way to store whole smaller fish or fish fillets in the fridge is to dry them well, lay them on a plate, then put the plate inside a large plastic bag, which you tuck under the plate, but otherwise leave unsealed. Larger whole fish can be wrapped in a damp tea towel, then loosely in a plastic bag or two.

Smoked fish stored in the fridge should be sealed properly in a bag or cling film, or they'll permeate the whole fridge with their smoky, fishy aroma. Generally, salted, smoked and other cured fish don't thrive in the fridge for too long, unless they are vac-packed, stored in Tupperware, or fully sealed in some other way. Cured fish will dry out more quickly in chilled air, as you'll know if you've ever left a tin of anchovies open in the fridge – they quickly harden as

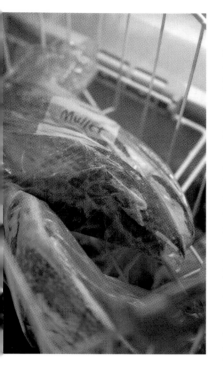

In this context, the natural mucus on very fresh fish is no bad thing. It actually protects the fish while it is frozen. So, when freezing a very fresh whole fish, don't feel the need to wipe away every last trace of its slime. This applies only to fish that have not been descaled, however – that process will already have removed most of the benign gunk. Freezing fish with scales (and some slime) still on is generally not a bad plan – except that you will really struggle to descale a defrosted fish. So if you know you want to end up with a nicely descaled fish, or fillets, then that's what you should put in the freezer.

2. WRAP AND BAG WITH CARE We tend to 'double wrap' most of our fish. A fairly tight binding of cling film acts as a second skin, protecting the first one and the cut surfaces of fillets from both freezer burn and condensing moisture – two or three layers will do the job. We'll then bag the wrapped fish or fillets in strong transparent freezer bags.

Don't freeze fish in carrier bags, bin bags or any other kind of bag that you lugged it home in. It doesn't matter whether you caught the fish yourself or bought it from a supermarket fish counter: you still need to unpack, dry, cling-wrap and re-pack it before freezing.

The thicker the bag, the more protection it provides. If a bag gets ripped by a sharp fin and doesn't seal properly, then air and ice crystals will get inside, causing the flesh to dehydrate. Ideally you should snip off all fins and spines before wrapping and bagging fish for the freezer.

3. DON'T FREEZE LARGE AMOUNTS OF FISH TOGETHER There is so much water within fish flesh that there is always a certain amount of 'expansion' during freezing. If you put a large single pack crammed with lots of fish into the freezer, the exterior layers will freeze first, with the centre of the pack remaining unfrozen for considerably longer. As the fish on the outside freeze and expand, they will begin to crush the unfrozen fish at the centre, and bruise and damage their flesh.

4. FREEZE QUICKLY The quicker you freeze fish, and the colder the temperature that you keep it frozen at, the longer and better it will last. If you remember, set your freezer to 'boost' or 'super-chill' a couple of hours before you put your fish in it. And ideally keep it at least −15°C at all times. Don't pile up a batch of fish to be frozen in the same part of the freezer, as the ones in the middle of the pile will freeze too slowly. Spread the bags around, amongst other items that are already frozen, to speed up the chilling.

5. LABEL, DATE, ROTATE Proper labelling is a pain, especially when you're dog-tired or in a hurry, but it's essential. You might think, 'I don't need to label this, I'll never forget what's in such a distinctive package!' Two months later, someone could beat you repeatedly around the head with the very same package and you still wouldn't have the foggiest idea what was inside. A label stating what's in the bag and when it was frozen may seem a touch obsessive for some, but you'll be glad you took the trouble.

It makes sense to use fish in the same order it went into the freezer. Once you've decided to favour an item that was only recently frozen over one that's been in there for a couple of months, the chances of your coming back to that older fish and doing something good with it are ever-diminishing.

Freezing smoked and salted fish

Both smoked and salted fish freeze, and recover from freezing, extremely well, since much of the water has been removed by these processes. So the damage done by expanding ice crystals is greatly reduced. We often lightly salt pollack fillets (see page 124) before freezing them. But smoked and salted fish still needs to be thoroughly dried and carefully packed before freezing.

Many smokers actually like to work with frozen fish, provided it has been handled and frozen with care. After defrosting, the mild damage to the cellular structure of the fish flesh is partially 'repaired' by the subsequent brining process, as it draws excess moisture from the fish, and the flesh re-contracts somewhat. Nonetheless, the resulting fillets are more open grained, and the smoke will penetrate them more effectively.

Freezing sashimi and sushi fish

Freezing is stipulated by the Food Standards Agency as a part of the preparation of fresh raw fish for commercial sashimi and sushi. Its reason is that freezing kills off any parasites in the fish, making it safer to eat raw. But such safety-conscious behaviour will always be at the expense of that fresh-fish texture. Many UK sushi chefs find the law incomprehensible and infuriating, arguing that raw fish has been served for centuries in Japan without pre-freezing.

We take our lead from the sushi chefs, and don't pre-freeze our raw fish. Our sashimi and sushi are made with super-fresh fish we've caught ourselves, or bought direct from boat or fisherman. We clean it thoroughly and prepare it with great care (see pages 130–2), and to date it's done us nothing but good.

Defrosting

The way you defrost fish has consequences for its eating quality, and the key advice is *don't rush it*. In particular, don't use warm air (i.e. a low oven) or warm water in an attempt to accelerate the process. If you do, the outer layer will defrost and even 'cook' slightly, while other parts of the fish are still frozen solid. Fish flesh is very sensitive to heat and any temperature above 50°C will actually begin to cook the fish. Once your fish is a hotchpotch of frozen/part-frozen/thawed/warm flesh, it's impossible to get it all back to an equitable state.

The two best ways to defrost any fish are to put it in the fridge overnight or to immerse it completely in a large bowl of cold water. If you use the cold water method, which is much faster, you must keep the fish completely sealed inside a plastic bag: don't expose the flesh to the water or it will start to absorb it and become soft and fragile.

The overnight fridge method, though slower, is gentler in terms of limiting collateral damage. The temperature rise from −18°C in the freezer to about 5°C in your fridge will allow the ice to melt and the flesh to thaw gradually. Take the fish out of its bag and place it in a colander inside a larger bowl or on a tray, so that it doesn't marinate in its own melt water and start to absorb it.

Thawing fish naturally at cool room temperature, or outside in a shady place, is acceptable. But avoid direct sunlight, or temperatures much in excess of 15°C, especially for really big fish. They may take several hours to defrost, and the outside of the fish may even start to go off before the centre is defrosted. Always take measures to keep flies (and cats) off your fish while it is defrosting.

Shellfish skills

If you are starting to be swayed by our thesis that handling fish is both fascinating and rewarding (as well as speaking to your inner hunter-gatherer), then be assured that the same is true of shellfish – only several times more so. Compared with fin fish, there is sometimes more work involved in preparing shellfish (think crabs), sometimes less (think mussels). But in all cases, beholding the relevant creature in its entirety (preferably while it is still alive) adds hugely to the sense of occasion. There aren't many creatures that you have an opportunity to meet and greet before you eat.

As the term shellfish implies, we're dealing with marine animals here whose defining characteristic is that they have shells. Summarising the main families, in a not overly taxonomic fashion, we have crustaceans, such as crabs, lobsters and prawns, who tend to have claws and crawl around on a generous number of legs; bivalves, such as mussels, oysters and scallops, with their two-sided castanet-style shells that hide meat of very varying flavour and texture; molluscs, such as winkles and whelks, which are clearly underwater snails; and, out on a limb (quite a few limbs, in fact), the extraordinary squid, cuttlefish and octopus – they do have shells, but they're strictly vestigial.

Another defining characteristic, we would say, is the unusually intense feelings of involvement – physical and even emotional – that are evoked by their consumption. You can't eat a bowl of mussels as you might a bowl of cereal – with casual detachment and your mind on other things. To devour them, you have to engage with them, acknowledging their form and nature. It's a form of heightened awareness that, with luck, will stimulate your appetite and increase your pleasure. But not everyone can handle the stark reality of this carnivorous behaviour (more real to some than eating a fat steak). And we all know someone who says they can't/don't/won't eat shellfish. Some people have a genuine allergic reaction, others merely a physical aversion. But there is no doubt that in many cases, whether it's acknowledged or not, the problem is all in the mind. It's all too visceral, too near the knuckle – or the shell.

This is, of course, exactly what so many of us love about shellfish. There is not much indifference around it. You don't hear people say, 'Oysters, I can take them or leave them.' They either rave or they revile.

Well, we definitely count ourselves among the ravers. And we rave about the preparation of shellfish as well as its consumption. Although it is now possible to have much of the prep work done for you, by a fishmonger or a chef, we feel strongly that if you always take this route you will be missing out. The shucking of scallops, the evisceration of squid, the cracking of crab claws, the peeling of prawns, the picking of winkles – all of these acts will heighten the anticipation and stimulate the appetite for the meal to come.

Often, the benefits of tackling whole live shellfish are practical, too. If you want to eat certain shellfish at their best, you have no choice but to engage with their natural packaging. You can't buy fresh oysters, cockles or mussels without buying the shells they come in. Yes, you can buy a ready dressed crab, and you can buy a whole pre-cooked crab. But they will never come with the same guarantee of freshness as a living creature that is defiantly waving its claws at you even as you contemplate its purchase, its despatch at your hands and its consumption at your table.

Killing and cooking a crab

Most crabs that are sold alive for cooking at home will have had their claws clipped: a membrane between the two pincers is nicked with a blade to render the claws loose and harmless. But if you are in any doubt about this – especially if you happen to be buying a crab straight from a boat – check, and if necessary ask for it to be done. As a fish shopper, it's not worth running even the slightest risk of getting pinched. Having a hand or finger crushed by a crab claw is no laughing matter – it's not just painful, it can be seriously damaging to tissue and even bone. (Should you ever decide to take up casual crab and lobster potting, get a professional to show you how to nick a crab's claws, and bind a lobster's with rubber bands.)

Crabs have a simple nervous system but we still can't be sure they don't feel pain or distress. It is considered humane to kill them quickly before putting them into a pan of boiling water. So have a large pan of well-salted water (about 10g salt per litre) ready on a full rolling boil before you kill the crab. This is most effectively done by driving a sharp spike – a small pointed screwdriver or bradawl, for instance – into one of two points on the crab's body. We always spike both points, belt and braces as it were, to be completely sure the crab is dead before we cook it. So, to kill a crab, proceed as follows:

Lay the crab on its back. The first vital point is revealed by lifting the triangular tail flap in the centre of its undercarriage. Here you'll see a cone-shaped indentation in the shell. Push the spike firmly right into the middle of it and twist it a couple of times (see top picture). This will sever vital tissues in the crab's ventral nerve centre.

Remove your spike and immediately pierce the crab a second time, this time in the head at the top of the carapace: the spike must go in through the mouth, between and below the eyes (see lower picture). Lever the spike backwards and forwards a couple of times to destroy the vital nerve tissues here.

These two moves, in quick succession, will render the crab limp and lifeless in a matter of seconds. You can then lower it gently into your pan of boiling water. One advantage of killing your crabs before boiling them is that they won't usually shed their legs when they go in the boiling water – which they almost always do if you drop them in alive.

After the water returns to the boil, cook crabs weighing up to 1kg for 10–12 minutes; for larger crabs, add 3–4 minutes to the cooking time for every extra 500g. Small crabs such as velvets will take just 5 minutes. Remove your cooked crab(s) from the pan and leave to steam off and cool. If you want to accelerate cooling, take the crab outside into a cool breeze – but for heaven's sake don't dunk it in cold water, or this will seep back into the shell and make the meat wet. With careful cooking and cooling, your home-boiled crab should be better than anything you can buy ready cooked – such crabs are usually batch boiled, dozens at a time, in big kettles, and are often overcooked.

When a boiled crab has cooled off, it is ready to crack, pick and dress – or it can be put in the fridge on a plate (no need to wrap it up). It must then be eaten within 48 hours. The instructions that follow apply to pretty much all crabs, including spiders (page 557) and velvets (page 555). There are minor anatomical differences, variations in scale of course, and in the relative quantities of white and brown meat. But generally the approach, the tools and, most importantly, the sheer tactile joy are transferable across all species.

Picking and dressing a crab

There are two approaches to dressing a crab. One is the 'eat as you go' method, in which your guests are supplied with various hammers, crackers and picks, along with buttered bread, mayonnaise and a salad or two – plus wine, of course. It's a lively affair, as claws are cracked, legs pulled and nuggets of meat teased from the shell. Everything gets eaten as it is picked (see page 351 for our serving suggestions).

Then there's the 'hoarding' approach, in which an individual or team of pickers sets out to extract and save every last morsel of white or brown meat (separate bowls laid out for each) for use in some recipe, hot or cold, simple or sophisticated. Undertaken solo, this can be an almost transcendental experience, in which the picker is transported into a crab trance, cracking, picking, twisting and scooping until all that remains is an empty carapace, the hollow tubes of leg sections, and fragments of claw shell, like broken china, orange-brown on the outside, clean white on the inside. But it is also a pleasant pastime to engage in over a glass or two with a fishing buddy, or even a spouse (not that the two are mutually exclusive). There's no question that women are better – more thorough, more patient – at crab picking than men. (Or at least Marie is much better at it than Hugh, and it consoles him to generalise the point. If there is any rule here, Nick claims vociferously that he and Helen are the exceptions.)

Whether the kind of gratification you are aiming for is instant or delayed, a certain amount of method will serve you in good stead. To tackle a whole crab, you should first take off its legs and claws. Twist the legs off at the point where they meet the body, rather than just yanking them, and try to remove the articulated socket that they sit in too. By pulling this out, you'll expose hidden pathways to the Holy Grail of white crabmeat within the body.

When the legs and claws are off, you need to open up the crab by pulling the undercarriage (or 'body shell') away from the hard-topped carapace (or 'head shell'), as shown in the picture on the left. We find the easiest way to do this is to press your thumb into the mouth, just beneath the eyes, and prise the body apart from the front end. So, using the flat of your thumb protected against the sharp shell with a scrap of cloth, or the bowl of a teaspoon, crush the mouthparts and mandibles under the eyes back against the inside of the shell. This gives you an opening into which you can insert two thumbs, while holding the carapace and undercarriage with the spread fingers of each hand. Pull the two thumbs apart from each other, levering the carapace and body apart.

Now's a good time to identify the very few parts of the crab that you cannot eat. First, look at the carapace. The only bits you need to discard, apart from the shell itself, are the mandibles – the spiny, plastic-looking bits behind the eyes and around the mouthparts – and the small, yellow-white papery sac that attaches to them, which is the crab's stomach. What remains is the brown meat (see picture five of the sequence) – the rich, creamy, brown, orange and yellow goo, which is basically the crab's internal organs. Some of the brown meat is firmly set, even moulded to the contours of the shell; but some is quite soft, even semi-liquid. It may look weird but it's all good stuff, and can be scooped out of the carapace with a dessertspoon, either for instant gratification or, if you're a 'hoarder', to put in your dedicated 'brown meat' bowl. The only other thing to look out for, and discard, is a fine papery-white membrane that sometimes clings to the edges of the brown meat.

2. Fish cookery

A good piece of fresh fish, lightly seasoned, simply and accurately cooked, with perhaps just a few drops of lemon juice, will never be dull. That's the central message of this chapter. And although we are about to embark on an examination of the various methods by which a fish may be cooked, and look at the vast array of accompanying ingredients than can increase the pleasure of eating it, at the heart of pretty much all our recipes is a simple formula: some great seasonal ingredients on or around a lovely fresh piece of fish.

Some of the recipes in the chapters that follow may appear elaborate. But even if they look long, it doesn't mean they are hard. We tend to write long, dealing with the whys as well as the hows and anticipating questions, so that provided you don't mind tackling a little more of our prose, you should be well served to approach brand new recipes with the confidence of an old hand. But we certainly don't wish to bamboozle and confuse you. So first we'll deal very clearly with the basics here.

There's one point that needs making good and early: cooking fish is easy. Some people have a problem believing that, and seem to think that fish is an ingredient designed to catch them out and expose their shortcomings in the kitchen. Such anxieties can be borne of real experiences: poached or baked fish that turns out mushy or tasteless; barbecued fish that is burned on the outside but raw in the middle; fish that just doesn't taste *right*; and let's not forget rubbery squid. Such pitfalls exist, and experiencing them can sap confidence, but we have some suggestions that might help you to avoid these mistakes.

Raw, salted and marinated fish

Once you've got some bouncingly fresh fish in front of you – whether acquired by skilful fishing or clever shopping – one of the first questions you may want to ask yourself is, 'Am I going to eat this raw?' Taking the word 'raw' in a broad and flexible sense, there is an intriguing and exciting range of ways to answer, 'Yes'.

Your decision on whether to go the raw route will depend on many things: the type of fish you have, your mood, the weather, where you are and who's coming to dinner. Or, more practically, whether you have ready access to a bottle of soy sauce and some searingly hot wasabi (or hot English mustard – see page 130). If you decide that on this occasion you want to apply heat to the fish, then we hope you'll find inspiration elsewhere in this book. But assuming raw, or nearly raw, does take your fancy, we'll explore the possibilities here.

The raw approach

The first honourable mention should probably go to the oyster – perhaps the only item on the seafood menu for which, almost wherever you are in the world, the default setting for its preparation and consumption is raw, live, unadorned, straight from the shell. Sure, a squeeze of lemon is nice, and other embellishments – Tabasco, shallot vinegar, black pepper – are favoured by some enthusiasts, but an oyster with nothing but the briny juices of its own shell is by no means incomplete. It proves, if proof were needed, that eating seafood raw is not some folly or foible but a possibility to be taken seriously with any number of marine species – be they bivalves, crustaceans, cephalopods or fish.

When it comes to eating raw fish, some kind of seasoning undoubtedly enhances the experience. And none have come up with a better formula than the Japanese, in the form of sashimi, their purist raw fish creation. Sashimi is just neatly cut morsels of fish flesh, accompanied by two classic seasonings – wasabi and soy sauce. These are applied at the last possible moment, so there is no penetration, or marinating, of the fish. The flavours combine in the mouth as you chew the raw fish and the whole experience can be very stimulating. Paper-thin slices of pickled ginger are usually offered too, to clean the palate between mouthfuls. They literally wipe the taste slate clean, so you can start afresh with the next piece of raw fish.

Add sticky, vinegar-seasoned rice to the recipe and you find yourself in the realms of sushi. This has been one of the great cultural colonisers of the global food scene over the last twenty years – and quite rightly. At its best, it's a really outstanding way to enjoy good fish. At its worst – like so many attempts to cash in on a food phenomenon – it's awful. The only conceivable appeal of cheap smoked salmon and extruded 'ocean sticks' pressed on to lumps of fridge-cold rice must be its three-day shelf life. It really should be illegal to call that stuff sushi.

Not that we're sushi snobs. Some purists might cast aspersions on 'amateur' attempts to make sushi at home. Not us. We take the view that if you regularly catch your own fish, especially sea fish, you'd be mad not to. Fishing gives you access to fish that a master sushi chef would kill for. And simply being a good fish shopper also qualifies you to have a go – more so than any skills you may have with the filleting knife – because raw fish is all about choosing the right fish. The rest – provided you don't get stressed out by the quest for geometrical perfection in your presentation – is easy. See pages 130–7 for a relaxed River Cottage approach to sashimi and sushi preparation.

and ackee, or a Boston salt cod dinner. No wonder this robust and versatile source of protein has stood the human race in good stead for so long. It's indestructible – and you can't say that about many foods.

Salting fish at home

Both at home and in the River Cottage kitchen, we have co-opted this traditional technique and we now do a lot of salting. There are three slightly different approaches we use, and they all aim for a different effect.

Sometimes we want to preserve fish indefinitely, by salting it right down to that state of weatherproof, leathery desiccation. We do this when we have a surfeit of white fish (mainly pollack) to deal with – but it's not merely a matter of being frugal; we could use the freezer for that. As with all preserved food, salted fish has its own unique qualities. Even when soaked and restored to palatability, it doesn't 'become fresh' again. It has its own character – a denser, more resistant texture and greater depth of flavour, quite different from that of fresh fish – that has spawned a whole range of recipes. It holds its own in robust, spicy stews, and lends its distinctive tang to starchy staples such as rice and potatoes.

As well as this full-on salting and drying, which actually preserves the fish, we use a medium- or semi-salting technique, which cures and preserves fish for a short period (i.e. a couple of weeks), after which it can be eaten without the need to soak and/or cook it further. We're in the realms of gravad lax here, and indeed Gravad max (page 142) – our mackerel-based adaptation of the classic Scandinavian cured salmon.

We also use a very light salting process on fresh fish that's to be eaten straight away. This is more about modifying the eating qualities of a piece of fish than preserving it. It works wonders with very soft-textured white fish, and is a good way to 'restore' fillets of such fish if they have been frozen.

An outline of our basic fish-salting procedures follows, in ascending order of saltiness. In all cases, we're talking about fillets rather than whole fish. Whole fish can be salted and dried too, scales on and skeletons in, and in some parts of the world this is the standard approach. But salting fillets suits us much better, as they are easier to handle and to reconstitute through soaking, and ultimately easier to cook with. Moreover, if we do the filleting ourselves, we have the bonus of fresh heads and skeletons with which to make stock (see pages 252–3).

LIGHT SALTING OF POLLACK (AND OTHER MEMBERS OF THE COD FAMILY) When you start to experiment, as every ecologically minded fish shopper should, with alternatives to cod – pollack, pouting and whiting in particular – you will find their flesh is tender and delicate. When they are super-fresh, this is undoubtedly a virtue. But once they are a day or two old, though in no sense 'off', that delicacy is in danger of being interpreted as mushiness. Here's where a quick, light salting of a whole fillet serves as an excellent remedy to revive the eating qualities of the fish.

The idea here is not to preserve the fish for any significant length of time – though a lightly salted fillet will keep for a couple of days longer than a fresh one – but to draw out a little of the moisture and firm up the texture. White fish from the cod family, including pollack, ling, pouting and whiting, can all benefit enormously from a light salting before you cook them. As the salt extracts water

from the flesh, it condenses and concentrates it, lightly seasoning it at the same time. Once this is done, the fillet can be cooked as normal – floured, crumbed or battered, shallow or deep fried, or dropped into a simmering sauce or stew – but the result will be subtly different: firmer, lightly salty (obviously), but also slightly stronger in flavour.

Salt can vary in flavour from sea-breeze sweet to fiercely caustic. Your choice will have an effect on the taste of the fish, so it is important to use a good one. For light salting, you should go for a high-quality sea salt and choose coarse crystals or flakes. These will leach water away less aggressively than fine salt and are easy to rinse off the fish when the salting time is up.

It is very important not to over-salt fresh fish that you plan to consume immediately after salting, or you'll end up with a tough and unpalatably salty result. You'll need to soak it to make it palatable again. The amount of salt applied and the salting time depend on the size of fish, but always err on the side of caution. With a small, delicate fillet of less than 100g (pouting, for example), use just a sprinkling of salt (say, 2–3 teaspoons) that will cover the fish in a thin, even layer, then rinse it off after a matter of minutes – as few as five. With fatter fillets from bigger fish, use a more generous layer and leave it for longer – up

River Cottage sashimi and sushi

It might not sound very 'Dorset', but we eat a lot of sashimi and sushi. They are, after all, among the best ways to enjoy super-fresh fish, and we usually make them with specimens we've just caught, rather than bought. Our favourites for eating raw are mackerel, pollack, bream and bass – and, once in a while, wild salmon.

In case you were in any doubt, the difference between sashimi and sushi is simple: rice. While our sashimi is often eaten, as described below, on the hoof or on the boat, sushi is more of a sit-down affair – though some pre-made sushi rice can be taken aboard a fishing boat too, for the ultimate in fresh sushi assembly.

There is a degree of mystery associated with sushi, and it is rightly regarded as an art form when prepared by a master. However, it's unreasonable to suggest that only the highly trained professional is allowed to have a go. If you're capable of cutting a neat and skinless fillet from a fresh fish – and cutting it into a few bite-sized morsels – then you can delight your friends and family with a home-made version of this Japanese classic. And if the fish you are slicing and serving is one that you or your friends have caught within the last 24 hours, then there is every chance that you will delight them as much, or more, than any professional.

The accompaniments don't have to be super-exotic either, as you will see…

THE CORNER-SHOP SASHIMI KIT It's commonly thought that the *minimum* accompaniments to sashimi are wasabi, soy sauce and pickled ginger. In fact, only one of these is vital, and that's the soy. The ginger makes a nice palate cleanser between mouthfuls but it's not essential for flavouring the fish itself. The nose-searing, eye-watering wasabi is wonderful, of course, but the same job can be done by a properly peppy hot English mustard. So, if you take a bottle of soy sauce (light and Japanese, not heavy and Chinese – Clearspring and Kikkoman are good brands), and either a tube of wasabi or a jar of hot English mustard (good old Colman's does the trick) on a fishing trip, you are primed for some on-board Japanese raw fish action.

IMPROVISED ON-BOARD SASHIMI We almost always prepare a round or two of sashimi on the boat for our guests on every River Cottage Catch and Cook trip. Just-caught mackerel gets the most frequent outing, followed by pollack, bream and bass. Pollack is perhaps the biggest surprise. We didn't think it would be much of a sashimi fish until one day, in the absence of any alternative, we tried it more or less out of desperation. It was a knockout success.

It takes a calm, methodical approach to prepare a nice plate of sashimi on a moving boat with people fishing all around you, but it's a challenge that we now regard as a pleasure. We have devised a little system, which takes just-caught fish from a state of guts-in, scales-on wholeness to dainty finished sashimi in a few simple steps. It's called 'bucket, dirty board, clean board, plate', and it will serve you just as well in your kitchen as on the deck of a boat.

To expand: gut your fish (see pages 58–9) and rinse thoroughly in a bucket of fresh, clean seawater (or, if at home, under the cold tap in the sink). Discard the water and refill the bucket with more clean seawater. Wipe the fish with a clean cloth and put it on the 'dirty board' – it doesn't have to be dirty, of course, and should not be caked with fish guts, but it does not have to be pristine either. It's just the regular fish-prep or bait-cutting board that lives on the boat. A few sheets of wet newspaper over the board are no bad thing.

Salmon tartare *serves 4 as a starter*

You're probably familiar with the classic steak tartare, where finely chopped beef is combined with a range of piquant flavourings and eaten raw. You can do a very similar thing with spanking-fresh raw salmon – with excellent results. Raw salmon has a good, firm texture and eats best when cut fairly coarsely, in contrast to the almost minced texture of steak tartare.

Also works with:
• Sea trout
• Mackerel
• Scad

400g boneless, skinless organic farmed (or self-caught wild) salmon, cut into thumbnail-sized cubes
Juice of 1 lemon
A few shakes of Worcestershire sauce
A few scant shakes of Tabasco sauce

2 teaspoons finely chopped parsley
2 teaspoons finely chopped capers
2 teaspoons finely chopped gherkin
2 teaspoons very finely chopped red onion
Salt and freshly ground black pepper

Put the salmon in a large mixing bowl and squeeze over the lemon juice, followed by the Worcestershire sauce and Tabasco. Season with salt and pepper. Gently fold in the parsley, capers, gherkin and onion. Leave the mixture to stand for 10 minutes before serving, so the flavours get a chance to develop. Then mix again, leave to rest for another 10 minutes, and serve. Eat with buttered toast (granary or rye is best).

Brandade *serves 4 as a main course, 8 as a starter*

Brandade is a traditional Provençal dish, and a very rich and comforting one. The combination of buttery mash, salty fish and plenty of garlic really hits the spot. It's a versatile creation, too. You can serve it as a main course, accompanied by a crisp winter salad or braised greens, or turn it into a starter or snack, spreading it on slices of wholemeal toast. In fact, served in even smaller portions, it makes a lovely and very easy canapé. We also sometimes make it with smoked fish, poaching the fillet in milk until tender, then using some of the fishy, smoky milk in the mash.

250g hard-salted white fish (see page 127), such as pollack, ling, haddock, whiting or cod
500g floury potatoes, peeled and cut into chunks
25g unsalted butter

About 50ml hot milk
4–6 tablespoons olive oil
2–3 large garlic cloves, finely chopped
1–2 tablespoons double cream (optional)
Freshly ground black pepper

Soak the fish in cold water for 48 hours, changing the water at least twice a day.

Put the soaked fish in a pan, cover with fresh water and bring to a simmer. Cook gently for 10–15 minutes, until tender, then drain. Pick over the fish, discarding the skin and any bones, and break the flesh into flakes.

Boil the potatoes in lightly salted water until tender, then drain. Mash them thoroughly with the butter and hot milk to get a soft but not sloppy mash.

Heat 2–3 tablespoons of olive oil in a small pan over a low heat. Add the garlic and sweat gently in the oil for 2–3 minutes, without letting it colour.

Put the flaked fish in a food processor and pulse several times, trickling in the warm garlic and olive oil as you do so (or, more traditionally, pound everything together in a large pestle and mortar). Then add another 2–3 tablespoons olive oil, and the double cream (if you're feeling really greedy), and pulse/pound again. Transfer the puréed fish mixture to a large bowl and combine with the mashed potato, beating thoroughly so they are well mixed together (don't at any point process the potatoes in a machine, as it makes them gluey and spoils the dish). Season to taste with black pepper – you probably won't need any salt.

To heat before serving, spread the brandade in an ovenproof dish and bake for 15–20 minutes in a fairly hot oven (190°C/Gas Mark 5), until piping hot.

VARIATION

Gill's new potato brandade

This is a sort of deconstructed, summer version of brandade, invented by Gill, our chef at River Cottage, which is very simple and works particularly well with lightly salted fish (see page 124). It's one to improvise, using most or all of the following ingredients.

500g lightly salted, or smoked, white
  fish fillets, such as pollack, ling,
  haddock, whiting or cod
1kg new potatoes, scrubbed
A knob of butter

1–2 tablespoons olive oil
2 garlic cloves, finely chopped
2 tablespoons chopped parsley and/or
  chives
Freshly ground black pepper

Poach the lightly salted fish fillets in simmering water for 3–5 minutes, just until cooked (alternatively, use rehydrated hard-salted fish, prepared and cooked as above). Drain, leave to cool, then skin the fish. Break it into flakes, removing any pin bones.

Boil the potatoes in lightly salted water until tender, then drain well.

Heat a good knob of butter and a slug of olive oil in a small pan and gently sweat the chopped garlic in it for a couple of minutes, without browning. Take off the heat and stir in the herbs. Crush the potatoes lightly in a haphazard way with a potato masher or wooden spoon, to form a rough, chunky mash. Combine with the flaked salt fish and the herby, garlicky butter and oil. Season well with black pepper and serve, with a fresh lettuce salad on the side or to follow.

Smoked fish

It seems likely that smoked fish was not so much invented as discovered. It isn't hard to imagine how that might have come about. A good catch. A celebratory gathering of the clan around a roaring fire, over which the fish were grilled and toasted. Much crunching of crisply charred skin, snaffling of tender fish flesh and sucking of sticky, smoky bones. But a few spare fish laid on a stone in the dwindling fire prove to be more than the clan members can manage (even prehistoric eyes could be bigger than stomachs). They doze off, or wander back to their huts or caves to sleep off the feast, as the fish smoulder gently above the embers. The next morning the fish, now tawny gold but somewhat dried and leathery, are still sitting among the cold cinders. Though a little chewy, they turn out to be surprisingly palatable…

Harold McGee, in the ever-fascinating *McGee on Food and Cooking* (Hodder & Stoughton, 2004), suggests another very credible ancient scenario: fishermen wishing to dry and preserve their catch might have found the usual supply of sun, wind and salt inadequate for the task. Trying to dry fish over a fire perhaps began as an act of desperation, then rapidly evolved into a favoured solution, particularly at times when one or more of the other commodities was in short supply. This could also neatly explain the close cultural relationship between salt and smoke as preservatives of fish and other flesh, which remains to this day. If salt is available in any quantity at all, then fish are invariably salted before being smoked.

In fact, many anthropologists reckon that the discovery of smoking, like the discovery of fire for cooking, was made not once but many times, by different groups of prehistoric men and women in different parts of the world at different times. In coastal communities, fish would naturally have been the food that first got the treatment. In others, among the inland hunter-gatherer tribes, it would have been meat. We can't help thinking that the early fish smokers were, gastronomically speaking, getting the slightly better deal.

The observation that fish prepared in this fashion kept for a surprisingly long time was obviously key to the way smoking permeated global food culture. Initially, this only had to be observed, not understood. Now we know that smoking improves the keeping qualities of fish by killing off bacteria and partially drying it out. The process of burning wood produces a range of chemicals, several of which have antibacterial and antioxidant properties. What this means is that salting and then smoking fish is a kind of 'belt and braces' job in terms of preserving it. It also means that if you smoke fish, you need less salt to preserve it than if you were relying on salt alone. In any culture, salt is traditionally a valuable commodity, if not an expensive one, so the economic reasons for smoking fish have long been compelling. Also, a fish that was lightly salted but heavily smoked would not have needed soaking to make it palatable – and that can only have added to its appeal.

And so, for many centuries, in many cultures, fish has been smoked mainly to preserve it, and thereby extend its ability to feed a community. But in the modern world, certainly in the West, there's no doubt that the economics of the enterprise no longer stack up. This is largely because labour costs have skewed the figures. Before they can be smoked, fish have to be cleaned, descaled, gutted, sometimes filleted, then brined, racked or strung up. Even an industrialised version of the process requires expensive machinery. Consequently smoked fish is usually somewhere between three and ten times more expensive than the equivalent fresh fish.

Nor do we need to smoke fish any more. Domestic and industrial freezers offer a far cheaper and more efficient method of preserving fish. Even frozen fish fingers with the added charms of dayglo orange breadcrumbs are, kilo for kilo, cheaper than kippers. The sheer cost of production should theoretically price smoked fish out of the modern market. And it probably would, except for one important thing. We like eating smoked fish, a lot.

There is something beguiling and irresistible about that unmistakable tang of slowly infused wood smoke, and it finds one of its happiest, most alluring partners in the flesh of fish. To appreciate this, you only have to list the dishes that would disappear from the menu should the smoking of fish somehow be maliciously uninvented. Buttered kippers, smoked mackerel pâté, smoked salmon and cream cheese bagels, taramasalata, kedgeree... surely at least one of these would rate in your top ten ways to enjoy fish? And for those prepared to go the extra fathom, there's bloater paste sandwiches, Arbroath smokies, Japanese katsuobushi...

Buying smoked fish

If you're beginning to feel that the delights of smoked fish are under-represented in your kitchen, what can you do about it? Well, at the risk of stating the obvious, you can simply go and buy it more often. The UK is a particularly good place to do so, since we have long been a nation of virtuoso fish curers. Smoked herring, haddock and salmon, in all their many guises, are among the few traditional regional foods that continue to thrive in a culture that doesn't always value such gems as it should.

If you are near the coast, it shouldn't be too hard to find authentic types of smoked herring, whether kippers, bloaters or buckling. The Arbroath smokie, a small, whole-but-headless hot-smoked haddock, is thankfully alive and well – though not literally, obviously. And you can still find really good smoked salmon all over the UK if you look hard enough (if you're looking in the supermarket, you'll have to look very hard indeed).

This is the rub. There is unquestionably some good stuff out there. But, and it's a big but, there is plenty of mediocre stuff and some downright dismal stuff too. Consider smoked salmon, which was once the patriarch of the smoked fish family. It is now mass produced, using cheap, flabby, farmed fish, whose flesh is dyed orange by artificial additives in the food they eat. They are 'smoked', thousands of fillets at a time, lying on racks in computer-controlled stainless steel 'kilns', in a process that takes only a few hours.

Contrast the brick kilns of a traditional craft smokery, where wisps of smoke from gently smouldering oak chips curl around the hanging fillets, from head to tail, for the best part of a whole day. The two processes are worlds apart, and so, inevitably, are their products. One is a greasy, pappy, fake-tan, one-dimensional, cheap sandwich filler, the fishy equivalent of plastic ham. The other can be sublime.

Nor have the other traditional smoker's favourites, the herring and the haddock, escaped industrialisation. Kippers and smoked haddock fillets are also produced in huge modern kilns. The worst of the mass-produced versions are injected with brine and finished with a smoke-flavoured glaze containing artificial colouring. They can look enticing but the taste is one-dimensional and crude, with none of the subtle, layered notes and deep, lasting flavours of the real thing.

To enjoy top-quality smoked fish, it's worth seeking out products that have been cured by dedicated artisans, who put the pursuit of excellence before the pursuit of profit (not that the two ought to be incompatible). In the fishmonger's, always ask for undyed smoked haddock and kippers, and feel entitled to enquire about the origin of any smoked products. Good fishmongers should always be proud to tell you where they source their smoked fish.

Better still, buy direct from the best artisan smokehouses. For such small businesses, the regular custom of a few dozen enthusiasts, and the ensuing word of mouth, can make all the difference. We list several excellent smokeries in the Directory (see pages 590–1), most of whom have their own websites and deliver by mail order.

Buying from those who do things properly is one way to enjoy your share of good smoked fish. Another, and one we heartily recommend, as much for the pleasures of the process as the outstanding end result you can achieve, is to smoke some fish of your own.

We'll explain the rudiments here – and you'll soon see that ours is a rough and ready approach. Nonetheless, we reckon we can guide you to some very pleasing results. But if you want to pursue the art of home smoking on a higher plane, we highly recommend the book *Home Smoking and Curing* by Keith Erlandson (Ebury Press, 2003).

combine whole spices and seeds with your sawdust to achieve a highly flavoured smoke. Fennel seeds, dried chillies, cloves and allspice berries are good.

To get our bread bin smoker fired up, we simply scatter a 5mm layer of our chosen sawdust over the base, put the first rack in, with the larger pieces of fish (always lightly salted, rinsed, then pressed dry) on it, then add the second rack, with smaller fish or fillets, and put the lid on. The bin is then placed on whatever heat source is available – a gas burner, barbecue or the smouldering coals of a beach or riverside fire. The base of the tin heats up and the sawdust begins to smoulder, making smoke. The inside of the tin heats up, too – not to a very predictable temperature, given that our heat source varies, but with a bit of luck it will reach more than 80°C and not much more than 120°C. Depending on this temperature, and the thickness of the fish or fillets, it may take anywhere between 15 minutes and an hour to complete the job. But 30–40 minutes would be the desired range. Your judgement as to whether the fish is ready is effectively a judgement on whether it is cooked through, so testing its opaqueness by means of the knife test (see pages 113–14) is the way to go.

If the sawdust happens to burn out before the fish is cooked, you can add some more. But you will have to remove the racks and fish – with suitably protected hands – and start again.

If you don't rate your own DIY skills, or your old enamel bread bin is too precious to pimp, you can, of course, buy portable hot smokers. They are available in all shapes and sizes, and many of them come with little meths burners to place under the base and heat the sawdust to smouldering point. However, they are of variable quality, so take a good look around, and choose one that is robust and of simple design. If it can be used over other heat sources, such as fires and gas rings, so much the better.

Building a cold smoker

This is definitely a bit more of a project, not least because a cold smoker is not readily portable, even if it can be manhandled from one place to another, and the sessions take time – up to a day or more. But that doesn't mean it's hard. To reassure yourself on this point, it's worth remembering that for centuries, cold smoking was achieved by simply hanging fish in the column of smoke above an open fire, indoors or out. And it can still be done like that.

However, a modicum of DIY skills and a keen eye for salvage can produce a dedicated cold-smoking kit that will give you years of good service, without a great deal of technical know-how. Our own cold smoker (shown on page 155), which will be described fully in due course, is a case in point. Although it is based on a reasonable understanding of the principles involved, and a clear recognition of the right end results, it does not involve a great deal of, shall we say, *calibration*. We'll start, though, with some guidelines for crude cold smoking in an existing fireplace – as practised for generations by crofters and coastal dwellers all over the British Isles.

A fireplace smoker
If you have an open fireplace at home where you regularly burn logs, you may well be able to cold smoke fish and other foods above it. It simply depends on whether you can find a way to fix your fish a reasonable height above a gently

Smoked pollack with poached egg *serves 2*

According to Nick, this is the one dish guaranteed to calm and soothe his wife, Helen, after a particularly stressful day. Make sure you use very fresh eggs. As well as tasting better, they form smooth, round shapes in the poaching water.

2 fillets (about 400g) smoked pollack
  (or smoked haddock)
2 bay leaves
A few black peppercorns
Up to 500ml whole milk

400g fresh spinach, washed and coarse
  stalks removed
Olive oil
2 tablespoons cider vinegar
2 large, very fresh organic eggs
Salt and freshly ground black pepper

Cut the fish fillets in half and put them in a pan. Add the bay leaves and peppercorns, then pour on enough milk just to cover the fish. Put the lid on and bring to a simmer, then remove the pan from the heat. This should be enough to cook the fish through. If it isn't quite cooked – i.e. if it doesn't break easily into flakes – turn it over, cover again and leave in the hot milk (off the heat) for a couple of minutes. Remove the fish from the milk and keep warm.

Meanwhile, put the spinach in a large pan with a little salt and pepper and a glug of olive oil. Set the pan over a medium-high heat and sweat the spinach briefly in its own juices until completely collapsed. Drain off any excess liquid.

Bring a small pan of water to the boil for poaching the eggs. Add the cider vinegar. Stir the water with a spoon to create a whirlpool. Crack the eggs into the whirlpool (or break them on to saucers first, then tip them in), turn the heat down to minimum and cook for 3–4 minutes, until the whites are set. Remove the eggs carefully with a slotted spoon and drain on kitchen paper.

Put the fish fillets on warm plates and pile the hot, wilted spinach alongside. Top with a poached egg. Take to the table and let your guest – fractious wife or otherwise – break the egg so the golden yolk spills out.

Hot-smoked sea trout with Morello cherries

serves 4

This is a great combination, the punchy cherry compote giving a beautiful edge to the salty hot-smoked trout. It's a real summer treat, as both the fish and the fruit are in season for such a short time.

<u>Also works with:</u>
- Salmon (organic farmed or self-caught wild)
- Trout
- Mackerel

2 wild sea trout, weighing about 1kg each, descaled and filleted
Coarse sea salt
4 sprigs of tarragon (optional)
4 sprigs of thyme (optional)
Freshly ground black pepper

FOR THE CHERRY SAUCE:
200–300g fresh Morello cherries, stoned
Up to 50g light brown sugar

Lay the fish fillets on a large board and carefully remove the pin bones with tweezers. Salt the fillets with the sea salt, as described on page 167 – they will need 15–20 minutes.

Rinse the salt from the fillets and pat them dry. Using a sharp knife, cut the fillets in half. Grind some fresh black pepper over the fish and press the herb sprigs on to the flesh, if you like.

Gently hot smoke the fish, following the technique on pages 158–60. We've had a lot of success smoking trout over oak chips but you could try cherry wood or even a blend of cherry and bay. Ensure the temperature doesn't rise much above 80°C or the fish will cook too fast and may dry out. Fillets of this size should be ready in 40–50 minutes. When the fish is just cooked through, remove it and leave to rest in a warm place.

To make the sauce, put the cherries in a pan with a tablespoon of water and 30–40g sugar. Bring to a gentle simmer, then cook for 5–6 minutes, until the fruit is soft but still retains a little shape. Taste and add more sugar if you like, but it should remain slightly tart.

Serve the smoked fish on warmed plates with a spoonful of the warm sauce. A watercress salad and a slice of toasted walnut bread go very nicely alongside.

Open-fire cooking

Baked and grilled fish

In the mission to get fish hot, which we've established is the essence of most fish cookery, your oven is clearly going to prove useful. Just how far it can take you along the road of fish cookery may surprise you. Here are three simple approaches to get you started…

Put a whole large fish in your preheated oven and very soon it will be hot, and therefore cooked. A few slashes through the skin and flesh will speed up the transfer of heat to the thicker parts of the fish. They are also an irresistible opportunity to introduce some seasonings to the flesh – salt, pepper, a trickle of olive oil and maybe a sprig or two of thyme and some shards of chopped garlic; or perhaps some grated ginger and garlic, a little soy sauce and a pinch of sugar. With minimal time and effort, you'll have a crisp-skinned whole roast fish ready for the table. This kind of oven-bashing approach works for anything from whole cod to whole plaice, saddle of conger eel to the head of a large coley, ling or pollack. Our Roast pollack head with thyme, bay and garlic (page 380) has become something of a River Cottage 'house special'. Or…

Lightly oil a roasting tin and arrange half a dozen cleaned, gutted mackerel in it. Lay them out nose to tail, as if in a sardine tin. Sprinkle with garlic, salt and pepper, add a few torn bay leaves, a trickle of olive oil and a squeeze of lemon. Scrunch a foil lid over the tin and bung it into your hot oven. About 20 minutes later you've got yourself a fishy feast. It's a method that scales up well, if you use two big roasting tins, to what we call the mackerel 'triple 20' – feeding 20 people in 20 minutes for about 20 pence a head. (Yes, you really can buy twenty mackerel for £4, or maybe £5 if they are big ones, if you're buying them harbourside, straight from the boat, in the middle of summer. Though if you are reading this in the year 2020, those figures may well look absurd.) Or…

Imagine you have a magnificent fish of 3 or 4kg – a sea bass, or even a once-in-a-lifetime wild salmon you've caught yourself. Tear off a metre of foil, lay it on a baking tray and grease it with olive oil or butter. Put the fish in the foil and anoint it with some trusted flavourings: salt, pepper, parsley, a sliced onion, a squeeze of lemon. Wrap up the foil round the fish like the pastry of a giant Cornish pasty, adding a splash of wine before the final crinkle, then put it on a baking tray, and bake for an hour. When you open that parcel, prepare to be assaulted by a rush of aromatic steam. No need to knock up a sauce. It's there waiting for you, pooled around the fish at the bottom of the foil parcel. Just be careful not to lose a single precious drop.

This is how easy and joyous fish cookery can be when you turn to the oven. It's maximum payback for minimum effort. Not that you're shirking your responsibility to the fish. There's nothing remotely second best about any of the suggestions above. But the oven is a great friend to the weary cook, or indeed the weary fisherman. Imagine, for instance, that you've just come back from a day's fishing, you're tired, you're hungry and you want to eat some of that lovely fish you've caught with minimum further ado. Whatever you've caught, the oven can always see you right.

You'll see from our table on pages 116–17 that 200°C/Gas Mark 6 is our normal oven temperature for roasting fish. If in doubt, we would recommend defaulting to this. But there's no fixed rule: raising or lowering the temperature simply speeds up or slows down the cooking time, as you'd expect. We usually cook our foil-parcel fish at a slightly lower temperature – around 180–190°C/ Gas Mark 4–5 – otherwise it can suddenly be boiling rather fiercely in its pool of liquid. Higher temperatures – as much as 230°C/Gas Mark 8 – are good for rapid

roasting of unwrapped fish where you want to get good crisping and blistering of the skin. If you're roasting in a wood-fired pizza oven, the temperature may be up to 250°C or more, and small fish such as sardines or mackerel will be cooked through and crisped up, like a good pizza, in just a few minutes.

The oven/grill partnership

Most ovens now have an overhead grill built into them, which is why we've also included a handful of grilled fish recipes in this chapter. The overhead grill is rather marginalised these days, if not stigmatised – its thunder has been stolen by the chargrill and the ridged griddle pan (a very useful tool, which we discuss on page 298). But thirty or forty years ago it was a mainstay of British cooking, and eye-level overhead grills were all the rage.

If you have one, either at eye level or, more likely these days, at thigh level, do use it – because it is a very handy bit of fish-cooking equipment indeed. It's particularly useful when you are cooking whole fish and looking for that blistered, salty skin that can be so irresistible. Although you can get a good, crisp finish by starting your fish in a hot frying pan, then finishing the cooking in the oven (see opposite), it will never be quite the same as a proper grilling.

Indeed, an excellent alternative to the pan-with-a-hint-of-oven method is the oven-with-a-hint-of-grill approach. In other words, if you are roasting a fish and it's more or less done, but you feel the skin could use a little help to crisp up, then give it an extra brush of oil, and/or a quick baste with any pan juices, and put it close beneath a hot grill for just a minute. Watch it like a heron, though – nice brown blisters can turn to black charcoal faster than you can say, 'What's that burning smell?'

Of course, you can cook fish wonderfully by grill and grill alone, as our Grilled devilled sprats (page 245) and Grilled lemon sole with lemons (page 246) demonstrate. And the grill is often as handy as the oven when time is short and the crew is looking mutinous. To cook a few plate-sized (300–500g) whole fish, such as mackerel, trout, red mullet or small bream, start your grill heating up to medium-high while you get your coat off. Then line the grill pan with foil, brush the foil with some oil, sprinkle it with salt and pepper, plus a bay leaf or two if they're handy, and put your fish on top. Brush them with oil too, season them well, then give them 5 minutes on each side under fairly ferocious bars and you'll have a delicious supper in no time at all.

Beyond basic oven work

We use these basic oven methods – sometimes in conjunction with that flash under the grill – all the time. And sometimes we customise them to a slightly more refined level. The mackerel-in-a-roasting-tin, for example, can be expanded to create an entire meal by adding potatoes and onions to the tin and baking the fish on top of them. The juices from the mackerel mingle with the potatoes and onions; the effect is greedy and delicious, yet somehow rather chic – see page 218 for the full story.

There are many riffs on the foil-parcel theme, too: it can be used to cook a sandwiched pair of fillets – sea bass and bream are our favourites – as well as cooking whole fish. We might go for a more intense package of flavours: shaved fennel bulbs and lemon zest, for example, or a heady oriental mix of ginger, soy sauce, garlic and spring onions.

Even handfuls of small shellfish can be foil parcelled. A double layer of foil is best to protect against piercing by sharp shells – because, of course, you want to keep in those aromatic juices. Mussels, clams or cockles, scrubbed clean, can be parcelled up with a splash of wine, some garlic, some herbs and a good knob of butter, then baked at 220°C/Gas Mark 7. Within 10 minutes, they will have opened in the heat, allowing their juices to mingle with the other flavours and make a lovely, chin-dripping sauce. These one-per-person parcels can be opened on the plates, so everybody gets the benefit of that aromatic whoosh up the nostrils.

It is also to the oven that we turn when we want to create one of our most spectacular fishy set pieces: a whole hefty sea bass or bream baked in a thick, crusty jacket of salt (see page 226), or a saltdough crust (see page 225). The cracking and lifting of the crust to reveal the tender, aromatic flesh within creates a sense of occasion right up there with a whole poached salmon or a towering seafood platter. It's gone down a storm at various anniversaries and family birthdays – and it certainly takes the pressure off the cook.

The oven in a supporting role

When you have a fish to cook, whatever it is, the oven is so often the best option for getting the job done from start to finish. But it can also back up other cooking methods. The most obvious example, touched on above, is the use of the oven to finish off fish – usually whole ones – that have been started in a frying pan. The pan gets the seasoned skin nice and crisp, then the oven completes the job of getting the heat to the middle of the fish, which the pan might struggle to do on its own with a thick fish. We'll come to this very neat pan/oven double act again in the chapter on frying.

However, the role of the oven in fixing and finishing dishes that have been started somewhere else goes beyond this 'rounding-off' of whole fish in frying pans. There's a whole genre of fish-in-the-oven cookery that provides some of the most homely dishes in this book. These are what you might think of as 'composed' recipes, where fish is combined with other ingredients to make pies, pasties, tarts, gratins and bakes.

The baking of a fish pie (see page 236), with its crisp, browned topping of forked-up mashed potato, is a classic example of oven magic at work; the raising of a rich, creamy, smoked fish soufflé (see page 177) is another. We've even, in experimental mode, rustled up a crab bread and butter pudding. It turned out surprisingly well (see page 239). Gratins of fish and shellfish, or béchamel- and cheese-topped seafood crêpes, will also need a spell in a hot oven to crisp up their crumbs or bubble their cheese. Without the oven they would all be unfinished works: edible, maybe even delicious, but lacking a certain something – the ability not merely to satisfy appetites but to warm cockles and win hearts.

This kind of home-baking-with-fish may be a little more time consuming than the pared-down oven procedures we discussed at the beginning, but it's still enormously satisfying. Having started with a simply seasoned baked whole fish, we seem to have fetched up in the realms of creamy, indulgent fishy comfort food. It's not such a bad place to be.

Roasted whole plaice with cherry tomatoes

serves 2–4, depending on the size of your plaice

This is one of the best and simplest treatments for this wonderful flatfish. The crisp, blistered skin of the plaice is almost as delicious as the white meat beneath, and the unrivalled sweetness of little tomatoes, which burst in the mouth, sets it off perfectly.

This is definitely a dish to cook with one large fish rather than several small ones. Large plaice are, sadly, not as easy to find as they once were, but they are still out there. The fish we cooked for this photograph weighed nearly 2kg. If you aren't fortunate enough to come across such a monster, use a large brill, flounder, megrim or witch.

Also works with:
• Brill
• Flounder
• Megrim
• Witch

Olive oil

1 large plaice, weighing at least 1kg, descaled and gutted, but skin on

A large knob of unsalted butter, cut into small pieces

500g sweet cherry tomatoes, such as Sungold

About 6 sprigs of thyme

About 6 bay leaves

Salt and freshly ground black pepper

Oil a baking tray large enough to accommodate your plaice. Season the surface of the baking tray and place the fish on it, pale side (underside) down. Drizzle the fish with olive oil and massage it in. Season all over with pepper and lots of salt and dot the little pieces of butter over it.

Scatter the cherry tomatoes around the fish, along with the thyme and bay leaves. Bake in an oven preheated to 220°C/Gas Mark 7 for 20–30 minutes, until the fish is just cooked and the tomatoes are blistered and soft.

Once roasted, the flesh of the plaice should lift easily from the bone in neat fillets. Remove the top two fillets using a fish knife and fork. Ease the skeleton away to reveal the remaining two fillets from the underside. Serve the fish with the tomatoes and all their buttery, salty-sweet roasting juices.

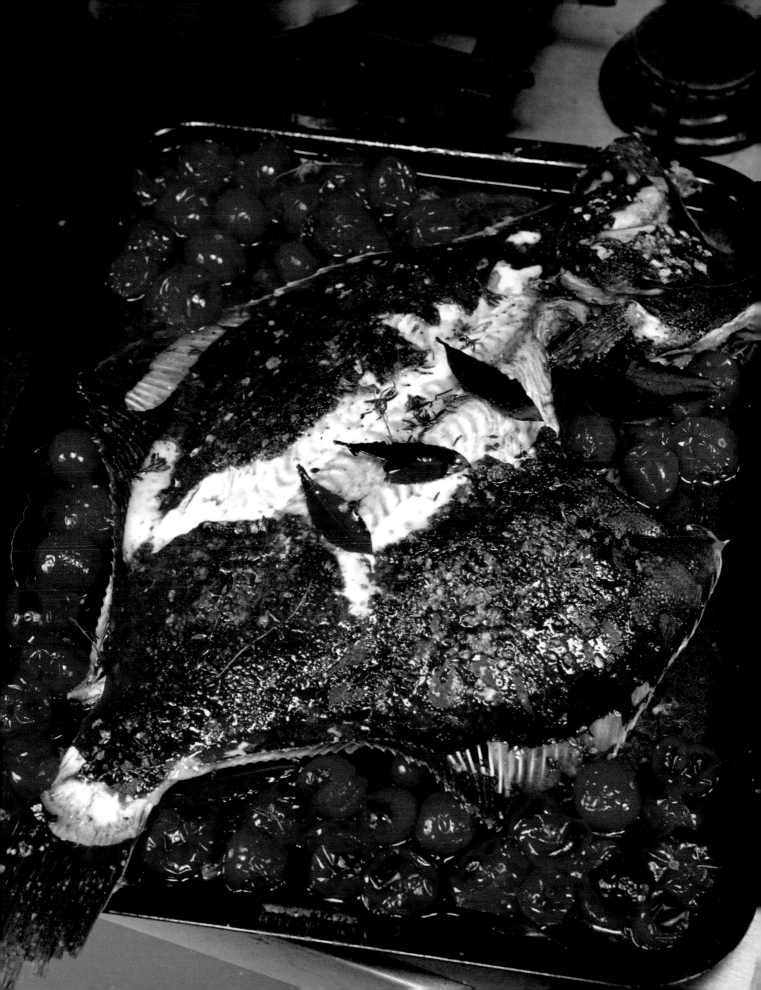

Mackerel on potatoes and bay

serves 4

This is a fantastic and very simple one-dish meal. The juices from the fish mingle with the olive oil and lemon juice to make a delicious, aromatic sauce that flavours the vegetables beautifully. Go for new potatoes if you can, but main-crop are fine too. Choose a waxy variety, such as Cara or Maris Peer, and parboil them for 5 minutes or so before you begin. Either way, keep all the veg nice and chunky – this should be a wonderfully rustic sort of dish.

For a more child-friendly version of this dish, use fillets from larger fish instead of whole fish.

Also works with:
• Sardines
• Red mullet
• Scad
• Garfish

Olive oil
1kg new potatoes, scrubbed and cut into rough chunks about 2cm thick
2 onions, thickly sliced
4 garlic cloves, very roughly chopped

2 lemons, halved and sliced into thickish pieces
4–6 bay leaves
2 sprigs of thyme
4 mackerel, gutted
Salt and freshly ground black pepper

Pour enough olive oil into a large, shallow roasting tin just to cover the base. Use your fingers to spread the oil all over the dish. Combine the potatoes, onions, garlic and lemons, season with plenty of salt and pepper and spread them out in the dish. Tuck the bay leaves and thyme in amongst the vegetables so they won't burn in the oven.

Put the roasting tin in an oven preheated to 180°C/Gas Mark 4 and bake for 30–45 minutes, until the potatoes are lightly browned and just about tender, taking the tin from the oven every 10 minutes and turning the vegetables over in their oily juices.

Meanwhile, season the mackerel well with salt and pepper. When the potatoes are ready, lay the mackerel on top, pour on another good splash of olive oil and return to the oven. Turn it up to 200°C/Gas Mark 6 and bake for a further 15–20 minutes (10 minutes if you're using fillets), until the mackerel is just cooked and the vegetables are beginning to catch and crisp up nicely. (If you like, take the fish out halfway through for a quick basting with the juices from the tin.)

Serve straight away. The dish doesn't really need any accompaniment but a green salad wouldn't go amiss.

Whole fish baked in a foil parcel *serves 2*

If you enjoy fish – and presumably you do, or you wouldn't be reading this now – this method should be part of your core repertoire. It is incredibly easy and very forgiving (even if you overcook the fish a little, it will still be delicious). Bream and bass work best, but you can extend and expand the technique to accommodate any whole fish for which your foil, and oven, are sufficiently capacious. You'll certainly need a double layer of foil for anything over 1.5kg. The biggest fish we've ever cooked this way was a salmon of about 3.5kg. It took just over an hour.

Also works with:
- Salmon (organic farmed or self-caught wild)
- Trout
- Mackerel
- Carp
- Pike
- Pollack
- John Dory
- Small whole flatfish

One 2-portion-size (or two 1-portion-size) black bream, sea bass or other whole fish, descaled and gutted
2 garlic cloves, peeled and lightly squashed with a knife
A few bay leaves

1 lemon
A few herb sprigs: fennel fronds, thyme and/or flat-leaf parsley (optional)
50g unsalted butter
A glass of white wine
Salt and freshly ground black pepper

Season the inside of the fish and put in the squashed garlic, along with a bay leaf or two and 1 or 2 slices of lemon. If you have other herbs to hand – some fennel tops, say, or a little thyme or parsley – you can pop some of those in too. (If you're using flatfish, sit them on top of these flavourings in the foil parcels.)

Take a sheet of foil for each fish, large enough to envelop it completely. Grease the inside (dull side) with a little of the butter. Put a fish in the centre and bring up the sides of the foil a little. Scatter a few more herbs over the fish and dot with the butter. Pour on the wine (you'll need a little less if you're cooking just one large fish) and add a good squeeze of lemon juice. Season again, bring the foil up around the fish and scrunch the edges together until the parcel(s) are completely sealed.

Put the foil parcel(s) on a baking tray and bake in an oven preheated to 190°C/ Gas Mark 5 for 20–25 minutes (small fish) or 30–35 minutes (larger fish). Small flatfish may take less time.

Bring the parcel(s) straight to the table and open them up on the plate to release a cloud of fragrant steam. The fish will be sitting in a pool of deliciously rich and aromatic juice – your sauce. Choose very simple accompaniments – perhaps roasted fennel or steamed spinach, and maybe a small pile of mash or rice.

Stuffed conger *serves 4–6*

We only cook a conger once a year, if that (see page 500) – so when we do, we really push the boat out. This is our take on an old Cornish recipe from Dorothy Hartley's *Food in England* (Macdonald, 1954). It sounded so bizarre that we felt we had to give it a go – and the results were really good. In fact, this fishy roast could easily take pride of place at Sunday lunch. The flesh of the conger is moist and full of flavour, and the juices make a lovely rich gravy. You probably won't find the skin palatable but it helps to hold the slices together as you serve the fish.

1.5kg section of a medium conger eel (a 5–10kg fish is perfect), cut from the middle of the fish, skin on
10 smoked streaky bacon rashers
1 small dessert apple, such as Cox's or Russet
35g unsalted butter
250ml medium cider, plus a little extra for the gravy, if necessary
1–2 teaspoons plain flour
Salt and freshly ground black pepper

FOR THE SAUSAGE STUFFING:
250g coarsely minced organic or free-range pork shoulder
1 small onion, finely chopped
50g fresh white breadcrumbs
A good pinch of ground mace
A pinch of cayenne pepper
A small handful of sage leaves, finely chopped
A small handful of thyme leaves, finely chopped
Grated zest of ½ lemon
2 tablespoons brandy
1 dessert apple, peeled, cored and cut into small cubes
½ teaspoon salt
Freshly ground black pepper

By hand, thoroughly mix all the stuffing ingredients in a large bowl, squishing everything together with your fingers. Then put the mixture in the fridge so the flavours can mingle while you prepare the conger.

Wash and dry the piece of conger. Open up the belly cavity and remove the section of backbone, teasing the flesh away from the bone with a sharp filleting knife until it comes free. Use tweezers to remove any other bones you find. Conger has a lot of tiny pin bones, so you do need to take your time over this. Run your fingertips up and down the flesh to locate the bones before pulling them out.

Now bring the sides of the fish together and sew them with butcher's string to form a cavity for the stuffing. Pack the pork stuffing into the cavity and season the fish all over, then place the bacon rashers over the top. Cut the apple in half and use the halves to plug the ends of the stuffed joint.

Melt the butter in a roasting tin over a gentle heat. Place the stuffed conger in the tin and pour over the cider. This will be your basting liquid and the base of your gravy.

Roast the conger in an oven preheated to 220°C/Gas Mark 7 for 10 minutes, then reduce the temperature to 180°C/Gas Mark 4. Cook for a further hour, basting regularly, until the stuffing is cooked right through (the tip of a skewer pushed into the middle of the stuffing should come out hot – a probe thermometer should read 70°C).

(continued overleaf)

As you remove the roast conger from the oven, transfer it to a warm platter and leave it to rest in a warm place, while you make gravy – in just the same way you would after roasting a joint of meat. If there is a lot of liquid, simply pour it into a saucepan and boil it down until it reaches the level of intensity you require. Alternatively, if there's not so much to play with, place the roasting tin over a gentle heat and stir the flour into the juices to thicken them. Allow to bubble for a few minutes to cook out the flour and finish the thickening. If you feel you need extra liquid, add more cider, or some fish stock. Either way, simmer the gravy for a minute or two, then taste and adjust the seasoning.

Remove the bacon and apple halves (which you can serve with the fish), and the string. Slice the conger fairly thickly, then serve with boiled, buttered potatoes or mash, some greens, such as Savoy cabbage or Brussels sprouts, and a jug of the hot conger gravy.

Brill baked with leeks and potatoes *serves 6*

Brill responds very well to a one-pot treatment, but because of its flat shape, it needs a slightly different approach. Strictly, this is a two-pot treatment, but still very straightforward.

A large knob of unsalted butter

3 tablespoons olive oil

4 medium leeks, white part only, cut into 2cm thick slices

4 large potatoes, peeled and cut into 2cm chunks

A couple of bay leaves

1 brill, weighing 1–1.5kg, descaled and gutted

A glass of white wine

Salt and freshly ground black pepper

Also works with:
• Plaice
• Turbot
• Sole
• Lemon sole
• Megrim
• Witch
• Flounder

Heat the butter and olive oil in a large saucepan over a medium-low heat. Add the leeks and potatoes, cover and sweat, stirring frequently, for 10–15 minutes, until the potatoes are almost tender.

Transfer the vegetables to a large roasting tin, so they form a shallow layer, and tuck in the bay leaves. Season well. Place the brill on top of the veg, then nestle it down so there are vegetables under, around and on top of it.

Trickle the wine and a glass of water over everything and cover the tin with foil. Put in an oven preheated to 180°C/Gas Mark 4 and bake for about 30 minutes, until the fish is cooked.

Mussel, spinach and bacon gratin

serves 4 as a main course, 6 as a starter

Moules marinière meets creamed spinach and gets an irresistible gratin top. This is the kind of simple but unexpected dish that gets people very excited.

Also works with:
• Cockles
• Palourdes

2 tablespoons white wine
1 shallot, diced
1kg mussels, scrubbed and debearded
  (see page 103)
1 tablespoon olive oil, plus a little more
  to finish
150g smoked bacon or pancetta, diced
  fairly small
1 fat garlic clove, finely chopped
About 400ml whole milk

50g unsalted butter
50g plain flour
500g fresh spinach, thoroughly washed,
  tougher stalks removed
A squeeze of lemon juice
75g fresh white breadcrumbs
50g Cheddar or Parmesan cheese, grated
  (optional)
Freshly ground black pepper

Place a large pan over a high heat and add the wine, 2 tablespoons of water and the diced shallot. Bring to a simmer, then throw in the mussels and cover with the lid. Let them steam open in the pan for 3–4 minutes, shaking the pan once or twice. Remove the mussels from the pan with a slotted spoon (discarding any that have remained firmly shut) and set aside until they are cool enough to handle. Pick the mussels from their shells and set aside. Strain all the cooking liquor through a fine sieve, or a coarse sieve lined with a cloth.

Heat the olive oil in a frying pan, add the bacon and sauté gently until starting to crisp up. Add the garlic and cook for a further minute or so, being careful not to let the garlic burn. Remove from the heat and transfer to a bowl.

Now you need to make a béchamel sauce. First, combine the reserved mussel cooking liquor with enough milk to make 500ml and heat gently in a pan. Melt the butter in a separate pan. When it is foaming, add the flour and stir well to make a smooth roux. Gradually add the warmed milk, stirring well after each addition to prevent lumps. Bring to a simmer and cook gently for 4–5 minutes to give a smooth, creamy sauce.

Drop the spinach into a large pan of boiling water and cook for just a minute, until wilted. Drain, leave to cool a little, then squeeze out excess water with your hands. Chop the spinach roughly.

Fold the bacon, mussels and spinach into the béchamel sauce. Season with freshly ground black pepper and a squeeze of lemon juice. Divide the mixture between 4 buttered shallow ovenproof dishes (or 6 ramekins if you're serving it as a starter) or spread it evenly into one large buttered gratin dish.

Sprinkle over the breadcrumbs, plus the cheese if using, and trickle over a little olive oil. Bake in an oven preheated to 200°C/Gas Mark 6 for 10–12 minutes, until golden and bubbling. Serve piping hot, with crusty bread.

Devilled spider crab in the shell *serves 2*

You might think of crabmeat as a very delicate thing, not suited to the rough and tumble of vinegar, mustard, chilli and other devilling ingredients – but it has a robust depth that can easily hold its own in a dish like this.

Baking the crab in its shell gives you the bonus of an extra shot of flavour. Crustacean shells are formed from concentrated proteins and sugars, and the heat of the oven causes them to release a nutty, rich flavour.

About 50g unsalted butter, plus a little
   extra for dotting on the breadcrumbs
1 large onion, finely chopped
100ml sherry
2 tablespoons cider vinegar
1½ tablespoons Worcestershire sauce
1 heaped teaspoon English mustard
1 teaspoon cayenne pepper or a generous
   shake of Tabasco sauce

200ml double cream
2 cooked medium spider crabs (about
   1–1.5kg), brown and white meat picked
   out, shells cleaned (see pages 89–93)
A squeeze of lemon juice
50g fresh white breadcrumbs
Salt and freshly ground black pepper

Also works with:
• Brown crab
• Blue velvet swimmer
  crab

Put a large, heavy-based pan over a medium heat and add the butter. Toss in the chopped onion and sweat gently until softened but not coloured – about 10 minutes should do it. Pour in the sherry, let it boil for a few seconds, then add the vinegar and Worcestershire sauce and let them come to the boil too.

Stir in the mustard and cayenne pepper or Tabasco, then add the cream. Let the mixture come to a simmer, cook for 2 minutes or until it just starts to thicken slightly, then remove from the heat.

Fold the crabmeat into the sauce. Season well with salt and pepper and a little lemon juice, then spoon the mixture into the cleaned crab shells or individual gratin dishes. Don't try and fill the shells up, just make a good mound of the mixture in the middle. Sprinkle with the breadcrumbs and dot a little butter over the top.

Place the crabs on a baking tray and bake in an oven preheated to 190°C/Gas Mark 5 for 20–25 minutes, until the breadcrumbs are golden and the crab bubbling devilishly. Serve piping hot, with doorsteps of thickly buttered toast and a green salad.

VARIATION
Devilled crab on toast

To ring the changes and speed things up a bit, you can make a lovely version of this dish with the bread on the bottom, in the form of toast, rather than on top, as breadcrumbs. It cuts out the baking stage, too.

After folding the crabmeat into the sauce, simply pile it on to hot buttered toast. A scaled-down version of this makes an excellent canapé: put generous teaspoonfuls of the hot (or cold) saucy crab on small squares of toast or little crostini and serve with drinks.

Hugh's mum's fish pie *serves 6*

This is a classic, creamy, comforting fish pie, which should delight fish eaters of all ages. The basic principle is to have some smoked fish, some white fish, some oily fish and some prawns. But, of course, you can vary the species according to what's available – and good value – on the day.

FOR THE FILLING:
400g cooked, shell-on Atlantic prawns
500g smoked white fish fillets, such as
   pollack or haddock
300–400g fresh white fish fillets
300–400g organic salmon fillets
1 onion, roughly chopped
1 large carrot, roughly chopped
1 celery stick, chopped
1 bay leaf
A few peppercorns
A bunch of flat-leaf parsley, leaves
   chopped and stalks reserved

About 750ml milk
3 large eggs, at room temperature
50g unsalted butter
75g plain flour
2 tablespoons chopped chives
Salt and freshly ground black pepper

FOR THE MASH:
1kg floury potatoes, such as Maris Piper
   or Désirée, peeled and cut into chunks
50g unsalted butter, plus extra to dot on
   top of the pie
100ml whole milk, warmed

Shell the prawns and put the shells and heads in a saucepan: they will help to flavour the sauce for the pie. With a sharp filleting knife, skin the fish (see page 73). Add the skins to the saucepan, plus the onion, carrot, celery, bay leaf, peppercorns and parsley stalks. Pour in enough milk just to cover, bring to a simmer, then take off the heat and set aside to infuse for at least half an hour. Remove any pin bones from the fish with tweezers and cut up all the fish into roughly 2cm cubes. Combine with the shelled prawns and set aside.

While the milk for the sauce is infusing, make the mashed potato. Boil the spuds in salted water until tender. Drain and leave them in the colander to steam for a minute or two, then return to the pan and mash with the butter and milk. Season to taste with salt and pepper.

Bring a pan of water to the boil, add the eggs and boil for 7 minutes. Take off the heat and put the pan under cold running water to stop the cooking. When the eggs are cool enough to handle, peel them.

To make the béchamel sauce, strain the infused milk into a jug and place by the hob. Melt the butter in a pan over a medium heat, add the flour and stir well to make a smooth roux. Cook this gently for a couple of minutes, stirring, then gradually add the infused milk, beating well after each addition so you don't get any lumps. Allow the sauce to cook gently for a couple of minutes, stirring occasionally so it doesn't stick. Remove from the heat, season to taste and add the chopped parsley and chives. Stir in the fish and prawns.

Cut the eggs into quarters and arrange them in a pie dish (about 30 x 20cm). Spoon over the fish mixture, then top with spoonfuls of mashed potato, spreading it evenly over the fish and raking the top into wavy lines with a fork to maximise crispness. Dot the potato with a little butter and bake in an oven preheated to 200°C/Gas Mark 6 for about 25 minutes, until the top is starting to brown and the sauce is bubbling up the sides of the mash. Serve with buttered peas.

Seafood pancake gratin *serves 12 as starter, 6 as a main course*

This follows the same kind of comfort-food principles as a really good fish pie: a rich combination of smoked fish, white fish and prawns, bound in a creamy béchamel sauce and all held together with a satisfying bit of starch – in this case, pancakes. The addition of a little bubbling cheese only adds to the feel-good factor.

1 quantity of fish pie filling (see page 236, but without the eggs)
2 tablespoons white wine
300–400g mussels, scrubbed and debearded (see page 103)
100g Gruyère or Cheddar cheese, grated

FOR THE PANCAKES:
250g plain flour
A pinch of salt
2 large eggs
250ml whole milk
Sunflower oil for frying

Make the filling according to the fish pie recipe but set aside 5–6 tablespoonfuls of the béchamel sauce before you add the fish. (You're saving it to pour over the pancakes, for a creamy, bubbling topping.)

Bring the wine and 2 tablespoons of water to the boil in a saucepan over a medium-high heat and add the mussels. Cover and cook, shaking the pan a couple of times, for 3–4 minutes, until the shells are open. Discard any that remain closed. When the mussels are cool enough to handle, remove them from their shells and add to the fish and béchamel filling.

For the pancakes, sift the flour and salt into a bowl, make a well in the centre and break in the eggs. Pour in half the milk and start to whisk, bringing the flour gradually into the egg and milk in the centre. Add the rest of the milk and 150ml water and keep on whisking until there are no more lumps. Stir in some more water (around 100ml) until the mixture is the consistency of thin cream.

Place a large frying pan over a medium-high heat and add 1 tablespoon of sunflower oil. Swirl it round the pan, then pour the excess out into a cup. Pour a small ladleful of batter into the pan and swirl it round quickly to form a crêpe. Cook for 1–2 minutes, until browned underneath, then flip over and cook the second side for a minute. Remove from the pan and set aside.

Repeat with the remaining batter, stacking the pancakes up between squares of greaseproof paper, then set them aside to cool. Add another swirl of oil to the pan after every 3 pancakes or so. You need 12 pancakes in all, and may have some batter left over.

Place a large spoonful of the fish and sauce mixture in the middle of one pancake. Roll up the pancake around the filling, fold in the ends to seal the filling in and continue rolling up the pancake. Place in a greased ovenproof dish in which the rolled pancakes will fit snugly (you might find it easier to use two dishes). Continue the filling and rolling with the remaining pancakes.

Gently reheat the reserved sauce, adding a little milk if it is very thick, then spoon it over the filled pancakes and scatter the grated cheese on top. Bake in an oven preheated to 200°C/Gas Mark 6 for 20–25 minutes, until bubbling hot and lightly browned.

Crab bread and butter pudding *serves 6*

This is a lovely comforting dish, based on a Jane Grigson recipe – ideal for the winter months, and cheap and cheerful too. It's not something you'd want to do from scratch with a couple of live crabs; they'd be better served really simply. It is more a way of spinning a clever crowd-pleaser from ready-picked brown and white meat.

125g softened unsalted butter

300g white and brown crabmeat

A good pinch of cayenne pepper

2 tablespoons chopped mixed herbs, such
  as parsley, chervil and chives

A squeeze of lemon juice

A day-old white baguette, cut into slices
  1.5–2cm thick

4 eggs

250ml milk

250ml single cream

Salt and freshly ground black pepper

Use some of the butter to grease a medium gratin dish generously. Combine the crabmeat with the cayenne, mixed herbs and lemon juice, and season well.

Generously butter the baguette slices. One good approach is to construct two giant, multi-decker, Scooby-snack style crab sandwiches, which will lie side-by-side in the gratin dish. Start with a buttered slice of baguette. Cover it with crab mixture. Add a second slice of bread, some more crab, then another piece of bread. Keep going till you have a sandwich long enough to fit the dish.

Place the sandwich in the dish on its side and then make a second one to lay beside the first. Use the remaining bread slices and filling to make smaller sandwiches to fit around the edge of the dish and fill any gaps.

Whisk together the eggs, milk and cream and season well to make a savoury custard. Pour this mixture all over the crab and bread and leave to soak for at least 10 minutes. Then bake in an oven preheated to 180°C/Gas Mark 4 for 25–30 minutes, until the custard is set and golden.

Serve warm, rather than hot, with something slightly bitter on the side, such as a salad of white chicory, radicchio, rocket or watercress with a citrus dressing – this helps cut the richness.

Also works with:
• Spider crab

Smoked pollack and spinach tart *serves 6*

This is one of the best savoury tarts we know. The balance of the lightly salty, slightly smoky fish, the sweetness of the onion, the greenness of the spinach and the just-set creaminess of the custard, all on crumbly pastry, is a kind of perfection. Is this the best recipe in the book? Arguably…

300–350g smoked pollack fillet
Up to 1 litre whole milk
A knob of unsalted butter
2 onions, finely sliced
400g fresh spinach, washed thoroughly, tough stalks removed
50g mature Cheddar cheese, grated
200ml double cream
2 eggs
2 egg yolks
Salt and freshly ground black pepper

FOR THE PASTRY:
200g plain flour
A pinch of salt
100g cold unsalted butter, cut into small cubes
1 egg, separated
About 50ml cold milk

Also works with:
• Smoked haddock and other smoked white fish
• Kippers
• Smoked salmon or trout

Start with the pastry. Put the flour, salt and butter in a food processor and pulse until the mixture has the consistency of breadcrumbs. Add the egg yolk and then, with the processor running, slowly add the milk, stopping as soon as the dough comes together. Tip out on to a lightly floured board, knead a couple of times to make a smooth ball of dough, then wrap in cling film and chill for half an hour.

Roll the pastry out thinly on a lightly floured surface and use it to line a 25cm loose-bottomed tart tin. Let the excess pastry hang over the edge of the tin. Prick the base in several places with a fork, line with a sheet of greaseproof paper and fill with baking beans or rice. Bake in an oven preheated to 160°C/Gas Mark 3 for 15 minutes, then remove the paper and beans and return the pastry case to the oven for 10 minutes, until it looks dry and cooked. Lightly beat the egg white and brush all over the pastry. Return the pastry case to the oven once more and bake for another 5 minutes, until golden. This helps to seal the pastry and prevent any filling leaking out. Trim off the excess pastry using a small, sharp knife.

Put the smoked fish in a pan, cutting it in two if necessary to make it fit neatly in a single layer. Pour in enough milk just to cover the fish, then cover the pan and bring to a simmer. Remove from the heat. The fish should be just cooked. If it isn't, turn it over and leave it in the hot milk for a minute or two more. Once it is done, remove the fish from the pan, strain the milk and set aside to cool.

Heat the butter in a pan, add the onions and fry gently until soft and golden brown – this takes a good 15 minutes. Drop the spinach into a large pan of boiling water and cook for just a minute, until wilted. Drain and leave until cool enough to handle, then squeeze out the water with your hands. Chop the spinach coarsely.

Flake the pollack into a bowl, discarding the skin and any bones, and add the cheese, onions and spinach. Mix well, then put the mixture into the tart case. Mix 200ml of the strained fish poaching milk with the cream, eggs and egg yolks. Season with salt and pepper and pour into the tart case. Bake at 160°C/Gas Mark 3 for about 40 minutes, until lightly set and browned. Serve warm or cold.

Crab tart *serves 8 as a starter*

With its creamy, soft-set filling, this tart is very rich and very gorgeous. You could use the recipe to make individual tarts, though a large one is less fiddly and avoids the potential pitfall of a too-high pastry-to-filling ratio.

1 cooked large brown crab or 2 spider
   crabs (or one of each), brown and white
   meat picked out (see pages 89–93), or
   300g fresh crabmeat
2 tablespoons olive oil
1 large onion, finely sliced
2 garlic cloves, finely chopped
½–1 fresh red chilli (depending on heat),
   deseeded and finely chopped
Juice of ½ lemon
2–3 tablespoons coarsely chopped
   coriander
50g Parmesan cheese, grated

2 eggs
2 egg yolks
200ml whole milk
200ml double cream
Salt and freshly ground black pepper

FOR THE SHORTCRUST PASTRY:
200g plain flour
A pinch of salt
100g cold unsalted butter, cut into
   small cubes
1 egg, separated
About 50ml cold milk

Start with the pastry. Put the flour, salt and butter in a food processor and pulse until the mixture has the consistency of breadcrumbs. Add the egg yolk and then, with the processor running, pour in the milk in a thin stream. Watch carefully and stop adding the milk as soon as the dough comes together. (You may not need it all.) Tip out on to a lightly floured board, knead a couple of times to make a smooth ball of dough, then wrap in cling film and chill for half an hour.

Roll the pastry out thinly on a lightly floured surface and use it to line a 25cm loose-bottomed tart tin. Let the excess pastry hang over the edge of the tin – don't trim it off. Prick the base in several places with a fork, line it with a sheet of greaseproof paper and fill with baking beans or rice.

Bake in an oven preheated to 160°C/Gas Mark 3 for 15 minutes, then remove the paper and beans and return the pastry case to the oven for 10 minutes, until it looks dry and cooked. Lightly beat the egg white and brush it all over the pastry. Return the pastry case to the oven once more and bake for another 5 minutes, until golden. This helps to seal the pastry and prevent any filling leaking out. Trim off the excess pastry using a small, sharp knife. Turn the oven up to 180°C/Gas Mark 4.

Loosely combine the brown and white meat in a bowl, taking care not to break it up too much or reduce it to a paste.

Heat a large frying pan over a medium-high heat and add 1 tablespoon of olive oil. Add the onion, sauté for 5–10 minutes, until soft and light golden, then remove from the pan and set aside.

Add another dash of olive oil to the pan and throw in the garlic and chilli. Fry until the garlic just begins to colour and gives off a nutty aroma, then immediately toss in the crabmeat. Stir to combine it with the chilli and garlic, then take the pan off the heat. Stir in the onion, along with the lemon juice, coriander and Parmesan. Season with salt and pepper.

Spoon the crab mixture into the baked tart case. Don't press it down or pack it in, just arrange it carefully with a fork.

Combine the eggs, egg yolks, milk and cream, season well and pour the mixture over the crab. A poke and a nudge might be required at this point to encourage the custard to spread evenly through the crab filling.

Bake the tart in the oven for 30–35 minutes, until the custard is just set, then set aside to cool slightly, for about 15 minutes before serving.

Grilled lemon sole with lemons *serves 2*

This is a great way to do justice to this lovely fish. You get the best of everything: a crisp, savoury top from the heat of the grill, a sweet, succulent middle from cooking on the bone, and a delicate lemon infusion from the base.

Also works with:
- Dab
- Flounder
- Witch
- Megrim
- Plaice

1 lemon sole, weighing about 750g, descaled and gutted, but skin on
1 lemon, plus extra wedges to serve

A few knobs of softened unsalted butter, plus extra for greasing
Sea salt

Preheat the grill to maximum. Trim the fins and tail from the fish. Cut the lemon into slices about 5mm thick – to make a bed to lay the whole fish on. Butter a grill tray and arrange the lemon slices on it, roughly forming a sole shape. Smear the butter all over the fish, season both sides with salt and lay it, dark side up, on the lemon slices. Score the top a few times, up to 5mm deep, with a very sharp knife – a herringbone pattern is nice, to mirror the shape of the head.

Now slide the tin under the fiercely hot grill. You need to keep an eye on it, and you may need to adjust your shelf height to achieve, after about 10 minutes' cooking, a deliciously browned and bubbled-up top skin and a just-cooked centre (test this by sliding a table knife in at the spine – the flesh should just pull away from the bone). Baste the fish with the buttery, lemony juices a couple of times during cooking.

Incidentally, if you're wondering, the heat conducted through the grill tray should have cooked the underside of the fish from underneath, but you can accelerate this by taking the tray out from under the grill about halfway through cooking and placing it on a hob over a high heat for just half a minute, then returning the pan to the grill.

When the sole is ready, slide it, sizzling hot, on to a serving platter – the lemon slices will probably come with it. Serve with nothing more than a few salad leaves and some plain boiled potatoes to squash into the juices, plus the lemon wedges to squeeze over the top.

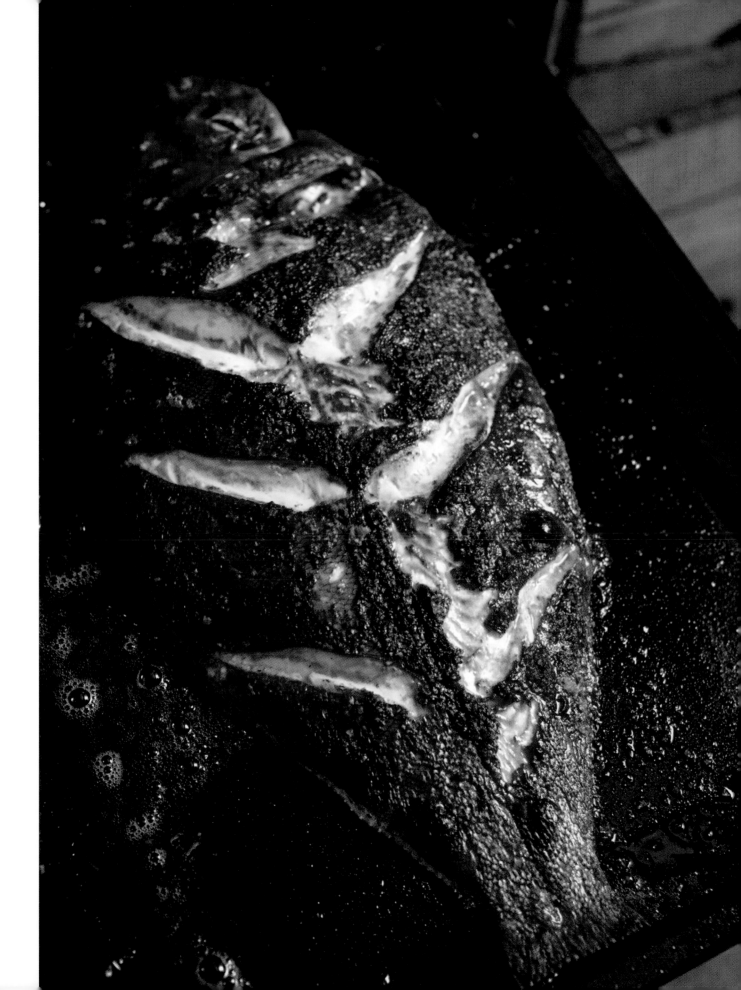

Soups, stews
and poaching

ingredients, vegetables, herbs and spices – before you add the fish. Your fillet of smoked pollack, or your fresh mussels, say, add the final touch to the delicious base you've already created. Our Fish (and chorizo) soup (page 260) is a good example of this: the greater part of the recipe is taken up with creating a rich, flavoursome base from onions, celery, fennel seeds, tomatoes, chorizo and fish stock (and maybe some potatoes or chickpeas if you want to make a hearty stew out of it). The fish element is added right at the end to complete the dish, giving texture and that little bit of fresh, sweet fishiness. It's not that it's an afterthought – far from it – but to get the best from fresh fish as an ingredient in a soup or stew, it's generally best to view it as the final flourish.

However, it would be misleading to suggest that most of these recipes do not see any fish at all until the end. Fish is often used early on in the proceedings to impart flavour to the brew – in the form of fish stock. Knowing how to make a good fish stock is useful – arguably essential – if you want to get the best from this chapter.

A good fish stock

Whenever you are left with a nice collection of fresh fish heads, skeletons and skins, it would be a crime to throw them away. Using them to make stock is economical (good ready-made fish stock is hard to find and never cheap) and also respectful of the fish itself. But above all, it's a great asset to your fish cooking. A fish stock on standby in your freezer means that when a bit of good fresh fish comes to hand you have access to a whole range of recipes beyond the simple fry/bake options.

Happily, good fish stock is even easier to make than good meat stock. And, in theory, every chance to buy good fresh fish is also a chance to pick up ingredients for stock. So whenever you visit the fishmonger's, it's worth asking for some fresh heads and frames – even if it's just to lay down some stock in the freezer.

A really good fish stock will bind together the elements of many of the dishes in this chapter and anchor them all with a base note of deep, savoury fresh fish flavour. Not that fish stocks need be 'fishy' in the negative sense. A good one, made with scrupulously fresh heads and frames from white fish, can be used as a base for non-fish soups, which won't taste fishy, just robust (we often make a nettle soup with fish stock, and nobody has ever guessed that it has fish in it). It goes without saying that fish stock is the liquid medium for fish risottos, too.

People often think that fish stocks are technical, the preserve of the experienced cook or even the professional chef. We know a few keen cooks who would never pass up the chance to make a chicken stock from the carcass of a roast bird, yet who remain hesitant about taking the plunge with a few fresh fish frames. It really shouldn't be like that. Fish stocks are easy – though you do, of course, need to understand what you're doing with your ingredients.

The key point is that a fish stock requires much less cooking time than a meat one. Because of the structure of the flesh and the fish's delicate bones, you can extract all the flavour and goodness in half an hour or so of gentle simmering. Vegetables used for flavouring should be chopped fairly finely or even shredded or grated, so they give up their flavour in a similarly short time. With chopped fish frames and shredded vegetables, plus a few fragrant herbs, a gentle sub-simmer is all that's required to turn tap water into great stock.

Overcooking fish stock, or boiling it too hard, will not only fail to extract further good flavours, it may start to generate some bad ones. A chalky flavour will arise as calcium salts in the bones start to dissolve into the stock. Next comes a strange, ammoniac taint – the sort of thing you'd associate with fish that's off – even if you're using spankingly fresh ingredients. Shellfish stock is the same: boil too long or too hard and, though it may still taste okay, you'll catch an offputting waft of ammonia. Bear all this in mind, and the simple recipe for fish stock on page 256 will stand you in good stead.

Simple poaching and court-bouillons

Not all poached fish is cooked in the liquid in which it will be served. It is sometimes better for whole fish and fish portions to be immersed in a relatively unseasoned liquid, such as lightly salted water or milk. A sauce to serve with such a simply poached fish – a salsa verde, perhaps, or a classic hollandaise – might be prepared separately, and bear no direct relation to the cooked fish until the two meet on the plate. There's nothing wrong with that. It's how fish is cooked and sauced in many respectable restaurants, but we think it's something of a missed opportunity.

Fish stock *makes about 1.5 litres*

This is our basic fish stock, a light, well-flavoured broth that we use as a base for all manner of soups, plus sauces and risottos. It's particularly good in 'green' soups – watercress, nettle or parsley, for example – even if no fish is being added to the soup.

Follow the general advice on preparing fish stock on pages 252–3. Get into the habit of freezing all your white fish trimmings and you can soon build up a good stash for making stock. You can use all of the fish frame: bones, skin, head, tail – anything that's not guts or gills. Not only is this good, thrifty cooking but making your own stock also gives you control over its flavour. Indeed, this recipe is only a guide. The more fish bits you pack into the pot, for instance, the more intense your stock will be. You can vary the vegetables too: trimmings of fennel bulbs, celeriac and shallots are all good candidates for inclusion.

The golden rule: *all* the fish trimmings must be scrupulously fresh (or fresh when they were frozen). A fish that only just passes the sniff test (see page 45) might have fillets that are just about worthy of the frying pan, but its bones will not be worthy of the stockpot.

2kg white fish trimmings, including
   at least 4 good heads
4 celery sticks, roughly chopped
2 garlic cloves, bruised but not peeled
2 onions, peeled and halved

2 carrots, chopped
2 bay leaves
5 thyme stalks
A handful of parsley stalks
½ teaspoon black or white peppercorns

Rinse the fish trimmings in cold water and put them in a large stockpot with all the other ingredients. Pack them in fairly well and add just enough cold water to cover everything. Bring up to a very gentle simmer. Skim off any scum that rises to the surface, then cover the pan and simmer for half an hour, taking care that the stock doesn't boil fast at any point. A gentle, popping simmer is all that is necessary – overcooking or boiling can make the stock cloudy and chalky tasting.

Let the stock cool slightly before straining it into a container. You can use it straight away, or refrigerate it for up to 2 days, or freeze it.

Shellfish stock

A stock made with the shells of crabs, lobsters, prawns or any of their kin makes a particularly rich and delicious base for soups and stews. You can get quite cheffy about it, using uncooked shells chosen specially for the purpose, sautéing them, then adding a splash of brandy and flambéing the whole thing before you add the water and aromatics. The result is an incredibly rich and intense broth, and well worth the effort.

However, a simpler version, employing the trimmings from shellfish that have already been used in other recipes, is perhaps more useful and practical for the lay cook. What's more, it's a great way to use up those thin back legs of a crab, lobster or langoustine. Though they contain flavoursome meat, these can be the very devil to crack open and deal with. But crush them and cook them in the stockpot and you can feel satisfied that you're wasting nothing. In fact, where large edible crabs are concerned, these little meaty morsels, along with the finer parts of the body shell, are preferable to big, thick chunks of carapace and claw. Not only are these very hard and therefore difficult to break up, but they can make your stock taste chalky.

Replace the white fish trimmings in the fish stock recipe opposite with mixed crustacean shells, legs and heads (excluding the main carapaces and large claws of big crabs) from any prawns, lobsters or crabs that you have already cooked and picked – you can always stockpile such leftovers in the freezer until you have enough to make a good stock. Including the shells and heads of some prawns or langoustines will make for a richer, better-balanced stock than crab trimmings alone.

You really need a good kilo of such trimmings to make a decent stock, but you can always supplement, say, half a kilo of shellfish trimmings with some frames and heads of fresh white fish.

Crush the shells with a rolling pin or meat mallet so they can release their flavour. If you like, you can sauté the shells in a little butter and oil for 2–3 minutes to create an extra layer of flavour, before adding the other ingredients, but it's not essential. Either way, add the stock vegetables, herbs and water and cook as per the fish stock recipe, making sure you don't go over the 30-minute mark. You can then simply strain the stock through a large sieve, pressing the shells hard with a ladle to extract as much juice as possible, or blitz the whole lot in a heavy-duty blender before straining.

A shellfish stock, or a mixed shellfish and fish stock, makes a particularly good base for any fish soup, stew, risotto or chowder to which other shellfish or crustaceans are going to be added.

Nettle soup with smoked fish *serves 6*

A soup made with the bright green tips of early spring nettles is a delicious and velvety affair. We've discovered that it's very successful when made with fish stock, which seems to enhance the nettle flavour without making the soup taste fishy. Add a generous sprinkling of smoked fish to finish it and you have a substantial dish.

Half a carrier bag full of nettles – tops or
   young leaves only
50g unsalted butter
1 large or 2 medium onions, finely sliced
1 small head of celeriac, peeled and cut
   into cubes
1 large garlic clove, crushed

1 litre fish stock (see page 256)
300g smoked pollack or haddock fillet
3 tablespoons cooked rice, or 3 rice cakes
2 tablespoons thick cream or crème
   fraîche, plus extra to serve
Salt and freshly ground black pepper

Wash the nettles thoroughly, checking them for unwanted extras – vegetable or animal – and discarding any tough stalks.

Melt the butter in a large pan over a low heat. Add the onion, celeriac and garlic, cover the pan and sweat gently, stirring occasionally, for 8–10 minutes, until softened but not brown.

Meanwhile, pour the stock into a separate pan and bring it to a simmer. Add the smoked fish and poach gently until cooked – no longer than 5 minutes, just until the flesh flakes easily. Scoop out the fish with a slotted spoon and keep warm. Pour the hot stock over the softened vegetables in the pan and simmer for 5 minutes or so, until the celeriac is almost tender. Pile in the nettles. Return to the boil, reduce the heat and simmer for 2–3 minutes, until the nettles are wilted and tender. Season with salt and pepper.

To keep the colour nice and bright, you'll need to purée the soup immediately – in batches if necessary. Tip it into a blender, add the rice or rice cakes and whiz to a purée. Pour into a clean pan, stir in the cream and reheat but do not let it boil. Check the seasoning.

Ladle the soup into warmed bowls. Flake the fish flesh from the skin, discarding any pin bones. Heap some flakes of hot smoked fish in the middle of each bowlful and finish with a swirl of cream.

Fish (and chorizo) soup *serves 5–6*

This soup has become a classic at River Cottage. We make it with all sorts of fish, from black bream to pouting. Many things can be added but the three basic ingredients are always the same: fillets of very fresh fish, sometimes lightly salted, roast tomato sauce and fish stock. You can make it a bit more 'deluxe' by adding squid and/or various shellfish. Usually, but not always, we add some of our homemade chorizo for an extra kick of spice and texture. And you can turn it from a starter soup to a main-course stew by adding potatoes, chickpeas or shredded greens, as suggested below.

The tomato sauce is an old favourite of ours, and very versatile. It's a brilliant way to deal with a glut of tomatoes, if you have one, as it freezes beautifully.

4 small, hot chorizo sausages, about
   250g in total, sliced on the diagonal
   (optional), or a little olive oil
2 garlic cloves, sliced
2 onions, sliced
2 celery sticks, finely chopped
A pinch of fennel seeds
200ml white wine
500ml fish or shellfish stock (see pages
   256–7)
500g lightly salted white fish fillets (see
   page 124), such as pouting, whiting or
   pollack (or unsalted bream or sea bass)
1 tablespoon finely chopped parsley
   (optional)

FOR THE ROASTED TOMATO SAUCE:
1kg ripe, full-flavoured tomatoes, halved
2–3 garlic cloves, finely chopped
2 tablespoons olive oil

OPTIONAL 'LUXURY' EXTRAS:
Up to 200g small-medium squid or
   cuttlefish, cleaned and 'butterflied'
   (see pages 97–102)
1–2 scallops per person, shelled, cleaned
   and sliced in half (see page 104–7)
½ dozen mussels per person, steamed
   open in a little wine (see page 262)

OPTIONAL 'BULKING' EXTRAS:
Up to 750g potatoes, peeled and cut into
   chunky cubes
Up to 500g pre-cooked or tinned (rinsed)
   chickpeas
Up to 250g spinach, Swiss chard or other
   greens, finely shredded

First make the tomato sauce. Arrange the tomato halves in an ovenproof dish so they sit snugly side by side, rather than on top of each other. Mix the garlic and oil together and trickle them over the tomatoes. Season lightly, then roast in an oven preheated to 180°C/Gas Mark 4 for 35–45 minutes, until the tomatoes are soft, pulpy and slightly browned. Rub them through a sieve, discarding the pips and skin, and set aside.

Put the chorizo (if using) in a large, heavy saucepan and fry over a medium heat until lightly coloured. Otherwise heat a little olive oil in the pan. Add the garlic, onions, celery and fennel seeds. If using potatoes, add them at this stage. Fry gently for 10 minutes, to soften the vegetables without browning them, then pour in the wine and simmer until reduced by half.

Add 250ml of the tomato sauce (you might have a little more than this, but any extra will keep well in the fridge) and the stock, plus the chickpeas if you are using them, then bring to a simmer and cook, covered, for 20 minutes.

Meanwhile, skin the fish fillets (see page 73) and remove any pin bones by slicing down either side of the bone line. Cut the fish into fairly large chunks – small pouting or whiting fillets can be used whole.

When the tomato soup base has had its 20 minutes, add the fish, together with the squid or cuttlefish and scallops if using. Cook briefly in the gently simmering soup for 2–3 minutes, adding any mussels and shredded greens after a minute.

Season the soup with pepper, adding salt only if necessary (with chorizo, you really shouldn't need it). Ladle into warmed bowls, garnish with chopped parsley if you like, and serve with crusty bread.

Cullen skink   *serves 4–5 as a starter, 2–3 as a hearty supper*

This is our version of a classic Scottish soup. We're not sure how it would go down in Cullen, the small village in the northeast of Scotland where the recipe originated, but we hope they'd find it passable.

Onions have always been a traditional part of this soup but our recipe uses more of them than is usual. We find cooking them down to a rich, sweet mass gives the soup a really wonderful depth of flavour.

50g unsalted butter

50ml olive oil

About 1kg onions, finely sliced

500g smoked pollack or other cold-
  smoked white fish

500ml whole milk

750ml fish stock (see page 256)

500g white potatoes, peeled and cubed

Salt and freshly ground black pepper

Heat the butter and oil in a large saucepan until the butter begins to foam. Add the onions and cook for 45–60 minutes, stirring regularly, until golden and buttery-soft. Don't let them catch on the pan.

Put the smoked fish fillet in a pan and pour over the milk. Cover the pan and bring to a gentle simmer. By the time the milk is simmering, the fish should be perfectly cooked and you should be able to remove it straight away. However, if you've got a particularly thick fillet from a monster fish, it might need to be left in the hot milk for a minute or two to finish cooking. Remove it when it's done.

Add the poaching milk, fish stock and potatoes to the onions, bring to a simmer and cook until the potatoes are tender. To thicken the soup slightly, crush some of the potatoes against the side of the pan with a wooden spoon and stir them back in.

Flake the pollack from its skin, discarding any bones. Add the fish to the soup, bring back to a gentle simmer and season to taste. Ladle into warmed bowls and serve with some good bread.

Smoked pollack and mussel chowder *serves 6*

Chowders can vary enormously, from tomato-based broths to flour-thickened, milky stews, but all should be soothing, rich and comforting. We favour the classic, creamy, New England-style chowder, based on potatoes – and the principle of balancing the sweetness of shellfish (mussels here, cockles in the recipe on page 264) with something salty (smoked pollack here, bacon there).

We've also specified different types of potato – the floury ones used in this recipe will crumble a little and help to thicken the soup, while the waxy ones called for overleaf will hold their shape much more and give a different, but just as delicious, texture. You can, of course, adapt either of these recipes, or mix and match between them. Cockles and mussels will work equally well in either, and the choice of potato is really up to you, too.

<u>Also works with:</u>
• Clams
• Cockles

1kg mussels, scrubbed and debearded (see page 103)
½ glass of white wine
1 tablespoon olive oil
2 leeks, white part only, quartered lengthways and thinly sliced
1 onion, finely diced
2 garlic cloves, finely chopped
30g unsalted butter

750ml fish or shellfish stock (see pages 256–7)
300g smoked pollack or haddock fillet
250g floury potatoes, such as King Edward, peeled and cut into 5mm dice
200ml double cream
A small handful of parsley, finely chopped
A small bunch of chives, finely chopped
Salt and freshly ground black pepper

Prepare the mussels first: heat a pan large enough to hold them all comfortably, add the wine and, when it's bubbling, tip the mussels in. Shake the pan well and cover. Steam the mussels over a medium-high heat for 3–4 minutes, until the shells are open. Remove them from the pan using a slotted spoon and discard any that haven't opened. Strain the cooking liquor through a fine sieve, or a coarse sieve lined with a clean tea towel, and reserve. Remove two-thirds of the mussels from their shells and set aside. Save the remainder for serving.

Place a large, heavy-based pan over a medium-high heat and add the olive oil, followed by the leeks, onion, garlic and butter. Reduce the heat and let the vegetables soften gently for 5 minutes. Pour in the stock and the mussel cooking liquid and bring to a gentle simmer.

Carefully lower the smoked fish into the pan. Poach for 4 minutes or until just cooked, then remove with a large fish slice. Add the potatoes to the simmering soup and cook until tender. Meanwhile, flake the fish off the skin, removing any bones you find along the way.

Add the cream to the soup, followed by the shelled mussels and the flaked smoked pollack. Stir gently, season with salt and pepper and add the chopped parsley and chives. Simmer gently for just a minute or two to reheat the fish – no more, or the potato will completely disintegrate.

Divide the shell-on mussels between warmed bowls and ladle over the hot chowder. Serve piping hot, with toasted sourdough bread.

Smoked pollack and sweetcorn chowder

If mussels are not to hand, you can make a really lovely smoked haddock chowder without them, using fresh sweetcorn kernels to complement the salty fish. Follow the recipe opposite, omitting the mussels. Slice the kernels from 2 corn cobs and add them to the soup just before the potatoes are cooked. Let them simmer for a couple of minutes before finishing the soup with the smoked fish and herbs.

Kipper, potato and spinach soup *serves 8*

This is simplicity itself, a kind of pared-down alternative to the more elaborate chowder opposite, but with the same soothing quality.

200g spinach, coarse stalks removed
1.5 litres fish stock (see page 256)
   or vegetable stock
250g kipper fillets
50g unsalted butter
1 onion, chopped

1 leek, white part only, finely sliced
1 large garlic clove, sliced
250g potatoes, peeled and diced
100ml double cream, plus extra to serve
Salt and freshly ground black pepper
Chopped chives, to finish

Also works with:
• Smoked pollack
• Smoked haddock

Bring a large pan of water to the boil, drop in the spinach and cook for 1 minute. Drain and allow it to cool a little. Squeeze all the excess liquid out of the spinach with your hands, then chop it finely and set aside.

Bring the stock to a gentle simmer in a large pan. Add the kipper fillets and poach for about 4 minutes, until the fish flakes easily. Take care not to overcook it. Remove the fish from the stock and flake the flesh away from the skin into a bowl, checking for bones as you go. Take your time over this, as kippers do have lots of little bones.

Melt the butter in a large pan over a medium-low heat. Add the onion, leek and garlic and sweat gently until soft. Add the fishy vegetable stock to the pan, along with the potatoes, bring to a simmer and cook for 20–30 minutes, until the potatoes are tender.

Purée the soup in a blender until smooth. Return to the pan and reheat gently. Add the flaked kipper flesh, spinach and cream and season well. Let the soup simmer very gently for 5 minutes, then divide between warmed bowls. Serve garnished with another swirl of cream and some chopped chives.

Cockle or palourde chowder *serves 4*

Like the recipes on the preceding pages, this chowder uses stock as the main cooking medium rather than the more traditional milk, but is finished off with a slosh of cream. The sweet shellfish component takes the form of cockles or palourdes (a nod to the classic clam chowders of New England) and the salty element is provided by the bacon.

Also works with:
• Other small clams
• Mussels
• Razor clams

1 tablespoon olive oil
2 knobs of unsalted butter
150g smoked bacon or pancetta, cut into small cubes or lardons
1 large leek, white part only, quartered lengthways and thinly sliced
1 onion, diced
2 small garlic cloves, finely chopped
1 large, waxy potato, such as Cara, peeled and cut into 5mm cubes

750ml fish or shellfish stock (see pages 256–7)
1kg cockles, palourdes or other small clams, purged if necessary (see page 103)
A glass of white wine
50ml double cream
Salt and freshly ground black pepper

Heat a heavy-based pan over a medium heat and add the olive oil and a knob of butter. When the butter is foaming, add the bacon and sauté until it starts to release some of its fat. Add the leek, onion and garlic, then cover and sweat gently for around 5 minutes, without letting the vegetables colour. Add the potato and sweat for 5 minutes more, then pour in the stock and bring to a gentle simmer. Cook, covered, for about 10 minutes, until the potato is soft – keep an eye on it, though, as you don't want it to disintegrate completely.

Meanwhile, scrub the cockles or clams under cold water, discarding any that are damaged or open. Put a large, wide pan over a high heat and add the wine, a glass of water and a knob of butter. Bring to the boil and add the cockles or clams. Cover at once with the lid, shake or stir after a minute or so, and cover again. Cook for 2–4 minutes, until the shellfish are open (discard any that remain firmly closed), then tip the contents of the pan into a colander set over a bowl to catch the juices. Set aside a few cockles or clams and pick the remainder from their shells.

Strain the juices through a fine sieve, or a coarse sieve lined with a cotton cloth, and add them to the chowder, along with the shelled cockles/clams. Stir in the cream, season to taste and reheat gently if necessary. Serve piping hot, garnished with the shell-on cockles or clams and accompanied by some bread.

Crustacean soup *serves 6*

This is an old favourite, which deserves to be included because it is so good. It's an endlessly flexible recipe – more of a guide, in fact, which you should use to your own ends, depending on what shellfish you have to hand. You can use just about any species of crab, though we favour velvet crabs for their sweet flavour.

1 large or 2 medium brown crabs or
    spider crabs
About 8 blue velvet swimmer crabs
    (optional)
About 6 large Dublin Bay prawns, or
    125g ordinary prawns
1 whole white fish, such as a gurnard or
    wrasse, gutted and skinned (optional)
2 tablespoons olive oil
1 onion, chopped
1 carrot, chopped
2–3 large tomatoes, chopped (or 250g
    cherry tomatoes)
4 garlic cloves, crushed
A few sprigs each of fennel, chervil and
    parsley, as available
2–3 bay leaves

A few parsley stalks or leek tops (optional)
A pinch of cayenne pepper
Salt and freshly ground black pepper
Croûtons and grated Gruyère cheese,
    to serve

FOR THE CHEATY ROUILLE:
1 garlic clove, peeled
1 hot red chilli, very finely chopped
¼ teaspoon coarse salt
1 teaspoon Dijon mustard
1 egg yolk
100ml olive oil
150ml groundnut oil
A squeeze of lemon juice
Freshly ground black pepper

Make the rouille in advance to allow the flavour to develop. Crush the garlic, chilli and salt to a paste with a pestle and mortar, then transfer to a bowl. Stir in the mustard, then the egg yolk. Combine the two oils in a jug and trickle them on to the yolk mixture as thinly as possible, whisking all the time with a balloon whisk, to create an emulsion. Once the mixture has thickened, you can add the oils a little more quickly. You should end up with a thick, wobbly mayonnaise. Taste and add lemon juice, pepper and more salt if necessary. Chill until needed.

Kill and cook all the crabs as described on page 89. Cook the prawns as described on page 96. Leave everything until cool enough to handle. Now break open the crabs and discard the dead men's fingers and stomachs, then remove as much brown meat as you can from the carapaces and all the white meat from the larger claws (see pages 90–3). Set the meat aside. Peel the prawns (Dublin Bay or otherwise) and set them aside, separately from the crabmeat. Cut the fish into chunks, if including.

Discard the main carapaces of the brown crabs. Put all the other heads, legs and shells of the crabs and prawns in a large bowl or heavy saucepan and pound them to pieces with a hammer or rolling pin.

Heat the olive oil in a large pan. Add the onion, carrot, tomatoes, garlic and herbs and fry gently for a few minutes to soften. Add the hammered shellfish, and the fish if using. Pour over enough water just to cover everything and bring to the boil. Simmer gently for 20 minutes (no more), then take off the heat.

This shellfish stock can then be processed in a number of ways. Either strain it through a heavy-duty conical sieve, pressing hard with the back of a ladle to extract as much fishy juice as possible; or, put everything in a heavy-duty blender, whiz it up and then pass through the sieve; or, if you are feeling strong, you could press the stock through a heavy-duty mouli-légumes or potato ricer.

Put the stock back in a clean pan over a low heat and stir in all the white and brown meat you saved from the crabs. Heat through but do not let it boil. Season to taste with salt, pepper and cayenne, then divide between warmed bowls. Add the prawns and serve with croûtons, grated Gruyère and the rouille.

Thai crab and fish soup *serves 4*

Here's an adaptable fish soup/stew. It begins life as a luscious crab soup but is easily adapted to take the fish and shellfish you have to hand. The idea is to create a creamy soup with just the right balance of salty, sweet, sour and hot flavours before adding the fish right at the end.

The crabmeat is literally a last-minute addition. The same would be true of just-steamed-open mussels or cockles. Raw additions, such as squid or white fish, will need a couple of minutes' simmering to cook them through.

1 tablespoon sunflower oil

1 onion, finely chopped

50g nugget of fresh ginger, cut into fine matchsticks or coarsely grated

3 fat garlic cloves, finely chopped

1 small, hot red chilli, deseeded and finely chopped

2 lemongrass stalks, tough outer layers removed, finely sliced

400ml well-flavoured fish or shellfish stock (see pages 256–7)

400ml tin of coconut milk

A dash or two of soy sauce

A dash of Thai fish sauce (optional)

Juice of 1–2 limes, plus lime wedges to serve

1 heaped tablespoon chopped coriander

FOR THE FISH:

Brown and white meat from 1 large brown crab (about 300–400g meat in total)

And/or 300–400g in total of raw prawns, squid rings, scallops, chunks of white fish fillet

And/or a dozen mussels or cockles, steamed open in a little water or wine (see page 262)

Heat the oil in a large saucepan over a medium heat. Add the onion, ginger, garlic, chilli and lemongrass and sweat gently, stirring from time to time, until the onion is soft and golden. Add the stock, bring to a simmer and cook gently for 10 minutes, allowing the stock to infuse with the lemongrass and garlic. Add the coconut milk, stir well and bring back to a simmer.

If you're adding any raw fish or shellfish, put it in now and cook at a gentle simmer for 2–3 minutes, until it's just done. Then add the crab, and the cooked mussels or cockles if using, and heat through gently for just 30 seconds or so. Taste the soup and season with the soy, fish sauce (if using) and lime juice. Serve straight away, scattered with the coriander and accompanied by lime wedges.

Leek, celeriac and oyster broth *serves 6*

This delicate broth is a great way to serve celeriac and oysters together – a pair that get on so well but meet so rarely. Well-flavoured fish stock is essential, so make some in advance. It's also important to cut the vegetables into small, neat, evenly sized pieces.

50g unsalted butter

1 tablespoon olive oil

About 400g celeriac, peeled and cut into small dice (like square petits pois)

1 small potato (about 100g), peeled and cut into small dice

2 tender inner sticks of celery, peeled and cut into small dice

1 large leek, white part only, quartered lengthways and finely sliced

1 small onion, finely diced

2 garlic cloves, very finely chopped

750ml fish or shellfish stock (see pages 256–7)

½ glass of white wine

18 fresh oysters

100ml double cream

Salt and freshly ground black pepper

Set a large saucepan over a medium heat and add the butter and olive oil. When the butter is foaming, stir in all the chopped vegetables and garlic. Cook gently for 5–10 minutes, until softened but not coloured. Add the stock and white wine and bring to a gentle simmer. Cover and cook for 20–25 minutes, stirring once or twice, until all the vegetables are tender.

Meanwhile, place a large pan over a high heat and add half a glass of water. When it's boiling, place 6 oysters in the pan. Cover and allow them to steam for 2 minutes. This will open the shells and allow you to remove the meat: you will still need to shuck them (see page 104), but it will be a much easier task. Repeat with the remaining oysters. Each oyster will have a little juice in its shell – make sure you don't spill this.

Finish the broth by stirring in the cream and the juice from the oysters and seasoning to taste. Divide the warm poached oysters between warmed bowls and ladle over the hot broth, making sure each person gets a fair share of vegetables along with the liquor.

Moules frites *serves 2*

Although this is quite a quick dish to make, it does require a little organisation, as the chips and mussels both need to be cooked at around the same time. It's also easier to cook in fairly small quantities, so this is a perfect two-person project, both in the cooking and the eating.

As with all the best chips, the *frites* are fried twice – once to cook the potato through, then again at a higher temperature to create the deliciously crisp, golden exterior every *frite* lover hankers after.

Also works with:
- Cockles
- Palourdes

1 tablespoon olive oil
A good knob of unsalted butter
1 garlic clove, finely chopped
4 small shallots, finely chopped
1kg mussels, scrubbed and debearded
  (see page 103)
½ glass of white wine
2 teaspoons double cream
1 tablespoon finely chopped parsley
Salt and freshly ground black pepper

FOR THE FRITES:
2 large, floury potatoes, such as
  Maris Piper, Désirée or King Edward
2 litres groundnut oil
Fine sea salt

Start with the *frites*. Peel the potatoes and cut them into matchsticks, about 5mm thick. Wash them in cold water to remove excess starch, then drain and blot dry with a clean tea towel.

Pour the groundnut oil into a deep-fat fryer or a deep saucepan and heat it to 130°C. Put the chips in the frying basket and lower it into the oil. Cook for 7–8 minutes, or until soft all the way through but not coloured. Remove the chips and drain on kitchen paper. If you wish, you can leave them at this stage and keep in the fridge for up to a day before their second frying. If you want to serve them straight away, increase the temperature of the oil to 190°C. Lower the chips in again and cook for 1–2 minutes, until light golden brown. Drain them again on kitchen paper to absorb any excess oil, then toss them in a little fine sea salt and put into a large bowl.

For the mussels, heat the olive oil and butter in a deep, wide pan over a medium heat. Add the garlic and shallots and cook for a few minutes, until softened. Add the mussels, increase the heat and add the wine and some salt and pepper. Cook, covered, for 3–4 minutes, shaking the pan a couple of times. Once all the mussels are open (discard any that remain steadfastly shut), stir in the cream and parsley and serve, juices and all, with your *frites*.

West Country cider mussels

serves 4 as a starter, 2 as a feast

Most ways of cooking mussels are variations of the recipe on page 272: steaming them open in a flavoured liquor, which becomes their sauce. And, of course, you don't have to serve them with chips – a hunk of bread, some pasta or rice can all be used to make a meal of them, or they can be served with just their broth, as a starter. This is our own locally inspired take on the classic *moules marinière*, using leeks, thyme and cider.

50g unsalted butter

1 or 2 leeks, white part only, finely
   shredded, or 1 onion, finely sliced

2 garlic cloves, finely sliced

1 teaspoon thyme leaves

1½ teaspoons cider vinegar (optional)

½ glass of real cider (medium is best;
   or use dry plus a splash of apple juice)

1kg mussels, scrubbed and debearded
   (see page 103)

2 tablespoons double cream (optional)

Sea salt and freshly ground black pepper

Also works with:
• Cockles
• Palourdes

Heat the butter in a deep, wide pan over a medium heat and add the leek or onion, plus the garlic. Cover and sweat for about 5 minutes, stirring occasionally, until soft but not coloured. Raise the heat and throw in the thyme. When its scent hits you, add the cider vinegar, if using, and cider, then the mussels and some salt and pepper. Give them a quick stir and a shake, then cook, covered, for 3–4 minutes, shaking the pan a couple of times. When all the mussels are open (discard any that remain closed), finish with the cream, if you like, and serve with some good bread and more cider (in a glass, this time).

VARIATION
West Country beer mussels

There's no reason to stop at cider. A good ale also makes a fantastic cooking medium for mussels. Avoid cheap, light lagers or very heavy stouts and instead go for a real ale with a bit of lightness and some floral, grassy, herbal notes. We would say this, but we have no hesitation in recommending our own organic Stinger beer, made with nettles (see the Directory, page 592). Proceed pretty much as above, but use beer in place of cider and leave out the cream. Serve with hunks of buttered bread.

Curried mussels *serves 4 as a starter, 2 as a main course*

Mussels can stand pretty robust spicing and, if you like your curry hot, feel free to play fast and loose with this recipe.

<u>Also works with:</u>
· Cockles
· Palourdes

A knob of unsalted butter
1 tablespoon olive oil
4 shallots or 2 onions, finely chopped
2 teaspoons mild curry powder
½ glass of white wine
750g–1kg mussels, scrubbed and
  debearded (see page 103)

3–4 sprigs of coriander, finely chopped
3–4 lovage leaves, finely chopped
  (optional)
2 tablespoons double cream
Salt and freshly ground black pepper

Heat the butter and olive oil in a large pan. Add the shallots or onions and sweat gently for 10 minutes, until soft. Add the curry powder and cook for a minute, then pour in the wine and half a glass of water and bring to a simmer.

Add the mussels to the pan, cover and let steam open over a medium-high heat for 3–4 minutes, until the shells are open. Remove them from the pan with a slotted spoon and discard any that stay resolutely shut. Pick all but a dozen mussels from their shells and put them into warmed bowls, reserving any liquid. Set aside the mussels in their shells.

Add the chopped coriander and the lovage, if using, to the liquor that remains in the pan, along with the cream and any liquid from shelling the mussels. Simmer for 2–3 minutes, then season to taste and ladle over the mussels in the bowls. Garnish with the shell-on mussels and serve straight away, with fresh bread.

Winkles in a court-bouillon *serves 6 as a snack or a canapé*

You can boil winkles in plain salted water or seawater, but if you add a few aromatics and a splash of wine, the flavour improves considerably. The following is just a guide – use as many of the court-bouillon ingredients as you have available. An onion and a bay leaf would be better than nothing – quite acceptable, in fact.

Winkles shouldn't need purging, unless they come from a particularly sandy place. If you think grit may be a problem, soak them in cold fresh water overnight before cooking.

3–4 dozen winkles, cleaned
  (see page 108)

FOR THE COURT-BOUILLON:
2 carrots, finely sliced
4 celery sticks, finely sliced
1 leek, finely sliced
2 onions, finely sliced

3 garlic cloves, bruised
2 bay leaves
A large sprig of thyme, if handy
A large sprig of tarragon, if handy
4 parsley stalks, if handy
2 teaspoons cracked black peppercorns
2 teaspoons salt
A glass of dry white wine

Start by making the court-bouillon. Put all the ingredients in a large pan and add 1.5 litres of water or seawater. Bring to the boil and simmer for 20 minutes. Add the winkles, bring back to the boil and simmer gently for about 5 minutes. Drain the winkles, discarding the court-bouillon and its bits. You can eat them hot or cold, but any you don't eat must be refrigerated and eaten within 24 hours.

Either way, to eat them you need some kind of winkle-picking device. The easiest thing to use is a large pin, with which you can remove the fingernail-like 'door' that seals the shell before skewering the little mollusc inside and hoicking it out. Eat them just as they come, without vinegar or any other accompaniment.

Whole fish poached in a court-bouillon

serves 8–10

You may have call for a fish kettle (see page 254) only a couple of times a year but you'll find it very useful for cooking a large fish for a big occasion – with minimum fuss and trouble.

Gentle poaching in a kettle is a fantastic treatment for species with firm, rich flesh that falls between what we conventionally describe as either 'white' or 'oily'. A large sea trout or small salmon is a case in point, but it works very well with sea bass, too. You can serve your fish hot, with a classic hollandaise sauce, as below, or cold, with mayonnaise (using the recipe on page 352, omitting the garlic and anchovies). You could even decorate a cold fish retro-style, with layers of cucumber 'scales'.

A court-bouillon is a light stock that usually contains some white wine, lemon juice or vinegar. This dash of acidity helps preserve the colour and texture of the fish as it cooks. To maximise the flavour, slice or chop everything quite finely. Once the fish is cooked, you will have a delicious fish stock that can be boiled down and made into a sauce or frozen and used later.

A 2.5–3kg sea bass, sea trout or organic farmed (or self-caught wild) salmon, descaled and gutted

FOR THE COURT-BOUILLON:
2–4 carrots, finely sliced
6–8 celery sticks, finely sliced
2–4 onions, finely sliced
1 teaspoon black peppercorns
4 teaspoons salt
400ml dry white wine

PLUS THE FOLLOWING, AS AVAILABLE:
1–2 leeks, finely sliced
4–6 garlic cloves, bruised
A couple of sprigs of thyme
A couple of sprigs of tarragon, or some fennel fronds
A few parsley stalks
Juice and pared zest (no pith) of 1 lemon

FOR THE CHEATY HOLLANDAISE:
1 egg yolk
150g unsalted butter
A squeeze of lemon juice
Salt and freshly ground black pepper

Also works with:
• Trout
• Carp
• Pike
• Zander

Start by making the court-bouillon. Put all the ingredients in a large saucepan or stockpot with 3 litres of water, bring to a simmer and bubble gently for 20 minutes. Strain through a fine-meshed sieve or conical strainer, preferably lined with muslin. If you're not using it straight away, the court-bouillon can be stored in the fridge for up to 3 days.

Pour the court-bouillon into a fish kettle and bring it to a simmer. Lay the fish on the kettle's trivet and carefully lower it into the court-bouillon, making sure the fish is covered by the liquid (add some more water if not). Bring back to a simmer and turn the heat right down. The liquid should just vibrate with the gentlest of simmers – anything more will damage the flavour and texture of the fish. You can even turn the heat off under the kettle and put the lid on. Reheat to simmering after about 10 minutes, then turn the heat off again.

Gently poached in this way, a fish of 2.5–3kg should be done in about 20 minutes, tops. Even a fish twice that size shouldn't take more than 30 minutes. Remember the principle that as soon as the heat reaches the middle of the fish, it is done

(continued overleaf)

Whole steam-baked brill *serves 6–8*

You may not have a turbotière – a giant, flatfish-shaped fish kettle – but you can still poach a whole large flatfish in a court-bouillon, or at least 'steam-bake' it, as described below. It's a lovely, simple way to cook the fish, and the sauce made from the cooking liquid is delicious. Obviously, the bigger the fish, the bigger the dish you'll need – something to bear in mind when you're sizing them up on the fishmonger's slab.

Also works with:
- Turbot
- Plaice
- Dover sole
- Megrim
- Witch
- Flounder

4 leeks, white part only, finely sliced
3 celery sticks, finely sliced
1 onion, finely sliced
2 sprigs of thyme
4 parsley stalks
2 bay leaves
A few strips of finely pared lemon zest

2–3 teaspoons black peppercorns
1 large brill, weighing 1–1.5kg, gutted
A glass of white wine
A large glass of water
100g unsalted butter, cut into small cubes
Salt and freshly ground black pepper

Place the vegetables, herbs, lemon zest and peppercorns in your chosen shallow baking dish. Put the fish on top, then pour over the wine and water. Don't expect it to cover the fish; it's just there to steam it through and give you a sauce at the end. Season with salt. Cover the dish with foil and place in an oven preheated to 160°C/Gas Mark 3. Cook for 45 minutes to 1 hour, until the flesh is just coming away from the bone.

Remove the fish from the dish using a couple of fish slices (have someone help you do this if the fish is big). Transfer it to a warmed serving plate. Strain the cooking liquid into a pan and boil until it has reduced by half. Remove from the heat and gradually whisk in the butter to make a sauce. Taste and adjust the seasoning. Pour into a warmed jug.

Serve the steam-baked fish with the sauce, steamed green vegetables and creamy mash.

Shallow and deep frying

Fried bream fillets with pea purée *serves 4*

Fillets from bream that you've just caught, served with a purée of peas that you've just picked... it must be July.

Also works with:
· Sea bass
· John Dory
· Red mullet
· Brill
· Lemon sole

Leaves from 1 **large** bunch of mint, chopped (keep the stalks)
400g freshly podded peas (or use frozen peas)
Olive oil
1½ garlic cloves – ½ finely chopped, the other clove skin left on and roughly bruised with a knife

75g unsalted butter
2 bay leaves
2 black bream, weighing about 450g each, descaled, filleted and pin-boned
Salt and freshly ground black pepper
Lemon wedges, to serve

Bring a pan of water to the boil and throw in the mint stalks. Add a pinch of salt and the peas and boil for 4–5 minutes, until the peas are tender (overgrown 'cannonball' peas may take a little longer). Drain and reserve the cooking water, but discard the mint stalks. Put the peas in a blender and set aside.

Set a small pan over a medium-high heat, then add 1 tablespoon of olive oil and the finely chopped garlic. Sizzle gently until the garlic just begins to colour, then quickly pour it into the blender with the peas. Add 50g of the butter, a pinch of salt and pepper and the chopped mint leaves. Add 2 tablespoons of the pea cooking water and blend the whole lot to a purée, adding a little more liquid if necessary, to give a consistency that is similar to coarse hummus. Taste and adjust the seasoning.

Put a large, non-stick frying pan over a medium-high heat. Add 1 tablespoon of olive oil and the remaining butter. Throw in the bay leaves and the bruised garlic clove to flavour the fat. Season the fish fillets all over and, when the fat is hot, lay them skin side down in the pan. Cook for about 3 minutes, until the flesh has turned opaque nearly all the way through, then flip them over and cook for a final 30 seconds.

Arrange the fish fillets skin side up on warmed plates, with a generous dollop of pea purée alongside. Serve with lemon wedges, plus a tomato salad.

Scallops with chorizo *serves 4 as a starter, 2 as a main course*

There are many ways to cook scallops, but few to beat this. It's one of the best possible expressions of the salty-spicy-pork meets sweet-succulent-shellfish concept so beloved of the Portuguese.

If you're cooking this dish in the summer when fresh broad beans are available, blanch some and toss them into the pan at the last moment. Sweet little fresh peas are another delicious addition.

To make this a more 'British' dish, you could substitute black pudding for the chorizo. Add 6 torn sage leaves to the pan with the scallops to bring out the flavour of the sausage.

12 large, hand-dived scallops
Olive oil
250g fairly hot cooking chorizo, cut into
  1–2cm thick slices
1 teaspoon fennel seeds (optional)
Few bay leaves (optional)
A squeeze of lemon juice
Salt and freshly ground black pepper

OPTIONAL EXTRAS:
Baby broad beans and/or garden peas,
  podded and blanched for 2 minutes

Open the scallops as described on pages 105–7 (reserve the frills for bream bait or to make fish stock). If the corals are plump and bright orange, leave them attached to the main muscle. Otherwise add them to the frills for stock. Pat the scallops dry with kitchen paper and set aside.

Heat a large, heavy-based frying pan over a high heat, add a little olive oil, then throw in the chorizo and, if you like, a sprinkling of fennel seeds and a few bay leaves. Fry for 3–4 minutes, stirring all the while, as the chorizo releases its salty, spicy fat.

Move the chorizo to one side of the pan. Check that the pan is still really hot, then add the scallops. Leave for about 45 seconds to 1 minute, then carefully turn them over. After another scant minute, using a sharp shake of the pan – or a light stir with a spatula – toss the chorizo and scallops together with all that lovely, flavoursome fat. (This is the moment to add the optional broad beans and/ or peas.) Cook for just another minute, tossing and shaking regularly.

Add a twist of pepper, a little bit of salt (the chorizo is already pretty salty) and a few drops of lemon juice, then divide the mixture between warmed plates and serve straight away, with bread and a green salad – for which the oil from the pan, with a few more drops of lemon juice, will make a sublime dressing.

Red mullet, woodcock-style *serves 2*

This recipe is loosely based on a traditional preparation for woodcock, where the bird is left ungutted during cooking, then the innards are removed and spread on a piece of toast, on which the bird is served. The flavour of the guts is creamy and mildly liverish, making it an excellent dish. Since the liver of the red mullet is also highly prized, it makes perfect sense to use the same approach. It works a treat. Indeed, it *is* a treat.

2 very fresh red mullet (350–500g),
   descaled and gutted, livers reserved
1 tablespoon olive oil
25g unsalted butter
1 small garlic clove, unpeeled

1 bay leaf
2 green olives, finely chopped
1 anchovy fillet, finely chopped
1 tablespoon white wine
Salt and freshly ground black pepper

Remove the livers from the fish and set aside. Season the fish. Place a large non-stick frying pan over a medium-low heat. Add the oil and butter, the garlic clove and the bay leaf, then add the whole fish. Sizzle gently for about 8–10 minutes, then turn them over and continue cooking for 6–7 minutes or so, until cooked right through (test the thickest part – see pages 113–14). Remove from the pan and keep warm.

Keeping the pan on the heat, remove the cooked garlic clove, then peel and chop it – it shouldn't be too burnt if you have cooked the fish gently. Combine it with the chopped olives and anchovy. Add this mixture to the hot pan, along with the fish livers and wine. Sauté for just half a minute to reduce the wine a little, then remove the pan from the heat and mash everything together with a fork.

Smear this paste over the skin of the mullet, and serve, accompanied by plain mash or sautéed potatoes and a tomato and chive salad.

Mackerel stuffed with salsa verde *serves 4*

This is a really impressive way of preparing mackerel. Fresh, vibrant salsa verde works beautifully as a stuffing and really complements the rich flesh of the fish. You can try the same technique with other stuffings, such as pesto or a piquant chilli salsa. The tail-on filleting technique suggested here gives you a very attractive little parcel. Remove the pin bones to create the all-important channel that holds the salsa verde, then simply sandwich two fillets together before tying with string.

Also works with:
- Trout (small)
- Sardines (large)

4 medium-sized mackerel, gutted
Olive oil
Salt and freshly ground black pepper

FOR THE SALSA VERDE:
A generous bunch of flat-leaf parsley,
   tough stalks removed
6–8 basil leaves

6–8 mint leaves
1 garlic clove, finely chopped
4 anchovy fillets
2 teaspoons capers, rinsed
1 teaspoon English mustard
Juice of ½ lemon, or to taste
Olive oil

Make the salsa verde first: put the herbs on a large board and chop them well. Combine the garlic with the anchovies and capers and chop/mash them together into a coarse paste. Bring the chopped herb and anchovy mixtures together and chop again. Pile the whole lot into a small mixing bowl and add the mustard, lemon juice and some black pepper to taste. Stir in just enough olive oil to make a thick green sauce (it shouldn't be runny or sloppy). Taste and adjust the seasoning, then set aside.

Now fillet the mackerel bait-cutter style, as described on pages 62–3, but leaving the fillets joined at the tail end. Make sure you remove all the pin bones. You should be left with a boneless, headless pair of fillets, still joined at the tail, and with one V-shaped channel in each fillet where the pin bones have been removed.

Run a good smear of the salsa verde down the V-shaped groove in each fillet of mackerel, then smear a little more over the flesh. Close up the fish and secure in a couple of places with kitchen string. You can do all this preparation several hours in advance and chill the fish until needed. In fact, the flavour will be better this way.

To cook, set a large, heavy frying pan over a medium heat. Brush the fish lightly with oil, season them and fry for 5–6 minutes on each side, until the flesh is cooked through. Alternatively, brush them with a splash of oil, season and roast in an oven preheated to 200–220°C/Gas Mark 6–7 for 12–15 minutes. They can also be barbecued.

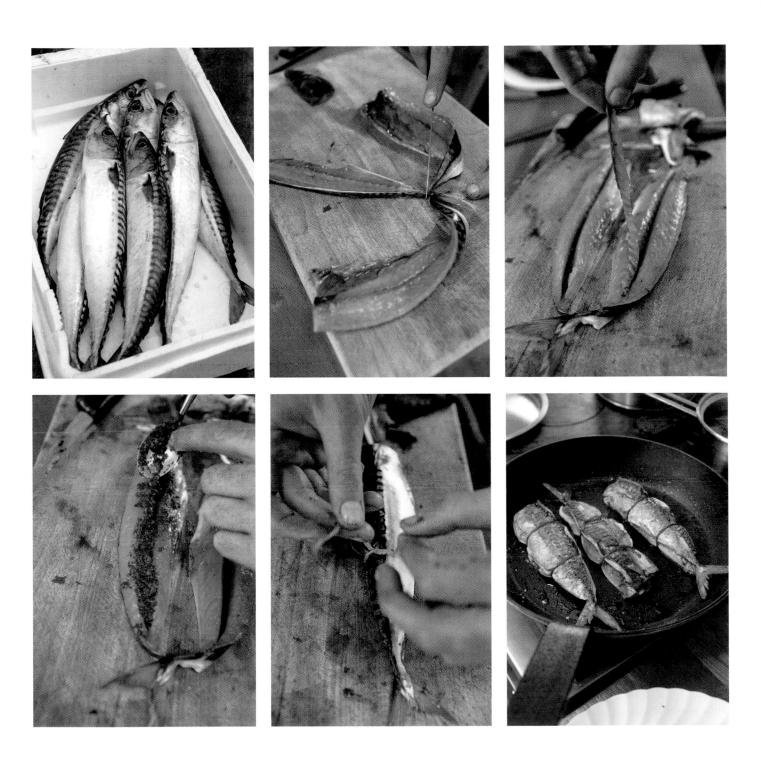

Brill with celeriac and crispy pork belly

serves 6 as a starter, 4 as a main course

This is further compelling evidence of the success of the pork/fish collaboration (see Scallops with chorizo, page 313). The first time we served this dish, it was a hit. Our friend and occasional fishing partner Paddy Rudd, who joined us for dinner that night, still talks about it.

Pork enthusiasts may notice that the procedure for the belly is really just an accelerated version of homemade bacon.

Also works with:
- Turbot
- Megrim
- Witch
- Flounder
- John Dory
- Black bream
- Sea bass

750g–1kg slab of organic or free-range boneless pork belly, cut from the thick end

1–1.5kg brill, skin on but descaled and filleted

FOR THE CURE:
100g fine sea salt
100g light brown sugar
6 juniper berries, bruised
4 bay leaves, finely shredded
1 teaspoon cracked black peppercorns

FOR COOKING THE BELLY:
½ head of garlic, lightly crushed with the back of a knife

2 celery sticks, roughly chopped
2 carrots, roughly chopped
2 onions, cut into quarters
2 bay leaves

FOR THE CELERIAC PURÉE:
1 small or ½ large head of celeriac
Up to 1 litre whole milk
50g unsalted butter
Salt and freshly ground black pepper

TO FINISH:
1 tablespoon lard or oil
2 garlic cloves, sliced
Leaves from 1 sprig of thyme
1 tablespoon olive oil

Mix all the cure ingredients together. Put the pork belly in a bowl and rub the cure mix all over it. Cover and place in the fridge for 12–15 hours. Revisit, and re-rub, once or twice during this time.

To cook the pork, wash it under gently running cold water to remove the cure, then pat dry. Place in a pan with the garlic, vegetables and bay leaves and cover completely with water. Bring to the boil, then cover and simmer very gently for at least 2, perhaps 3 hours, until the belly, including the skin, is very tender. Drain the meat and leave to steam off, so it dries a little as it cools. Discard the stock vegetables. If you're not serving the dish on the same day, you can cool and then refrigerate the pork at this point.

An hour before serving, peel the celeriac and cut it into cubes. Place it in a pan with enough milk to cover and bring to a gentle simmer. Cook until the celeriac is tender, then drain, reserving the hot milk. Purée the celeriac with the butter, adding enough of the hot milk to give a thick, but silky consistency. Season to taste and keep warm.

While the celeriac is cooking, finish the pork belly. Cut it into neat cubes about 2cm square. Heat the lard or oil in a large frying pan over a medium-high heat. Add the belly cubes and sizzle hard, turning them frequently, until browned and lightly crisp. Throw in the garlic and thyme for the last minute or two of cooking. Turn off the heat and leave the meat in the hot pan while you cook the fish.

Heat the olive oil in a large, non-stick frying pan over a high heat. Cut the brill fillets into neat pieces – enough to give each person 2 or 3 generous chunks. Season the brill, add to the pan, skin side down, and cook for 2–3 minutes, until the flesh has become opaque nearly all the way through. Turn the fish and cook for just a minute more.

Spoon some celeriac purée on to each warmed plate, then put 2 or 3 pieces of brill beside it. Scatter the browned pork belly over the fish and the celeriac, along with a trickle of its warm, aromatic cooking oil. Serve at once.

Fried mackerel in oatmeal with bacon *serves 2*

An oatmeal coating is traditional for fried herring, where it provides a lovely, crunchy contrast to the fish's oily flesh, but it works just as well with other oily fish, such as mackerel. The bacon contributes its own, salty-sweet savour, making the whole combination surprisingly rich and substantial.

2 mackerel, filleted
100g medium oatmeal
1 tablespoon sunflower or groundnut oil

4 streaky bacon rashers, cut into lardons
Salt and freshly ground black pepper

Also works with:
• Herring
• Sardines
• Garfish

Season the mackerel fillets well. Spread the oatmeal out on a plate. Coat the mackerel in the oatmeal, pressing it on to the fish firmly.

Heat a large, heavy-based frying pan over a medium heat and add the oil, then the bacon. Cook until crisp and golden, then remove the bacon with a slotted spoon, leaving the fat in the pan.

Keeping the pan on a medium heat, add the coated mackerel fillets, flesh side down. Fry for 1 minute, then turn over and fry for 1–2 minutes, until the skin beneath the oatmeal is golden brown.

Serve the fried mackerel straight away, with the crisp bacon, some bread and butter and a salad. Or, if you want to make a breakfast of it, serve with a fried egg on the side.

The FLT   *serves 1*

This is the ultimate fish sandwich: a fried fillet of plaice with lettuce and tomato in a bun. Make sure you use a decent bap – nothing too cotton-woolly – and good mayonnaise, and this becomes a delicious experience. You can make it for as many people as you like, of course, but somehow it's the kind of top-notch fast food that is particularly good cooked and eaten all by yourself, after a hard day, with a cold beer to hand.

Butter

A dash of olive oil

1 small plaice fillet (about 100g), skinned if you like

A little plain flour, seasoned with salt and pepper

1 large, white, floury bap

A few Little Gem lettuce leaves

1–2 ripe tomatoes, thickly sliced

1 tablespoon mayonnaise

Tomato ketchup (optional)

Salt and freshly ground black pepper

Also works with:
- Pollack
- Coley
- Whiting
- Pouting
- Megrim
- Witch
- Lemon sole
- Flounder
- Black bream

Heat a knob of butter and a dash of olive oil in a non-stick frying pan over a medium heat. Dust the fish fillet with seasoned flour and fry for about 2 minutes on each side. Alternatively, if you're a sucker for crisp skin, fry it skin side down for about 3½ minutes, then give it a quick 30 seconds on the other side to finish.

Slice and generously butter the bap. Lay the lettuce leaves on the base of the bun, followed by the sliced tomato, then the fish. Season well. Spread a generous amount of mayonnaise on the top half, add ketchup if you feel like it, then close up the bap and eat straight away, while the fish is still warm.

Fish tacos *makes 5–10, depending on size*

This is the classic street food of Baja California and the other coastal resorts of Mexico. There, the fish is often battered and deep fried. However, good fish can get a bit lost if enveloped in batter and a tortilla, so we prefer just to dust the fillets with a little seasoned flour – which also means they can be shallow rather than deep fried. Use boneless fillets of absolutely any fish, from whiting to dogfish, plaice to bass. There's no need to use extravagant fish, unless you've had some good fishing and happen to have a surfeit of it. You can mix up the fish with scallops and/or squid as well.

The soft tortillas do take a bit of work but they are fun to make, and really not at all difficult.

A handful of plain flour
Roughly 1kg boneless, skinless fish
    fillets, cut into 2-bite-sized pieces
Groundnut or sunflower oil for frying
Salt and freshly ground black pepper

FOR THE TORTILLAS:
500g plain flour
A generous pinch of salt

FOR THE TOMATO SALSA:
1 teaspoon sugar
1 tablespoon wine vinegar or cider vinegar
10 ripe tomatoes (about 500g), skinned,
    deseeded and diced
2 small red onions, finely diced

FOR THE GUACAMOLE:
2 ripe avocados
1 red chilli, as hot as you like, finely
    chopped
A small bunch of coriander, finely
    chopped
Lime juice, to taste

OPTIONAL ACCOMPANIMENTS:
Soured cream or crème fraîche
Chilli sauce or Tabasco

First make the tortillas: mix together the flour and salt and add enough water to make a soft but not sticky dough – probably 300–325ml. Knead for a few minutes, until silky and smooth. Take one small piece of dough at a time (a lime-sized lump is good, but you can make them any size you like), shape it into a ball (the rounder your ball, the rounder your tortilla), then use a rolling pin to roll it out into as thin a circle as you can.

Heat a heavy-based frying pan (a flat griddle or a pancake pan would be even better), without any oil, until hot but not smoking. Quickly but carefully lay a tortilla in the pan and cook on both sides until it is bubbly and ever so slightly charred, but still soft and floppy. Roll out the next one while the first one is cooking. Stack them on a plate as they are done, covering with a cloth.

To make the tomato salsa, simply toss all the ingredients together, leave for a few minutes, then toss again before serving.

To make the guacamole, halve, peel, stone and mash the avocados. Stir together with the chilli and coriander, plus as much lime juice as you like.

When you are ready to eat, reheat the tortillas, wrapped in foil, in a low oven (120°C/Gas Mark ½). They will probably have gone a little hard on cooling, and this will soften them up again.

To cook the fish, season the flour generously with salt and pepper, toss the fish pieces in it, then shake off the excess. Heat a shallow layer of oil in as large a frying pan as you have and fry the fish over a medium to high heat for a minute or so on each side. The pieces should be lightly browned and just cooked through. Do this in batches if necessary – don't overcrowd the pan.

As soon as the fish is cooked, it's time to serve: simply load a warm tortilla with a bit (or a lot) of everything, including soured cream and chilli sauce if you like, then roll it up. Eat messily.

Garlic-sautéed Billy Winters *serves 4 as a starter*

'Billy Winters' is affectionate West Country parlance for the fat local prawns – the same kind you find in rock pools all around the coast, but bigger – fished with special prawn pots from around November until February. They make extremely good eating, especially when cooked in this simple but intensely flavoured way. It's all very quick and simple – the prawns go from hot water to hot fat in a matter of seconds, and are ready to eat about two minutes later.

25g unsalted butter

A dash of olive oil

500g live Billy Winters, or very fresh
 raw Atlantic prawns

2 fat garlic cloves, finely chopped

A pinch of cayenne pepper

1 tablespoon cider brandy (optional)

Salt and freshly ground black pepper

Lemon wedges, to serve

Bring a large pan of heavily salted water to the boil. When it's bubbling, heat a large frying pan over a medium heat next to it on the hob and add the butter and olive oil.

Throw the live prawns into the rapidly boiling water to kill them instantly. After no more than 30 seconds, fish them out with a large slotted spoon or a small sieve and tip them into a waiting tea towel. Shake them in the towel to dry them a bit (this helps stop them spitting madly in the frying pan), then transfer immediately to the pan of hot butter and oil, adding the garlic at the same time. Cook them for 2–3 minutes, stirring and shaking from time to time. Add a little salt, plenty of black pepper and a pinch of cayenne as they cook.

If you feel like it, you can add the cider brandy and set it alight at the end of the cooking time, tossing the prawns vigorously until the flame dies down. This gives another rich layer of flavour, but it's really not essential. Tip the hot prawns out on to a warmed plate and tuck in straight away, peeling them with your fingers. Have some brown bread and butter to eat with them, and more black pepper, cayenne and lemon wedges to hand.

Crumbed plaice fillets with tartare sauce

serves 4

Crisp, golden, breaded plaice fillets occupy the same kind of cherished niche in our fish-eating culture as battered cod. The crunchy crumb and soft, white fish make an incredibly successful marriage, especially when attended by a freshly made, creamy but piquant tartare sauce. Forget those awful plastic sachets of flavoured salad cream, which are an insult to the name; instead, take the time to make your own mayonnaise as a base and you'll find that proper tartare sauce is a thing of joy. Don't reserve it for this recipe alone – it will enhance almost any kind of battered, crumbed or fried fish.

Also works with:
• Pollack
• Whiting
• Pouting
• Megrim
• Witch
• Flounder

4 fillets of plaice, weighing about 200g each
100g plain flour
2 large eggs, lightly beaten
150g fairly fine fresh white breadcrumbs
250ml groundnut oil
Salt and freshly ground black pepper

FOR THE TARTARE SAUCE:
2 generous tablespoons mayonnaise (preferably homemade, see page 332, omitting the garlic and anchovy)
1–2 hard-boiled eggs, finely chopped
1 tablespoon roughly chopped parsley
1 teaspoon chopped dill
2–3 gherkins, finely chopped
2 teaspoons capers, finely chopped
Juice of ½ lemon

Make the tartare sauce first by simply stirring everything together in a bowl. Set aside.

Put the plaice fillets on a board and skin them (see page 73), then give them a quick bone check with your fingertips.

Put the flour in a deep plate and season it with salt and pepper. Put the beaten eggs and the breadcrumbs in two separate deep dishes.

Lightly coat one fillet of fish in the flour, shaking off any excess. Dip the floured fish in the egg, making sure it's well coated, then roll it in the breadcrumbs so it's generously covered. Repeat with the remaining fillets.

Set a large, fairly deep, non-stick frying pan over a medium heat and add the oil – it should be about 1cm deep. When it's hot, fry the breaded fillets, in batches if necessary, for 2–3 minutes on each side, until golden brown and crisp. Serve with the tartare sauce, along with buttered peas or creamed spinach (see page 309) and sautéed potatoes, chips or mash.

Whelk fritters *serves 8–10*

Not everyone is instantly enamoured of the whelk, but we love these chunky, humble sea snails. We therefore see it as our mission to lead a whelk revival. The following recipe has been known to convert even the most diehard whelk sceptic.

Also works with:
• Winkles

10–12 whelks
1 celery stick, roughly chopped
1 carrot, roughly chopped
1 bay leaf
3–4 rashers of fatty bacon, diced
1 onion, chopped
2 medium eggs, separated

2 garlic cloves, very finely chopped
1 tablespoon chopped parsley
½ teaspoon thyme leaves
A good pinch of curry powder
40g fresh breadcrumbs
Sunflower or olive oil for frying
Salt and freshly ground black pepper

Scrub the whelks under the cold tap. As you handle them, you may find that some of them release a certain amount of slime – don't worry about this, just rinse it away. Put the cleaned whelks in a large pan, cover with cold water and add the celery, carrot and bay leaf. Bring to boiling point and cook at a gentle simmer for 8–10 minutes. Drain, discard the vegetables and leave the whelks to cool.

Extract the cooked whelks from their shells, using a fork to twirl them out. Remove the coarse cap or 'trap door' (like a black fingernail) from the front end and the dark digestive sac from the tail end. Roughly chop the whelks.

Gently cook the bacon in a frying pan until it releases its fat and is lightly cooked. Add the onion to the pan and fry until soft, then set aside to cool.

Put the egg yolks into a bowl and lightly break them up with a fork. Stir in the chopped whelks, bacon and onion, garlic, parsley, thyme, curry powder, breadcrumbs and salt and pepper to taste.

In a separate bowl, whisk the egg whites until they form soft peaks. Gently fold them into the whelk mixture. Form the mixture into even-sized patties, around 5cm in diameter.

Pour a 1cm depth of oil into a large frying pan and set over a medium-high heat. When hot, add the patties (be careful, as they can spit ferociously) and fry for 3–4 minutes per side, until crisp and golden. Serve the fritters hot from the pan, with a little lemony mayonnaise dabbed on top if you like.

Pike fishcakes with caper sauce *serves 4*

This is more than just a thrifty way to use up leftover pike. So distinctive is the taste of the pike, and therefore the fishcakes, that this is a dish worth planning for. So when you have a decent-sized pike in your kitchen, think in terms of poaching or baking it for your first meal, but having enough left over to make these fishcakes the following day.

Lightened up with egg whites and enriched with cream, they're a cross between a traditional fishcake and a more cheffy quenelle. You can vary the quantities a bit, depending on how much pike you have, but make sure there's never more potato than fish.

Also works with:
- Perch
- Zander
- Grayling
- Sea bass
- Gurnard
- Black bream

250g floury potatoes, such as King Edward, peeled and cut into large chunks
500g cooked, boneless pike
1 tablespoon each chopped chervil, chives and parsley
2 egg whites
100ml double cream
A little flour for dusting
Groundnut oil for shallow frying
Salt and freshly ground black pepper

FOR THE CAPER SAUCE:
150g unsalted butter
1 egg yolk
1 teaspoon mild mustard
1 tablespoon finely chopped capers
1 tablespoon chopped chives
A squeeze of lemon juice

Cook the potatoes in boiling salted water until tender, then drain and leave to steam-dry for 10 minutes. Mash them and leave to cool.

Mash the cooked pike meat with a fork, double checking for any bones, then put in a bowl with the herbs and plenty of seasoning and combine well. Lightly whisk the egg whites – you just want them loose and foamy, not meringuey – then stir them into the cooled potato, along with the cream. Finally, combine the potato mixture with the pike. Leave in the fridge for at least 2 hours to firm up.

With lightly floured hands, shape the mixture into little cakes – it will be quite difficult to handle but this results in a lovely, light texture.

Heat a thin layer of groundnut oil in a large, non-stick frying pan over a medium heat. Fry the cakes, in batches, for 3–4 minutes per side, until golden brown. While they're cooking, make the sauce.

Melt the butter in a small pan until gently sizzling. Have the egg yolk ready in a small bowl. Gradually trickle the butter on to the egg yolk, whisking vigorously to form an emulsion. Whisk in the mustard and plenty of seasoning, then stir in the chopped capers and chives, plus a squeeze of lemon juice to taste.

Ideally serve the hot fishcakes straight away with the sauce. If it has to stand for a while, keep the sauce warm by placing the bowl in a larger bowl of hot but not boiling water.

Saltfish and parsnip rösti fishcakes

serves 4–6 as a starter, 2–3 as a main course

Saltfish and parsnips appear together in various medieval recipes, but they tend to be complicated. Charmed by the idea of the combination, we improvised this very simple recipe, which absolutely hits the spot. A fried egg (or two) per person, and a bit of salad, makes a good supper of them.

1 large or 2 medium parsnips (about 250–300g), coarsely grated

1 small onion, coarsely grated

100g hard-salted fish, such as ling, pollack, pouting, whiting or cod, rehydrated (see page 127), or 200g lightly salted fresh white fish fillets (see pages 124–5), cut into 1cm cubes

1 garlic clove, finely chopped

Leaves from 1 small sprig of rosemary, finely chopped (optional)

1 large egg, beaten

Groundnut or sunflower oil for frying

Freshly ground black pepper

Mix all the ingredients except the oil together in a bowl. Heat a thin layer of oil in a large frying pan over a medium heat and when it is hot, put a handful of the fish and parsnip mixture into the pan. Squash it into a cake roughly 8cm in diameter and 1cm thick. Repeat until you have 4 or 5 cakes in the pan.

Fry fairly gently, so the heat has time to penetrate into the centre of the cakes without the outside burning. Press each cake down with a spatula from time to time. After 5–7 minutes, when they are nicely browned on the underside, flip them over and continue until the second side is browned. Remove and drain on kitchen paper.

Serve the fishcakes piping hot, with a green salad on the side.

Fried squid rings with garlic mayonnaise

serves 4 as a starter

This is delicious and very easy. The mayonnaise is a doddle if you use a food processor and the squid takes seconds to cook, so you can get it all on the table very quickly. Served with a cold beer, there are few better summer meals.

Use medium-sized squid, about 15–25cm body length (i.e. not including head or tentacles). They tend to be less chewy than their larger fellow cephalopods and therefore more suited to quick cooking methods.

4 medium-sized squid, cleaned
  (see pages 97–100)
100g plain flour
About 1 litre groundnut or sunflower oil
  for deep frying
Salt and freshly ground black pepper

TO SERVE:
Coarse sea salt
Lemon wedges

FOR THE GARLIC MAYONNAISE:
2 very fresh egg yolks
2 small anchovy fillets or 1 salted
  sardine fillet
2 garlic cloves, roughly chopped
1 heaped teaspoon English mustard
A small pinch each of salt, sugar and
  black pepper
1 tablespoon cider vinegar or lemon juice
100ml olive oil
200ml groundnut oil

Start by making the mayonnaise. If you're a purist, you can do it by hand, crushing the garlic and anchovies and mixing them with the egg yolks and seasoning before slowly whisking in the oil. If not, put the egg yolks, anchovies, garlic, mustard, salt, sugar, pepper and vinegar or lemon juice into a food processor and process until smooth. Combine the two oils in a jug. With the processor running, start pouring in the oil in a very thin trickle. When the oil starts to emulsify with the yolks, you can add it a little faster. By the time you've added all the oil, you'll have a thick, glossy mayonnaise. Adjust the seasoning and, if it seems too thick, thin it slightly with a little warm water. Cover and chill until needed.

Prepare your squid into rings about 1cm thick (as described on page 100). Cut each ring of tentacles in half at the base. Put the flour in a bowl and season it well.

Heat the oil in a deep-fat fryer or a deep, heavy pan to a temperature of 180°C. To test this, drop a cube of white bread into the oil. It should turn golden brown in about a minute.

Toss a handful of squid, say 7 or 8 rings, into the seasoned flour. The best way to do this is to place the squid in a sieve with a few tablespoons of the flour. Shake the sieve until the flour has evenly coated the squid and any excess has dropped through.

Put the squid gently into the hot oil and fry for 1–1¹/₂ minutes, until golden. Transfer to a tray lined with a few sheets of kitchen paper. Continue in this way, flouring and frying a handful of squid at a time, until it's all cooked.

Serve straight away, sprinkled with coarse salt, with lemon wedges and a dish of the mayonnaise alongside.

Fish in beer batter *serves 4–6*

What makes a good batter? What creates that crisp, savoury, golden coating that seals in all the moisture of the fish it covers? The answer, or at least one answer, is beer. It not only contributes a wonderful lightness to the mixture but adds flavour, too: a nutty, wheaty edge to the crunch. But beer isn't the only important element. A good batter also needs to have the right consistency: too thick and floury and you'll end up with a pancakey, chewy result; too thin and it won't stick to the fish.

This recipe is one of the most useful in the book because you can use it when you're deep frying almost any fish or shellfish. As well as the obvious fillets of white fish, such as plaice, pollack, coley, cod, haddock and whiting, we've had great success with beer-battered dogfish goujons, squid rings, even scallops.

We've included our tried and tested recipe for homemade tomato ketchup here too, as it never fails to please with battered fish. The recipe is based on one by Lindsey Bareham in *The Big Red Book of Tomatoes* (Michael Joseph, 1999).

200g plain flour

Groundnut oil, including plenty for
   deep frying

About 250ml good beer – anything really,
   including stout, but preferably not cheap
   lager

Mixed fish of your choice

Salt and freshly ground black pepper

FOR THE TOMATO KETCHUP:

3kg ripe tomatoes, roughly chopped

4 onions, sliced

1 large red pepper, seeds and white
   membrane removed, chopped

100g soft brown sugar

200ml cider vinegar

¼ teaspoon dry mustard

A piece of cinnamon stick

1½ teaspoons allspice berries

1½ teaspoons cloves

1½ teaspoons ground mace

1½ teaspoons celery seeds

1½ teaspoons black peppercorns

1 bay leaf

1 garlic clove, peeled and bruised with
   a knife

Paprika to taste (optional)

Salt

For the ketchup, combine the tomatoes, onions and red pepper in a large, heavy pan over a medium heat. Bring to the boil, then simmer, stirring occasionally, until very soft. Push the lot through a coarse-meshed sieve and return the purée to the pan with the sugar, vinegar and mustard. Tie the spices, peppercorns, bay leaf and garlic in a square of muslin and drop it into the pan. Bring to the boil, then reduce to a slow simmer. Allow to bubble gently, for at least an hour, stirring often. The time will depend on how juicy your tomatoes are, but you should cook the sauce until it is really thick and pulpy. Taste it a couple of times during cooking and remove the spice bag if you feel the flavour is getting too strong.

Once cooked, season to taste with salt and paprika, if you're using it, then leave to cool. Pour the ketchup through a funnel into suitable bottles and seal. Stored in the fridge, it will keep for a month.

To make the batter, sift the flour into a bowl, or put it in a bowl and whisk it (which is almost as effective a way to aerate the flour and remove lumps). Add 2 tablespoons of groundnut oil, then gradually whisk in the beer, stopping when you have a batter with the consistency of thick emulsion paint. Beat it well to get rid of any lumps, season generously, then leave to rest for 30 minutes or so.

Heat the oil in a large, deep, heavy-based pan until it reaches 160°C, or until a cube of bread dropped into it turns golden brown in 1½–2 minutes.

Dip your chosen piece of fish into the batter so it is thoroughly immersed, then lift it out and hold it over the bowl for a few seconds so any excess batter drops back in. Now lower the battered fish into the hot oil. Do this one piece at a time, if using large portions, or in small batches for smaller pieces, so as not to crowd the pan. Fry large pieces of fish for 4–5 minutes, and smaller items, such as squid rings, for 2 minutes or so, until golden brown and crisp. Scoop them out with a wire basket, or 'spider', and transfer to a warm dish lined with kitchen paper. Keep them warm while you fry the remaining fish, then serve straight away, with your ketchup or perhaps some tartare sauce (see page 324).

Deep-fried whole fish with citrus salsa *serves 2*

A deep-fried whole fish (such as the one shown on pages 292–3) may seem a bit of a curiosity but it works very well, as you get lovely, crisp skin and tender flesh through to the bone. When you or your fishmonger are preparing the fish, leave the fins on. They become deliciously crunchy when cooked.

It's worth pointing out that you do need a large cooking vessel to make this dish successfully. A proper deep-fat fryer with a lid is ideal but, failing that, you'll need a pan long and deep enough to accommodate a whole fish submerged in oil, bearing in mind that for safety's sake the oil should come no more than a third of the way up the sides of the pan.

Groundnut or sunflower oil for deep frying
2 single-portion-size red gurnard, black
   bream, red mullet, grey mullet or sea
   bass (500–750g each), descaled and
   gutted

2 tablespoons plain flour
Salt and freshly ground black pepper
Citrus salsa (see page 327), to serve

Heat the oil in a deep-fat fryer or a very large, deep heavy-based saucepan until it reaches 190°C. You can test this by dropping in a cube of white bread. It should turn golden brown in about 25–30 seconds.

Dry the fish well inside and out, using kitchen paper. Use a sharp knife to slash the sides of the fish, going almost down to the bone, 5 or 6 slashes on each side. This helps the heat penetrate the flesh and speeds up the cooking. Season the flour well with salt and pepper and use it to dust the fish all over. Lower the fish into the hot oil and cook for 5 minutes, until the skin is puffed up and crisp and the slashes have opened up a little. Remove and drain on kitchen paper.

Take a little of the salsa and spoon it on to the fish, so the flavours penetrate via the slashes in the flesh. Serve straight away, with the remaining salsa on the side. The flour-dusted, deep-fried skin will be lovely and crisp. Dab a little salsa on each forkful and eat everything but the bones.

Smoked pollack croquetas *makes about 20*

This is a dish for those who don't mind a little bit of a fiddle, and are not afraid of the deep-fat fryer. Crispy on the outside, creamy and lightly smoky in the middle, they're worth every ounce of the effort spent in preparing them.

75g unsalted butter, plus a little extra
  for frying
25g smoked bacon, finely chopped
250g smoked pollack (or haddock) fillet
About 500ml milk
½ onion, sliced
1 bay leaf

75g plain flour
25g mature Cheddar cheese, grated
1 heaped teaspoon chopped parsley
1 egg, lightly beaten
75g fresh white breadcrumbs
Groundnut or sunflower oil for deep frying
Freshly ground black pepper

Heat a little butter in a frying pan over a medium heat and fry the bacon in it until crisp. Set aside.

Put the smoked pollack fillet in a saucepan just large enough to hold it (cut the fillet in half if necessary). Pour over enough milk to cover the fish and add the onion, bay leaf and a few twists of black pepper. Cover the pan and bring the milk to a gentle simmer. By the time the milk is simmering, the fish should be perfectly cooked and you should be able to remove it straight away. However, if you've got a particularly thick fillet from a monster fish, you might need to leave it in the hot milk for a minute or two longer.

Flake the flesh off the skin of the fish into a bowl, checking for bones as you do so. Strain the milk and reserve it, but discard the flavourings.

Heat the 75g butter in a saucepan over a medium heat. Stir in the flour to make a roux and cook gently for a couple of minutes. Gradually stir in about 300ml of the reserved fish poaching milk and cook, stirring, until it becomes very thick – it needs to bind the croquetas together, so it must be robust. Bring this fishy paste to a simmer and cook very gently for 5 minutes, stirring constantly. This ensures there's no taste of raw flour in the finished sauce. Remove from the heat and stir in the grated Cheddar, flaked fish, chopped parsley and cooked bacon, being careful not to break up the fish too much. Leave the mixture to go cold, then chill until firm.

Put the lightly beaten egg in one shallow bowl and the breadcrumbs in another. Take dessertspoonfuls of the chilled fish mixture and, with lightly floured hands, roll them into short, fat, thumb-sized sausages. Roll each one in the beaten egg, then the breadcrumbs. Cover and return to the fridge for another hour.

When you're ready to fry, heat the oil in a deep, heavy pan or a deep-fat fryer until it reaches 180°C. To test this, drop in a cube of white bread. It should turn golden brown in about 1 minute. Fry the croquetas in small batches for about 3–4 minutes, until deep golden brown and crisp. Alternatively, you can shallow fry them in a 1cm depth of oil, turning regularly. Either way, drain them on kitchen paper and serve straight away.

Deep-fried fish calzone *serves 2 as a hearty snack or light supper*

Deep-frying fish within a thin wrap of pizza dough is an excellent way to cook fillets from more robust, well-flavoured species. Unlike the usual batter, pizza dough absorbs very little oil, so comes out satisfyingly crispy – like a spring roll, but with more substance. The fish inside cooks delicately in its own steam. We serve it with a spicy tomato sauce.

Once you have the cooking method down pat, the variations are endless. You could flavour the dough (finely chopped rosemary would be good), or add a smear of salsa verde (see page 316) to the fish fillet before wrapping it.

You can also ring the changes by baking the dough-wrapped fish instead of deep frying. About 10 minutes at 230°C/Gas Mark 8 should do very nicely.

Also works with:
- Brill
- Red mullet
- Grey mullet
- John Dory
- Gurnard
- Sea trout

2 fillets of salmon, sea bass or bream, weighing about 200g each, descaled if necessary (or four 100g mackerel fillets)
Groundnut or sunflower oil for deep frying
Salt and freshly ground black pepper

FOR THE DOUGH:
7g dried yeast
160ml warm water
125g plain flour
125g strong white bread flour
5g salt
1 tablespoon olive oil

FOR THE CHILLI-SPIKED TOMATO SAUCE:
1 onion, finely chopped
1 garlic clove, finely chopped
1 tablespoon olive oil
5–6 large tomatoes (about 600g), skinned, deseeded and chopped (or a 400g tin of tomatoes in their own juice)
½–1 fresh red chilli (or a pinch of dried chilli flakes)
A squeeze of lemon juice
A good pinch of sugar (optional)

First make the dough: dilute the yeast in a little of the water, then mix all the dry ingredients together in a bowl and stir in the yeast mixture, the olive oil and the remaining water. Mix until evenly combined.

Turn the dough out on to a lightly floured work surface and knead until smooth, silky and stretchy. This combination of plain and strong flour with a dash of olive oil produces a good, soft, elastic dough that is easy to roll.

Return it to the bowl, cover and leave to rise in a warm place until doubled in size – or longer, if you want. It will happily ferment all day – just knock it back every now and then to stop it getting too big. It will even keep in the fridge for a couple of days.

You can make the sauce while the dough is rising. Sweat the chopped onion and garlic in the olive oil for 5–10 minutes, until soft but not coloured. Add the tomatoes and chilli and cook gently until thick and pulpy. Season with salt and pepper, a little lemon juice, and a pinch of sugar if it needs it, then set aside.

Take a lemon-sized ball of dough, or slightly bigger, dust it lightly with flour, then roll it out to about 2mm thick. Cut a rectangle long enough to wrap around a single fish fillet (or a sandwich of two fillets, in the case of mackerel) and wide enough to overlap by a centimetre or two, so you can seal it. (You can either make a 'jacket', with just half a centimetre of fish poking out at each end, as in the pictures opposite, or a sealed parcel, which will protect a more fragile fish.) Roll out a second piece of dough and cut a rectangle in the same way.

Season the fish on both sides, lay a fillet (or two, for mackerel) on each rectangle and fold the dough around it. Seal the lip along the length of the fillet by pressing it to the dough underneath – and the overlapping ends too, if you're going for the sealed parcel. Leave to prove for 5 minutes – time for a few small but significant air pockets to form in the dough.

Heat the oil for deep frying in a deep-fat fryer or a large, deep, heavy-based saucepan to 180°C or until a cube of white bread dropped into it turns golden brown in 50–60 seconds. Now lower one of the wrapped fish into the oil and cook for about 5 minutes. The parcel will puff up and float to the top pretty quickly, after which you will need to turn it every now and then to ensure even cooking.

When it is done, drain the calzone on a few layers of kitchen paper, then keep warm while you cook the second one.

Serve with a good spoonful of chilli-spiked tomato sauce on the side. As soon as the calzone are cool enough to touch, pick them up and eat with your hands, dabbing the fish into the sauce as you go.

Shallow and deep frying

Frying fish is rarely a bad idea. In fact, we can't think of a single species that doesn't respond well to this treatment, which is why reaching for the frying pan is, or should be, second nature to the keen fish cook. It is to us. In fact, when we've been out fishing, and finally got home with some nicely prepped fish (assuming we've been both lucky and conscientious), we can find ourselves placing the frying pan on the hob and trickling in a little oil even before switching on the kettle, or opening the fridge and reaching for a beer.

Basic shallow frying is such a simple, reliable and effortless way of cooking fish that it's worth mastering this technique before any other. Incidentally, we won't call it 'pan-frying', as some modern chefs do, because not only is this a tiresomely tautological term but it also rather smacks of bogus industry inside-knowledge, claiming credit for a level of expertise where none is due. You really don't need to be a trained chef to fry fish, any more than you need to be trained

in the use of a knife and fork to enjoy it. So for anyone who likes to eat fish but is (temporarily) stuck in the mindset that it's difficult to cook, this chapter is a good starting point.

The joy of frying lies not just in its simplicity but also in its results. There are few more pleasing sensations than biting into a crisp skin, crumb coating or batter to find tender, delicate, lightly steaming fish flesh within. The merest dab of a simple relish – a homemade tartare sauce (see page 324), for example – elevates it to the gastronomic heights. You find yourself asking, 'Could this be done better, and enjoyed more?' and the answer is usually, 'No'.

Simple shallow frying

All you need is a decent pan, a bottle of olive or groundnut oil, some salt and pepper – plus perhaps a scrunched bay leaf or two and a bit of garlic. Just heat a layer of oil a scant millimetre thick in your frying pan, season your fish, or fish fillets, and fry until crisp. Once you've got the knack, you won't need a cookbook, not even this one.

With the acquisition of that knack in mind, it's just as well to get the theory straight. One important thing is to banish the idea that every pan you put a bit of fish in should be searingly, smokingly hot. Certainly, it should be on the hotter side of medium but, if you put a very fresh fillet into a very hot pan, the heat will quite often shock it into curling up. This happens because the fibres on the outside of the fish contract rapidly on contact with the fierce heat, while those on the inside are unaffected. This curling can make it difficult to cook the fish evenly, and indeed to get a good, crisp exterior, as it's hard to achieve even contact between the curled fillet and the flat pan. The trick is to start the fish over a medium heat at a gentle sizzle, pressing it lightly with a spatula if it shows an inclination to curl. Then turn the heat up a couple of minutes into the cooking time to achieve that toothsome exterior.

You might have noticed that we've already made an assumption that it's fillets you're putting in the pan. Much as we love to cook whole fish, it's well-trimmed fillets that lend themselves best to shallow frying. They naturally lie flat in the pan, and cook quickly and evenly in a matter of minutes. You'll be wanting a crisp skin, of course, and most fish – including sea bass, bream, salmon and pollack – will require descaling to prepare the skin for this treatment. Mackerel is one of the very few that will not. Its scales are tiny, and by the time you've got it into the kitchen it's lost most of them anyway. The few that remain cook imperceptibly into the skin as it crisps up.

The classic way to fry a fillet of fish is to season the skin with salt and pepper first, then put the fillet skin side down on to that layer of hot oil, keeping it there at a nice sizzle. If at any point it buckles up, gentle pressure of the spatula should be applied. Only when the skin is crisp and the edges of the fillet on the upper side look opaque should you flip the fillet over – for just a minute or two to finish it off. This method guarantees a good crisp skin and, because the fish is skin side down most of the time, it stops the flesh absorbing too much oil.

Once you've achieved that irresistible crisp skin on your fillet, you obviously want to enjoy it – or have your guests enjoy it – at its best. Always serve the fillet crisp side on top. If it's served the other way up, the skin will quickly soften and become soggy.

Shallow frying whole fish

Shallow frying a whole fish – say, a plate-sized bream, bass, trout or mackerel, or a small flatfish such as dab or lemon sole – is a slightly different business from frying a fillet. For a start, you have that uneven, round-bodied shape to contend with (less so with flatfish, obviously). A whole round fish, such as mackerel or bass, does not have two obligingly flat sides, so the contact between fish and pan is limited. In other words, frying one is more like frying a sausage than a burger. Indeed, with really round-bodied fish – mackerel is the best example, but it applies to small grey mullet and gurnard too – the sausage comparison is useful. They can, like sausages, be turned in the pan several times rather than just once, and you can try to balance them on their bellies and backs as well as their flanks. Another way to address the issue is to use considerably more oil in the pan – a centimetre rather than a millimetre, to increase the amount of contact between hot oil and fish. You're on your way to what we call 'deep shallow frying', which we will come to later.

Incidentally, some species benefit from a neat procedure of trimming and de-finning that prepares them for shallow frying, making them a little more manageable in the pan and tidier to eat. It works particularly well with spiny and relatively two-sided fish, such as bream, bass, red mullet and, should you find yourself somewhere exotic, snappers and their ilk. It's described in detail on page 61. But however well trimmed, a whole fish is always likely to be thicker than a boneless fillet, and therefore take a little longer to heat through – and of course you are aiming to get the skin crisp on both sides of the fish. With an overheated pan, and an overzealous attempt to get that skin crisp, you may find that it's frazzled on the outside but, on applying the knife test (pages 113–14), still raw in the middle. Best to go for a steady sizzle over a medium heat, aiming to give the fish 3–5 minutes on each side, depending on size. A total cooking time of 6–10 minutes should see you right for most single-portion fish.

However, if you are frying a larger fish – a fat, 1kg-plus specimen that challenges the size of your pan, perhaps to the extent that you have decided to remove its head and/or tail (not to mention dignity) to help you fit it in – then you will have to slow things down a bit in the pan, as it may take as long as 15–20 minutes' total cooking time to be hot through to the bone.

Alternatively – and this is a trick you may come to rely on quite a bit if you're a regular shallow fryer – you can deploy the oven to finish the job of cooking the fish through (if you have an Aga, this makes perfect sense as you have always got the oven on anyway). Fry a whole fish for a couple of minutes on either side over a fairly high heat to get that seasoned skin nicely crisped, then lay it in a preheated ovenproof dish or roasting tray and put into the oven. If your frying pan has a heatproof handle, you can just transfer the whole thing to the oven. So: fish into pan, 2 or 3 minutes each side; pan into oven at 200°C/Gas Mark 6; 8–10 minutes later, fish out. This sequence works beautifully with flatties such as brill, plaice or Dover sole weighing around 1–1.5kg, as well as bass, bream and large red mullet.

A word of warning: if you go the pan-into-oven route, the chances are that, one minute after the pan comes out again, you'll pick it up by its burning-hot handle. So you should always wrap a folded tea towel several times around the handle as soon as it comes out of the oven – and leave it there until the empty frying pan is deposited safely in the sink, preferably under a cold running tap.

Shallow frying tranches and cutlets

Between the boneless fillets and the whole fish is the portion of cut fish often called a tranche. As described (and pictured) on page 72, this is a portion of fish cut from a larger specimen – usually a chunky flatfish – often (but not always) with some bone. It may be a whole middle section from a medium-sized brill or turbot, or a half or even a quarter of such a piece if taken from a really big fish – a 5kg-plus turbot or a huge halibut.

A good tranche is roughly square in cross-section – or at least more or less rectangular. It therefore has two skin-covered sides with a good surface area, and shallow sides of cut flesh, with a bit of backbone running down the length of the third, middle side that helps to hold the tranche together. Obviously tranches will vary in shape according to where they are taken from, but if you're cooking several, you'll want them to be more or less the same weight.

You can see immediately how such a fish portion would lend itself well to shallow frying: four fairly flat sides, each of which can have a turn in contact with the hot pan base. You will want to concentrate on the two skin sides, of course, getting them as crisp as possible. The two flesh sides, as with the flesh side of a fillet, will need just a brief searing to give them a little colour and a nice savoury surface.

The other kind of bone-in portion of fish is the cutlet: a sliced cross-section of a round-bodied fish, such as a sea bass, salmon or large grey mullet (see page 71). Cutlets can also be shallow-fried, but it's the flat flesh sides, rather than the rounded, skin-covered edges, that will come into contact with the pan (as shown above left). They're easy to cook, though, and hold their shape well in the pan, so should not be overlooked.

Ridged griddle pans

We should mention here another bit of kit, which, at least superficially, is related to the frying pan. A heavy ridged griddle pan is a very useful tool for the fish cook, helping to create a crisp skin and beautiful, seared stripes on your fish, which you would normally only achieve on a barbecue. In fact, food cooked in a griddle pan is really being subjected to a form of indoor barbecuing. It's not being shallow fried at all but, since there is a natural link between a flat pan and a ridged one, we're sure you'll forgive us for discussing it here.

We particularly like griddle pans for cooking squid or scallops because the charring created by the ridges gives a special flavour that you won't get from using an ordinary frying pan. But a really hot griddle pan is a good place for any piece of fish to find itself – flattish fillets or portions being the optimum choice because they will lie flush against those searing ridges.

The secrets of griddle cooking success are largely the same as those for barbecuing (see pages 189–91). The basic idea is to oil the fish (not the pan) lightly and get the pan fiercely hot before you introduce the fish to it. Once you've added the fish, resist the temptation to move it until it's ready to turn over – many griddled fish have shed their skin through impatience. These steps should ensure that you can griddle your fish successfully without any of it adhering to the pan… well, not much anyway.

Dustings and coatings for extra crispness

Let's return to shallow frying, and the pursuit of that crisp exterior, which can become mildly obsessional. If it's not part of your plan to achieve it then, frankly, the 'steam-braise' technique described on page 255 is more forgiving and reliable (and offers that nice little spoonful of juices as a by-product). But assuming you want to maximise crispness when shallow frying your fish, it's a simple matter to enhance the results by dusting it with a starchy flour or grain of one sort or another. The idea of such coatings is not merely to lead to the holy grail of crispness – though it should certainly help achieve that. They also provide a fine but significant protective layer for the fish beneath, keeping it moist and tender.

The first obvious option is a simple dusting of seasoned flour. This alone is enough to create the most delicate of crusts, and is particularly useful when you're dealing with thin-skinned white fish, such as pollack, whiting and coley. There are alternatives to flour, which all have their own charms – semolina works well, as does matzo meal. It's worth ringing the changes to explore the

subtly different textures created by these starchy granules. Go further and dip your floured fish in beaten egg and you'll get a lovely, slightly pancakey jacket over your fillet – the result is not so crisp but for some reason children seem to love it. The next step is to press your lightly egged fillets into a plate of breadcrumbs – only a few minutes' more work, but resulting in that crunchy exterior that is perhaps the apex of crispness (see page 324 for the ultimate in crisp-crumbed, shallow-fried fillets).

A crumb coating, being thicker and more absorbent than mere flour, will require you to add a little more oil to your frying pan – to about 5mm depth, say – but you're still in the realms of shallow frying. It's only when you start using thick batters that it becomes necessary to turn to the deep-fat fryer. But that does open the door to some particularly delicious recipes, so we'll be wheeling out our fryer shortly.

Battered or breadcrumbed fish dishes are usually the ones that people who are not out-and-out fish lovers (poor things) tend to go for. Or, to put it another way, plenty of people who say they don't like fish will happily eat fish fingers. And, with these recipes, you can use that natural liking for the crisp and crunchy, to branch out into slightly less familiar but nevertheless crowd-pleasing versions of fried fish. Fish fingers don't have to come from the freezer. They don't even have to be finger-shaped. The breadcrumbs don't have to be dayglo orange. The reinvented, homemade fish finger, or crumbed fillet, is almost invariably an improvement on the mass-produced big-brand version. By jingo, you can even call it a goujon.

So this is, if you like, the Trojan horse chapter; you can use it to wrong-foot the fish phobic. 'Don't worry,' you can say, 'it's only a bit of fried fish.' Just don't tell them that it's a pouting, a whelk or a piece of squid! The familiar crunch of batter or breadcrumbs will lull them into a false sense of security, which will have them conquering a whole new dish, or fish, before they know it.

Deep frying fish for ultimate crispness

We know and love deep-fried fish mainly, of course, through our experience of the Great British Fish and Chip Shop (300 million portions of fried fish are sold every year in the UK, so they must be doing something right). The deep-fat fryer will always be a delightful way of cooking fish fillets and other crumb- or batter-coated morsels of seafood, including prawns, squid, scallops and even oysters. And there is no reason why we can't reproduce the chip-shop effect at home, if we set our minds to it. Nor does it require a custom-built deep-fat fryer. A deep, wide, stainless steel pan will do the job. The great thing about doing it at home is that we may somehow feel less compelled to drown our lovingly made fish supper in a vat of vinegar and a kilo of ketchup.

However, successful deep frying does require a little more skill – or at least attention to detail – than shallow frying. To paraphrase the marriage service (not for the first time in a River Cottage book, according to our editor), to enter into it lightly or wantonly, without a little forethought, may well lead to disappointment or, far worse, outright danger. It is therefore understandable that many fish cooks, even experienced ones, make the decision that they will leave the whole business of deep frying to the professionals, and concentrate on exploring other areas of fish cookery. If you are inclined to put yourself in that category, and particularly if you have young, inquisitive children who like to be around and involved when you are cooking, then fair enough. On the other hand, if you consider yourself a responsible, well-organised cook, or at least one with a built-in sense of self-preservation, there is no reason why you can't explore the delights of deep-frying fish at home. In terms of kit, you will want to go one of two routes: you can either purchase a plug-in, domestic 'safety' deep-fat fryer or, if you're sure you know what you're doing, you can deep fry in a suitable large saucepan – something robust and solid (stainless steel is preferable to aluminium), and at least 25cm in diameter and 20cm high. And it should *never* be more than a third full of oil.

At home we both still use the large-saucepan-of-oil approach, with a selection of wire baskets and 'spider' spoons for removing the cooked food from the oil (the ones we like best have heatproof bamboo handles, and can be found in Chinese grocers). However, we know from fellow cooks that the plug-in domestic fryers are very useful, especially if you plan to deep fry more than once in a blue moon. Although they can be pricey, they give consistent results and are a particularly safe way to deep fry. If you're shopping for one, don't be tempted by a bargain or anything secondhand. Get something new that smacks of quality – and ideally comes with a clear set of instructions and an unambiguous warranty.

If you are planning to do as we do and use a saucepan, one small investment you should make is a fire blanket (domestic size). It's the only safe way to smother and put out a chip pan fire. Keep it close to the cooker, and know where it is. You'll never have to use it, of course, but its very presence will make you a safer fryer.

Such a belt and braces attitude to safety will stand you in good stead, because the secret of successful deep-fried fish is good preparation and a little bit of confidence. It's all about having everything ready – and especially having your batter right and your oil hot enough (but not too hot, as we'll see). All fish for deep frying should have some kind of coating, and usually that means breadcrumbs or a liquid batter into which the fish is dipped. Even more than with shallow frying, the function of the coating is not only to create that delectable crunchy crust but also to protect the delicate fish inside from the fiercely hot oil. By inflicting severe heat damage on the breadcrumbs or batter, it just so happens that you make them rather delicious. Do the same to a piece of unprotected fish fillet and you would dry it out and spoil it.

Battered and breadcrumbed fish fillets are the stock-in-trade of deep-fat frying, but occasionally it may be rewarding to deep fry a whole fish, with bones still in, that has simply been dusted in seasoned flour (see page 337). You'll need a fish of the right size (not too big for your pan of oil), with a skin that, after descaling, is robust and prone to very satisfactory crisping (small bream and gurnard spring to mind).

The effects of temperature and timing

When you place a piece of battered fish in a pan of hot oil, the heat causes the water in the batter to boil and evaporate (that's why you see that mass of tiny bubbles). Once all its moisture has vaporised, the batter becomes crisp. You can tell this is happening because the bubbles slow down and the batter changes colour to that appealing golden brown. But if you go on frying much beyond this

point, the batter will start to take in oil and become greasy – particularly if it's a batter made with wheat flour, as the gluten it contains is absorbent. So, since you don't want to leave your fish frying for too long, you need a high temperature that will cook it right through to the centre, before the batter on the outside starts soaking up lots of oil.

Fortunately, as we've discussed, fish conducts heat pretty well. And although the batter coating provides a protective and somewhat insulating layer, the surrounding heat will cook the fillet through fairly fast. If all goes well, the effect is almost as if the fish is steamed inside its batter crust – when it happens, that's chip-shop nirvana.

Things can go wrong, though. If the fillets are too thick and come straight from a very cold fridge, they may still be uncooked in the middle when the batter reaches perfection. If they're too thin, they may be soft and mushy. Success therefore depends on working within the right parameters of oil temperature, fillet size and frying time. As it happens, 2–3cm is about the right thickness for a fillet, and 3–4 minutes about the right cooking time. And the right oil temperature, most professional fish fryers would concur, is between 160°C and 180°C. Whole fillets in a thick batter need the lower temperature to give them time to cook through; smaller pieces, or those coated in only a thin dusting of flour or breadcrumbs, can happily take a higher heat.

Fortunately, it is not difficult to monitor your oil temperature. The best way, if you're using the big-pan-of-oil approach, is with a cook's thermometer. Most domestic deep-fat fryers have a thermostat that you can set to a desired temperature. But you can also make a good estimate of the temperature by using the old cook's trick of dropping a cube of white bread into the hot oil. If it turns light golden brown in about 90 seconds, your oil is at around 160°C; 50–60 seconds signifies a temperature of around 175–180°C. If it takes about 25–30 seconds, you've got very hot oil – about 190°C – appropriate for the final frying of chips and just about okay for flour-dusted squid rings, which will cook in barely a minute, but a bit too hot for a battered fish fillet. If it takes any less than that for the bread to colour, your oil is dangerously hot and you should cool it down before you think of cooking anything in it. Otherwise you might be reaching for that fire blanket.

If you've made a good batter that coats the fish well and you've got the temperature of the oil right, you'll have a lovely, deep golden crust around your moist white fillet. But you will still need to drain the fish well. Lift it from the hot oil with a wire basket or a spider spoon and give it a little shake. Prop the basket or spider over a drip tray or bowl and leave for half a minute. Give it another tap or a shake. Then lay it on several layers of absorbent kitchen paper for another half minute or so, turning once. It's now ready to serve – still crisp and piping hot.

There's no denying that, however well it's done, deep-fried crumbed or battered fish will always be a relatively fatty food. That, combined with the skill and care required to get a perfect result, means that it is best seen as something of a treat. However, fried at the right temperature for the right time, and well drained and blotted, your fish should never be oil-logged or greasy, and certainly no more calorie-laden than a blob of homemade mayonnaise or even a slab of cheese on toast – and who would ever quibble with everyday treats like those?

The all-important oil

What you fry your fish in is important, and some oils are quite unsuitable. Volatile oils, including seed or olive oils described as 'cold pressed' or 'extra virgin', are simply too fragile and unstable at high temperatures, and will smoke long before they reach the required 180°C. Smoking oil not only releases toxins into the air, it also taints the flavour of the food you're frying. We tend to use groundnut oil, though sunflower oil is also a good option. Both are very stable at high temperatures – in other words you can get them very hot before their molecular structure changes and they start to smoke.

Some sources will tell you that once you've deep-fried fish in oil, you should discard the oil straight away because the flavour will be tainted. We think that's unnecessarily extravagant and wasteful. In fact, if your fish was good and fresh to start with, and encased in a protective batter, you should be able to reuse that oil several times, as long as you filter it between frying sessions to remove any solids. At home, passing the oil through a funnel lined with a coffee filter is a good way to clean it. But, obviously, never pour it back into a plastic bottle until it's cooled right down.

You can't go on using the same deep-frying oil forever, though (and changing the oil regularly marks the difference between a good chip shop and a bad one). If you've reused some oil a few times, then left it sitting around in a jar or bottle for a month or two, and you want to see whether it's still good, then the best test is a taste test. Just heat a tablespoon of the oil in a small frying pan and shallow-fry a cube of bread in it until golden. Taste it. If it's fishy, or a bit musty, or unpleasant in any way, then discard the oil and start with fresh. If the fried bread tastes fine, then the oil is good for another go.

A middle path: deep shallow frying

If you feel nervous about deep frying, for whatever reason, bear in mind that there are very few dishes in this book, and even in this chapter, that absolutely have to be cooked that way. Only quite large pieces of fish, completely coated in batter, need total immersion in hot oil to give the right results. A viable alternative for many recipes, including anything coated in breadcrumbs, is what we like to call the deep shallow fry, where you need only about a 5mm depth of oil in your pan. You are still deep frying, really, but you're deep frying one side at a time.

The vast majority of recipes in this chapter are not about using great panfuls of oil at all. They're about using just a little bit – a tablespoon or so – to get very quick, very good results. Sometimes there will be something coming between the fish and the oil, a variation on the theme of flour, egg or breadcrumbs; and sometimes the fish will be cut into small pieces and mixed into a fritter batter or made into some kind of fishcake before being fried. But there are many recipes here in which the fish remains naked, or wears nothing but its own skin, and is just placed directly on to a thin film of hot fat and flipped over after a couple of minutes. These are among the fastest, most instantly gratifying fish recipes you'll find. So if in doubt, or a hurry, reach for the frying pan.

Quick-fried mackerel fillets with garlic and bay

This is perhaps the simplest way to enjoy a catch of fresh mackerel when you get home, tired but elated after a few good hours at sea. It's super-quick and very family friendly.

Also works with:
- Sardines (large)
- Herring
- Trout (small)

Fresh mackerel, 1 per person
Olive oil
A few garlic cloves, thickly sliced

A few bay leaves, roughly torn
½ lemon
Salt and freshly ground black pepper

Cut the fillets from either side of the mackerel, bait-cutter style (see pages 62–3). Season them with a little salt and pepper.

Put a large frying pan over a medium heat and add a thin film of olive oil. When the oil is fairly hot, scatter in the garlic and bay leaves, then lay the mackerel fillets over them, skin side down. You're looking for a gentle sizzle rather than a fierce flash-fry. As it cooks, the mackerel flesh will change from translucent pink to opaque white. When the fillets are almost completely white, turn them over for just a minute to finish cooking. The whole process won't take longer than 5 minutes. Let the garlic and bay just sizzle in the oil under and next to the fish, flavouring it gently.

Lift the mackerel fillets from the pan, leaving the bay and garlic behind (they're probably just starting to burn a bit). Give the fillets a squeeze of lemon juice and serve straight away, with salad (a sliced tomato salad is delicious with mackerel) and either new potatoes or buttered bread.

Black bream with herbs *serves 2*

This dish is really about the preparation of a whole fish of a certain size (a one-portion fish), especially for the frying pan. It's descaled, beheaded, de-spined and trimmed, so it's easy to cook, easy to get a nice crisp skin and deliciously easy to eat. The removal of the fin line along the spine and tail allows the oil, butter and herbs to penetrate deep into the centre of the flesh. It works best with bream and their near relatives.

2 black bream, weighing 500–750g each
A small bunch of thyme sprigs
2 small, tender sprigs of rosemary
25g unsalted butter
3 bay leaves

2 tablespoons olive oil
2 garlic cloves, skin left on, bruised with
    a knife
Salt and freshly ground black pepper

First you need to descale your fish (see pages 55–6) and then remove the bream's spiny fins (see page 61). Use sharp kitchen scissors to snip off the small pectoral fins on the underbelly and gut the fish (see pages 58–9). Decapitation is optional, but it will give you more room in the pan. If you're going to do it, cut the head off just behind the pectoral fin. Trim the tail, too, if you think you're tight for space.

Slash the fish two or three times on each side. Stuff a little thyme and rosemary into the slashes and cavity of each fish, along with the butter. Put a bay leaf into each cavity. Season the fish all over with salt and pepper.

Heat the olive oil in a large, non-stick frying pan over a medium heat, then add the other bay leaf and garlic so they can gently release their flavour as the fish cooks. Lay the fish in the pan and fry for 5–6 minutes on each side, until cooked through to the bone. You can turn the heat up towards the end of cooking, if necessary, to help crisp the skin. Serve at once, with a leafy salad and sautéed or boiled new potatoes.

Also works with:
• Red mullet
• Sea bass

Witch with lemon zest mash *serves 2*

Witch is a ghostly looking little flatfish that makes surprisingly good eating, fully deserving its place alongside its cousin megrim on our list of the top ten most underrated fish (see page 49). It's great simply flashed under a grill or gently fried. The goujon treatment – filleted, dipped in seasoned flour, egg and breadcrumbs, then fried – would also be a good option. A citrus-infused mash works beautifully as an accompaniment.

Also works with:
- Lemon sole
- Dab
- Flounder
- Megrim
- Plaice

1 tablespoon olive oil
2 witch, weighing about 500g each, gutted
25g unsalted butter
Juice of 1 lemon
1 tablespoon marjoram leaves (optional)
Salt and freshly ground black pepper

FOR THE LEMON ZEST MASH:
500g floury potatoes, such as Désirée, Pentland Javelin or Wilja
2 bay leaves
50ml whole milk
25g unsalted butter
2 tablespoons extra virgin olive oil
Finely grated zest of 1 lemon

First prepare the mash. Bring a large pan of salted water to the boil. Peel the potatoes and cut them into roughly equal pieces. Pour cold water over them, stir, then drain (this removes some of the starch). Add the potatoes and bay leaves to the pan of boiling water, bring back to a steady simmer and cook until they are completely tender. Tip them into a colander and leave for at least 3 minutes to 'steam off' (this helps to reduce the water content). Discard the bay leaves.

Put the milk, butter, olive oil, lemon zest and some black pepper into the warm pan and place over a low heat to melt the butter (but don't let it boil). Pile the potatoes into a potato ricer and rice them directly into the seasoned hot milk and butter mixture (or push them through a sieve if you don't have a ricer). Stir well with a wooden spoon to get a smooth, even texture, then taste to check the seasoning. Keep warm while you cook the fish.

Heat a large non-stick frying pan over a medium heat and add the olive oil. Season the fish on both sides, add to the pan and cook for 4–5 minutes on each side. Divide the mash between two warmed plates and put the fish next to it. Return the pan to the heat. Add the butter, lemon juice, and marjoram if using, and allow the butter to foam for a minute or so. Spoon over the witch and serve.

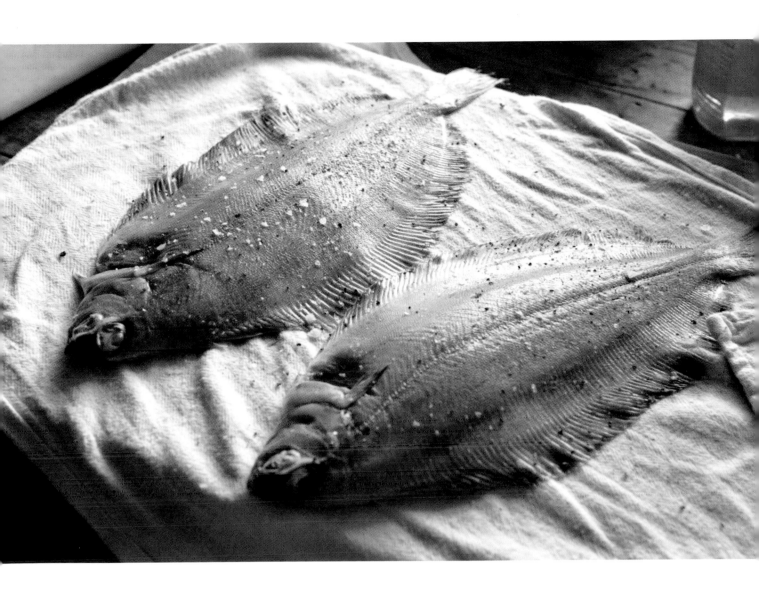

Sea trout fillet with sorrel sauce *serves 4*

Larger than brown or rainbow trout, sea trout is a relatively rare treat – a fish that's available only during spring and summer, when it returns from the sea to our rivers to spawn. Its oceanic journey seems to give it a fantastic extra depth of flavour.

You can cook sea trout whole, in many of the same ways you'd cook other trout, or salmon, but a big fish will yield lovely meaty fillets, which are quite delicious with a velvety sorrel sauce.

In fact, the sauce – which is extremely quick and easy to make – should be a mainstay in any fish cook's repertoire. Somewhere between a herb and a salad leaf, sorrel has a startlingly lemony flavour, which makes a perfect foil for everything from barbecued mackerel to steamed brill or fried pollack (or indeed a poached egg on toast). Be warned, though, that the leaf undergoes a dramatic change of colour when cooked, turning from vibrant green to a dull, army-fatigue khaki. Don't worry – the taste remains bright and fresh.

Also works with:
- Salmon (organic farmed or self-caught wild)
- Trout
- Sea bass
- Mackerel

4 thick, roughly square, fillet pieces (200–250g each), cut from large sea trout fillets, skin on but descaled
1 tablespoon olive oil
1 tablespoon groundnut or sunflower oil
4 bay leaves
2 garlic cloves, skin left on, bruised with a knife
Salt and freshly ground black pepper

FOR THE SORREL SAUCE:
50g unsalted butter
1 large bunch of washed sorrel (about 200g), stalks removed, leaves coarsely chopped
1 egg yolk
1 tablespoon double cream (optional)

Heat a large non-stick frying pan over a medium-high heat. Season the sea trout fillets all over. Add the two oils to the pan, along with the bay and garlic, which will subtly perfume the fish. Place the fish, skin side down, in the pan and cook for 5–7 minutes, by which time the skin should be crisp and the fish cooked at least three-quarters of the way through. Flip the fish over and cook for a further minute, until opaque, but only just, all the way through. Transfer to warmed plates (discarding the bay and garlic) while you make the sauce.

Sorrel cooks very fast, so this sauce can be whipped up in minutes. Put the butter in a small pan over a medium heat. When it is frothing, throw in the sorrel, which will quickly wilt and turn a dull greeny-brown. Give it a quick stir to make sure all the leaves are wilted. Remove the pan from the heat, let it cool for 30 seconds, then beat in the egg yolk, which will thicken the sauce. Season to taste with salt and pepper. If you like, enrich the sauce by stirring in the double cream. You can re-warm it, ever so gently, over a low heat, but be careful not to scramble the egg in it.

Serve the fish fillets with the warm sorrel sauce and some waxy new potatoes.

Sea trout with creamed spinach

If sea trout with sorrel sauce is a light, peck-on-the-cheek of a dish, then the same fish with wilted spinach in a creamy béchamel sauce is a comforting hug.

To serve four, blanch 500g trimmed fresh spinach in salted water. Refresh in cold water, then squeeze out as much liquid as you can. Roughly chop the spinach. Grate a small onion and $\frac{1}{2}$ carrot and put in a pan with 250ml whole milk, a bay leaf, some ground black pepper and a few gratings of nutmeg. Bring almost to boiling point, then leave to infuse for 10 minutes. Strain into a warmed jug, discarding the herbs and vegetables.

Melt 50g butter in a pan and stir in 25g plain flour to make a loose roux. Cook gently for a couple of minutes, then stir in half the milk. When the sauce is thick and smooth, stir in the rest of the milk. Simmer gently for just a minute, then stir in the chopped spinach. Heat through until thoroughly hot, but don't let it bubble for more than a minute. Taste and adjust the seasoning with salt, pepper and a touch more nutmeg if you like. Serve at once, with your fried sea trout fillets. Note that this creamed spinach is also a very good accompaniment to crumbed, fried fish fillets (see page 324).

Fried bream fillets with pea purée   *serves 4*

Fillets from bream that you've just caught, served with a purée of peas that you've just picked… it must be July.

Also works with:
• Sea bass
• John Dory
• Red mullet
• Brill
• Lemon sole

Leaves from 1 large bunch of mint, chopped (keep the stalks)
400g freshly podded peas (or use frozen peas)
Olive oil
1½ garlic cloves – ½ finely chopped, the other clove skin left on and roughly bruised with a knife

75g unsalted butter
2 bay leaves
2 black bream, weighing about 450g each, descaled, filleted and pin-boned
Salt and freshly ground black pepper
Lemon wedges, to serve

Bring a pan of water to the boil and throw in the mint stalks. Add a pinch of salt and the peas and boil for 4–5 minutes, until the peas are tender (overgrown 'cannonball' peas may take a little longer). Drain and reserve the cooking water, but discard the mint stalks. Put the peas in a blender and set aside.

Set a small pan over a medium-high heat, then add 1 tablespoon of olive oil and the finely chopped garlic. Sizzle gently until the garlic just begins to colour, then quickly pour it into the blender with the peas. Add 50g of the butter, a pinch of salt and pepper and the chopped mint leaves. Add 2 tablespoons of the pea cooking water and blend the whole lot to a purée, adding a little more liquid if necessary, to give a consistency that is similar to coarse hummus. Taste and adjust the seasoning.

Put a large, non-stick frying pan over a medium-high heat. Add 1 tablespoon of olive oil and the remaining butter. Throw in the bay leaves and the bruised garlic clove to flavour the fat. Season the fish fillets all over and, when the fat is hot, lay them skin side down in the pan. Cook for about 3 minutes, until the flesh has turned opaque nearly all the way through, then flip them over and cook for a final 30 seconds.

Arrange the fish fillets skin side up on warmed plates, with a generous dollop of pea purée alongside. Serve with lemon wedges, plus a tomato salad.

Cold fish and salads

'Cold fish' isn't perhaps the most inspiring phrase in the English language – you wouldn't want to be seated next to one at dinner. But having one in front of you on a plate wouldn't be quite so bad. Because cold fish can be absolutely delicious.

Just to be clear, we're not talking about raw or marinated fish – though sushi, ceviche and a good rollmop are examples of just how appealing cold fish can be. We've already shone the spotlight on them, however. Nor are we dealing with leftover fish. We'll tackle that rich topic with great glee later on. No, our focus here, believe it or not, is on fish that you cook with the *deliberate intention of letting it go cold before you eat it*. It's not really such an eccentric thing to do. Think of a quick snack of potted shrimps on toast, or a full-on feast of cold poached sea trout with homemade mayonnaise, and perhaps you'll realise you're already quite at home with the idea of cooked fish served cold.

The tastes and textures offered by cold fish are quite different from those you get when eating it hot – and that's part of its charm. When fish is potted or made into a pâté, the different flavours will merge as it ripens and, if it's a good recipe, the combination will have a subtle harmony that often eludes warm, sauced fish. When cold poached (or even tinned) fish is tossed in a salad of fresh vegetables, leaves and herbs, the ingredients remain separate, yet together. Every mouthful offers a different combination – Salade niçoise (page 360) is the apotheosis of this phenomenon. But even when fish or shellfish is simply cooked and left to cool, then eaten at room (or garden) temperature with minimal adornment – a dressing of good oil and lemon juice, perhaps – there is a clarity of flavour about it that can be very satisfying.

The chef at any half-decent pub knows that there is no more sure-fire winner on a summer menu than half a pint of cold, shell-on cooked prawns served with a blob of mayo. Even with a relatively indifferent salad on the side and mayonnaise from a jar, it's still something of a treat. But if the pub chef goes the extra yard – whips up a homemade mayonnaise, offers leaves from a freshly torn lettuce, some buttered brown bread and half a lemon, he or she will have the customers in clover. And why stop there? How about a freshly boiled lobster or cracked crab with homemade garlic mayonnaise? Consider other shellfish – langoustines, winkles, whelks – and you'll see why 'cold fish' needn't be a term of derision. In fact, serving these delightful shellfish cold, with some kind of simple dressing or mayonnaise, is the obvious default setting for enjoying them at their best.

The two ends of the spectrum are the *grande assiette de fruits de mer* at a *fin de siècle* Parisian brasserie, and the cup of whelks from a seafront stall in one of Britain's bucket-and-spade holiday resorts. One may be gilt-edged and glamorous, the other plebeian and packed in polystyrene, but affection for both runs deep – and so it should.

It's not just shellfish that tastes good cooked and served cold with a light dressing. Many fish are fabulous this way too, though you should opt for those with a reasonably robust flavour. The oilier varieties – mackerel, salmon and trout, for instance – are the most obvious examples. In fact, when they've been smoked – either hot or cold smoked – then eating these species cold is the norm. But they certainly don't need to be smoked to shine in or around a salad. Baked, poached or even barbecued, then left to cool and served with a suitable dressing – lemony or garlicky, or perhaps both – they are outstanding. The same is true of a whole bunch of other less obvious, yet still robust, full-flavoured fish: sea bass, bream, gurnard, red mullet and scad, to name but five. They may rarely be given the chance to display their charms at room temperature, but they will certainly not disappoint when they do.

This cannot be said of all fish. There are some species that definitely don't float the boat as cold cuts. White fish such as pollack, pouting, haddock and cod, and the more delicate flatfish such as plaice, tend to be better in hot dishes. Since the flavour of any food is a little muted when eaten cold, a very delicate bit of fish flesh can become insipid when the warmth has left it. There's a fine line between subtle and dull, and with fragile white fish it's often crossed when the fish goes from warm to cold.

How cold is cold?

Coldness is, of course, relative, but we know roughly what it means in the context of food. No doubt somebody somewhere has served an anchovy ice cream (and if it was Heston Blumenthal, it was no doubt delicious). But on the whole, we are talking about serving fish somewhere between fridge temperature (4–6°C) and room temperature (20–25°C). Even this 20° window offers quite a range of sensations for the palate to explore.

Food at 4–6°C is *really cold* – a full 30°C colder than the temperature inside our mouths. Any food served at that temperature, or at anywhere up to about 10°C, is going to taste distinctly chilly. Generally speaking, this is not the temperature range to which we are referring when we suggest a dish can or should be served cold. In fact, the word to use for food served at this temperature is 'chilled' – and you would only choose to serve food, including fish, this way if you wanted the distinct effect of putting something cold in a warm mouth. That might be because it is simply intended to cool or refresh the palate; or because, like a set mousse or jelly, it is meant to melt in the mouth, releasing new and perhaps surprising flavours as it does so.

The traditional fish cookery canon does include such dishes: fish jellies, aspics and mousses abound in the works of Mrs Beeton, Mrs Marshall and Escoffier – not to mention their latter-day champion, Fanny Cradock – and they still have their followers amongst the starry-eyed chefs of today. But we don't have much time for such concoctions, not least because more often than not they involve a great deal of fuss: the puréeing and sieving of fish flesh, the mixing with egg yolks, the whipping of cream, the creaming of butter, the whisking and folding in of egg whites, the reducing of fish stock and/or the dissolving of gelatine. Frankly, who needs it? It shouldn't take an army of sous-chefs and a truckload of gizmos to extract the joy from a fish. So our soufflé on page 177 is as far as we're prepared to go along this route. It's half the fuss of any fish mousse recipe and, we would say, twice the pleasure of most. It is meant to be eaten hot from the oven, of course, though we've found the leftovers quite passable straight from the fridge.

Generally, the recipes in this chapter are best served at, or perhaps a little below, room temperature – say, 12–20°C. This is easy enough if they are created at room temperature, or cooled to it immediately after cooking, and then served without delay. But sometimes – the Potted mackerel on page 357 springs to mind – refrigeration is part of the preparation of a dish. In this case they will benefit from an hour or two out of the fridge before serving, to take the chill off them. In dishes where no refrigeration is prescribed, however – i.e. where a fish is simply cooked and left to cool – common sense should prevail. If it's a baking-hot day, or just baking in the kitchen, then a short spell in the fridge is in order.

What we're trying to avoid here is wedding-salmon syndrome. The point is that the temperature at which we propose you serve most of the dishes in this chapter is not one at which they should be allowed to hang around for long. Room temperature is also bug-breeding temperature (and so is garden/marquee temperature in the summer months). So if you need to store a cold fish dish before serving it, the best place is in the fridge (or, for al fresco feasts some distance from the kitchen, a properly chilled cold box).

The window for serving such dishes should be kept to an hour or two at most, and any leftovers should be refrigerated without delay and consumed within a day or two, max. If in doubt, use leftovers to make fishcakes or kedgeree and make sure in both cases that they are thoroughly heated through – beyond the magic 70°C for 2 minutes, which kills those bugs.

Tinned fish

One often unsung 'family' of fish that offers a useful set of ingredients for the cold-fish enthusiast is the kind we like to buy in tins. Everyone should have a shoal of well-chosen tinned fish in their larders. They are invaluable stand-bys for any keen composer of what Tom Norrington-Davies, a food writer we both enjoy, calls 'larder salads'. They're quite handy for larder sarnies, too.

Most notable by far – because they are the most delicious, and also the most versatile – are the mighty tuna and the diminutive sardine. One is so huge that a single fish might find its way into a thousand tins; the other so small that it might require half a dozen bedfellows to occupy just one.

Both may be eaten hot or cold, but on balance we prefer cold. Good sardines in good oil, forked straight from the tin on to buttered toast, with a couple of sticks of celery or maybe a raw carrot, make a classic stand-up lunch. It's the kind of meal you eat hovering in the kitchen while waiting for the kettle to boil (and very much the kind that has fuelled the writing of this book).

Tinned tuna offers similarly instant gratification – all the more so when it's tinned in oil rather than brine. The pleasure, though, comes increasingly at a price to the conscience, as discussed on pages 447–51. So, whether you're bashing out tuna sandwiches for the kids' lunchboxes or putting together a well-balanced classic Salade niçoise (page 360) for an outdoor summer lunch, always think beyond the tin, to the finned blue torpedo that travels the oceans of the world – increasingly in flight from our technology-laden boats (and even helicopters). We're sure you wouldn't want any fish to be hounded and harried to extinction, but especially not one that tastes so good. Please, only buy sustainably sourced tinned tuna – the Fish4Ever brand is the one we recommend (see the Directory, page 591).

There are other fish in tins, of course, and among them we particularly enjoy mackerel fillets and whole pilchards (which are really just big sardines and can be used in many of the same recipes). The tinned mackerel in oil will readily stand in for any recipe that calls for tuna – and so can certainly help in any bid to keep one's fish shopping sustainable.

Anchovies

We certainly mustn't leave the subject of tinned fish without mentioning one fabulous little contender. All hail the anchovy, without whose intense piquancy – sheer essence of fish – some of the recipes in this book would fail to reach the dizzy heights we expect of them.

Anchovies come preserved in various forms, including salt, vinegar and oil. Some cooks, and many restaurant chefs, like to buy them in bulk – packed and pressed in a tub of salt, headless but otherwise whole, with the backbone still in. These need to be lifted carefully from their crusty salt bed and split open with a small knife (or, if you've got the knack, a fingernail), so the fragile backbone can be removed and discarded. They then need gentle rinsing to remove the excess salt. After that they can be used straight away – or transferred to a smaller jar or plastic box and covered in oil.

Most of us, though, buy anchovies in small jars or tins of oil. These have already been salted, rinsed and filleted before being packed in oil. They are ready to use in any recipe that calls for anchovies, as several of ours do. (If you only ever cook one of them, we'd recommend it's the Anchovy and chilli dressing on page 398. Here we suggest it as an accompaniment to purple sprouting broccoli or curly kale, but you'll soon find it has a million and one uses.)

In many ways the greatest charm of the anchovy is its ability to lend its potent fishiness at short notice to some impromptu culinary experiment. A salad of new lettuces and hard-boiled eggs makes a simple and charming summer supper. But crack open a tin of anchovies (and a bottle of rosé while you're at it) and suddenly you're dining like kings. With anchovies added, a gratin dauphinois becomes less a greedy, creamy side dish, more a meal in its own right. It's on its way to what the Scandinavians call Jansson's temptation. Similarly, a pile of Puy lentils – simmered until just tender, left to go cold, then dressed with olive oil and lemon juice – make a lovely accompaniment to a cold fish dish (see page 355). But with some leftover cooked mackerel and a tin of anchovies roughly chopped and mixed through, they *are* a cold fish dish (see page 400).

Anchovy fillets come in various oils and vessels under a bewildering range of brands, mostly Italian or Portuguese. They vary slightly, and aficionados can exhibit fierce brand loyalty. We're a bit more happy-go-lucky, taking what comes our way. We've rarely, if ever, felt seriously let down by an anchovy, except the ones that come in vinegar. The Spanish call these *boquerones*, and they are emphatically not what is called for when a recipe asks for anchovies. They taste only of vinegar and are rarely as good as a decent rollmop. Unless you're sitting in a bar in Spain, with a glass of chilled Manzanilla to hand, they are bordering on pointless.

Fresh anchovies, on the other hand, should be snapped up at every opportunity. Tossed in seasoned flour and rapidly shallow or deep fried in olive oil, they can be munched head, guts, tail and all. You'll sometimes find them in fishmongers during the winter months, as boats out fishing for sprats occasionally get amongst huge shoals of anchovies (which are related to the sprat, as it happens). Sam and Sam Clark, who run the lovely Spanish/Moorish restaurant Moro in London, are always on the lookout for fresh anchovies. And when they get them, they cook them quite beautifully, coated in a coarse Spanish flour called *harina de trigo*, then deep fried.

Cooking fish for serving cold

When your cold fish doesn't come from a tin, you'll need to cook it yourself first. To do this, you won't need much in the way of special techniques – the various methods described in previous chapters will serve you in good stead. It's worth making a bit of a fuss over the fish as you cook it, just as you would if it were to be served steaming hot, because you still want to get as much flavour into it, and then out of it, as you possibly can.

The cold salmon, sea trout or sea bass on page 355, for instance, is poached in an aromatic court-bouillon before cooling, while Potted mackerel (page 357) is first baked in foil with garlic and bay leaves. These recipes illustrate the two main ways of cooking fish for serving cold – poaching and baking – both of which give you plenty of opportunity to infuse that fish with lots of flavour.

It's worth noting that a slightly shorter cooking time is usually in order if you're going to let the fish cool completely after baking or poaching. This is because, even after you've taken the fish away from the heat source, the heat will continue to travel to the middle of it.

Cooking shellfish for serving cold

When it comes to serving shellfish cold, the various species each have their own cooking processes. These are described either in specific recipes or in the relevant sections of the chapter on Shellfish skills (page 86). It's often easy enough to buy them ready cooked but we'd urge you to buy them live and boil them up yourself whenever possible. It's the best way to ensure the job's done well – not least because some fishmongers err on the side of over-boiling their crabs and lobsters.

Once you've got the cooked, cooled crustaceans in front of you, don't be daunted by the cracking and picking part of the deal. The way we look at it, the bashing of shells and wrenching of claws and legs is all part of the sense of occasion that befits the arrival of these armoured marine aliens at the table. It's also the best possible way to appreciate them in all their glory. You'd be cheating yourself, and your guests, if you didn't take the opportunity to marvel at their otherworldly bodies. The process of dismantling them and removing their flesh is both a ritual and an education.

You'll need the right equipment, of course, and the toolbox may be as useful a place to look as the kitchen drawer. Nutcrackers and rolling pins, small screwdrivers and tweezers will all come in handy. Even if you've never done it before, you'll soon be at it, almost literally, hammer and tongs.

Lobster with herb mayonnaise *serves 4*

Generally speaking, the less you do to the sweet, pearly flesh of a lobster, the more impressive it will be. But anointing your freshly cooked crustacean with a little homemade mayonnaise laced with fresh herbs is one of the best treatments imaginable – simple, luxurious and somehow the epitome of summer.

2 live lobsters, weighing about 750g each

FOR THE HERB MAYONNAISE:
2 very fresh egg yolks
1 anchovy fillet, chopped
1 small garlic clove, chopped
1 teaspoon English mustard
A small pinch each of salt, sugar and
  freshly ground black pepper

Juice of ½ lemon
100ml olive oil
200ml groundnut or sunflower oil
1 tablespoon small capers, rinsed and
  finely chopped
2 tablespoons mixed very finely chopped
  parsley, chives and basil

Begin by putting the live lobsters into the freezer for around 2 hours. This is the RSPCA-sanctioned method of reducing them to a state of unconsciousness, which means they will know nothing about it when you then drop them into a large pan of well-salted boiling water. Cook according to the instructions on page 93. Allow them to cool completely but don't try and speed this up by dunking them in cold water – they'll get waterlogged. Just let them steam off naturally.

While the lobsters are cooling, make the mayonnaise. Put the egg yolks, anchovy, garlic, mustard, salt, sugar, pepper and a squeeze of lemon in a food processor or blender and blitz until smooth – 30 seconds or so will do it. (Alternatively, whisk the ingredients together in a bowl.) Combine the two oils and start adding them, trickling them in a thin stream through the hole in the lid of the processor (or by hand into your bowl). Keep whizzing (or whisking) all the time, to emulsify the oil with the egg yolks. When you have a thick, smooth mixture, you can add the oil a little faster. Keep going until all the oil has been added and you have a thick, glossy mayonnaise. If it's too thick, add a tablespoon of warm water to 'let it down' slightly.

When you're happy with the consistency of the mayonnaise, fold in the capers and chopped herbs. Taste and adjust the seasoning with salt, pepper and lemon juice, then cover and put in the fridge until you're ready to serve.

Split the cooked lobsters in half (see page 94), then give each person half a lobster with a good dollop of the mayonnaise. A new potato and marsh samphire salad goes well with this. When everyone's finished eating, don't forget to save the lobster shells for stock (see page 257).

Cold fish with salsa verde mayonnaise *serves 8–10*

This recipe is a fond tribute to Hugh's days as a sous-chef at London's River Café, where one of the many dishes he served was cold poached sea bass with a piquant salsa verde. We've just taken the idea and mellowed it a little by folding the salsa into a homemade mayonnaise. As a celebratory summer feast, you'd be hard-pressed to do better than this.

Don't poach your fish a day ahead and refrigerate it, as some would suggest, as the fish will dry out too much, and anyway, it's better eaten at room/air temperature rather than chilled. Ideally, cook it about 4 hours before serving and leave it to settle in a draughty kitchen or cool larder.

1 quantity of court-bouillon (see page 281)
1 sea bass, black bream, sea trout, or
   organic farmed or self-caught wild
   salmon, weighing about 2.5kg,
   descaled and gutted

FOR THE SALSA VERDE MAYONNAISE:
2 very fresh egg yolks
A small pinch each of salt, sugar and
   black pepper

1 teaspoon mustard
1 tablespoon lemon juice
200ml olive oil
300ml groundnut oil
2 anchovy fillets
1 large garlic clove, very finely
   chopped
1 tablespoon capers, rinsed
A good handful of flat-leaf parsley
   leaves

Put the court-bouillon in a fish kettle and add the fish, placing it on the kettle's trivet. Bring to a simmer, put the lid on, then turn the heat off underneath the fish and leave for about 40 minutes, until the fish is cooked through and the kettle is only hand hot. Remove the fish and transfer it to a platter. Don't skin it until it has cooled, or it will lose precious moisture.

To make the mayonnaise, put the egg yolks, salt, sugar, pepper, mustard and lemon juice into a food processor or blender and process until smooth. (Alternatively, whisk by hand in a bowl.) Combine the two oils in a jug. With the processor running (or with your whisk arm working), start pouring in the oil in a very thin trickle. When the oil starts to emulsify with the yolks, you can add it a little faster. By the time you've added all the oil, you should have a thick, glossy mayonnaise.

Combine the anchovies, pre-chopped garlic, capers and parsley on a board and chop them all together as finely as you can, then stir them into the mayonnaise. Taste and adjust the seasoning with more salt, pepper or lemon juice as needed. Chill until ready to serve.

To serve the fish, peel off the skin from the upper side and bring the whole fish to the table. Gently ease portions of the fish away from the backbone with a spatula or fish slice and place on serving plates. When you've done the first side, lift off the backbone, head and tail, and gently break the remaining side into portions. Accompany the fish with the salsa verde mayonnaise, plus some cold, cooked Puy lentils that have been tossed with olive oil and plenty of seasoning. Buttered new potatoes or a potato salad, and a leaf salad or a salad of shaved fennel, also make fantastic accompaniments.

Potted mackerel *makes about 500g*

Potting is another of those preserving techniques borne of necessity that have survived into the age of fridges and freezers because the results are so delicious. This is our much-used recipe for potted mackerel, which is perfect served on hot brown toast.

4–5 medium mackerel (about 300g each), gutted
4–5 garlic cloves
4–5 bay leaves
1 teaspoon ground mace
½ teaspoon cayenne pepper

1 tablespoon chopped parsley
1 teaspoon chopped thyme
250g unsalted butter
Juice of 1 lemon
Salt and freshly ground black pepper

Put the mackerel side by side in an oiled roasting tin. Crush the garlic cloves roughly and put one inside each fish cavity, along with a bay leaf. Season the fish well with salt and pepper. Bake in an oven preheated to 180°C/Gas Mark 4 for 12–15 minutes, turning the fish over halfway through, until they are just cooked. You can check this by gently lifting the flesh from the bone; it should come away without any resistance.

When the fish are cool enough to handle, flake the flesh into a large bowl, carefully checking for bones as you go. Discard the skin, heads, bay leaves and all but one clove of garlic. Add the mace, cayenne, parsley and thyme to the flaked mackerel.

Melt the butter in a pan over a gentle heat. Finely chop the reserved garlic clove and add it to the butter. Leave the butter to settle (it will separate into a clear, golden layer on top and a whitish layer on the bottom). Pour two-thirds of the clear butter over the mackerel mixture. Add the lemon juice and season well with salt and pepper. Toss together gently, so as not to over-process the mixture.

If you're going to serve the potted mackerel within a day or two, you can pot it in individual ramekins. However, we make large batches to keep for several days, so we like to use sealable glass jars such as Le Parfait. Either way, make sure your pots/jars are spotlessly clean and pack the mixture in so there are no air spaces. Leave a little room at the top of each. Top the mackerel mixture with a layer of the clear, golden butter (discard the milky white solids left in the pan). This butter seals off the mackerel from the air and will help it keep a little longer. When cold, seal the jars (if you're using them).

Store your potted mackerel in the fridge and use open ramekins within a day or two, sealed jars within a week.

Also works with:
• Herring
• Scad
• Sardines (large)
• Trout

Kipper, orange and carrot salad *serves 4 as a starter*

This is a lovely recipe. It's cheap and cheerful, yet it poshes up nicely for a dinner party. You can get all the main ingredients from your average corner shop (yes, in desperate circumstances, frozen boil-in-the-bag kipper fillets can be used).

4 double kipper fillets (about 400g)

2 large oranges

1 tablespoon good wine vinegar or cider vinegar

Juice of ½ lemon

2 large donkey carrots (about 500g)

2 tablespoons good olive oil

Freshly ground black pepper

The kippers and oranges need to macerate together, so prepare them a good couple of hours in advance. Peel the oranges with a sharp knife, slicing off the rind and all the pith. Cut between the membranes to release each segment – do this over a bowl so you catch all the juice, dropping the segments into the bowl as you go. When you've finished, add the wine vinegar and lemon juice to the bowl.

Skin the kipper fillets, removing any bones you come across, and cut them at a slight angle into slices 1–2cm thick. Add them to the orange segments and toss gently but well. Leave to macerate for an hour or so, tossing once or twice.

Peel the carrots and cut them into fine matchsticks, using a food processor or mandolin if you have the right blade, or by hand if you don't (grated carrots are not what you want here – they're too soggy). Toss the carrots with the kippers, oranges and olive oil and season with black pepper. Leave for another half-hour or so, gently turning once or twice. Serve with buttered brown bread.

Tuna, white bean and red onion salad
serves 4 as a starter or light lunch

This shows why it's always a good idea to have a couple of tins of tuna and a tin of white beans in the cupboard. It takes all of 10 minutes to knock together and makes a delicious, sustaining and very healthy light lunch.

Two 120g tins of sustainably caught tuna in oil

1½ tablespoons olive oil

2 tablespoons lemon juice

1 teaspoon English mustard

A pinch of sugar

400g tin of white beans, such as butter or cannellini beans, drained and rinsed

1 small red onion, finely sliced

1 heaped tablespoon chopped flat-leaf parsley

Salt and freshly ground black pepper

Drain the tuna, keeping 1½ tablespoons of the oil. Mix this oil with the olive oil, lemon juice and mustard. Season with salt, pepper and a pinch of sugar and whisk or shake together to make a creamy dressing.

Break the tuna into large flakes and put into a bowl. Add the rinsed beans, the onion and parsley and toss together. Re-whisk or shake the dressing, add to the salad and toss together again. Serve straight away, with crusty white bread.

Thai whelk salad *serves 4 as a starter*

Experience has taught us that this is another fine way (in addition to the Whelk fritters on page 328) to win round a whelkophobe. We first made this dish several years ago to sell at the Lyme Regis regatta and it was a roaring success. To get the most from it, make sure you chop the ingredients for the salsa really finely.

2 dozen large or 3–4 dozen smaller
  whelks, plus a couple extra for the cook

FOR THE STOCK:
Large knob of fresh ginger, sliced
3–4 garlic cloves, crushed
1 tablespoon salt
Stalks from a bunch of coriander
  (used for the salsa)

PLUS, IF THEY ARE TO HAND:
3–4 lemongrass stalks, sliced
2 onions, sliced
A few bay leaves

FOR THE SALSA:
1 small red onion, very thinly sliced
3 medium-hot fresh red chillies, deseeded
  and very finely chopped
½ small garlic clove, very finely chopped
1 small or ½ medium cucumber, peeled,
  deseeded and cut into pea-sized dice
Leaves from a large bunch of coriander,
  chopped
2 tablespoons sunflower, groundnut or
  light olive oil
Juice of 1 orange
Juice of 1–2 limes
A few drops of Thai fish sauce (optional)
Salt

To make the stock, put all the ingredients into a large pan (plus any extras you have to hand) with 3 litres of water and bring to the boil.

Meanwhile, scrub the whelks under cold running water. As you handle them, you may find that some of them release a certain amount of slime – don't worry about this, just rinse it away.

Drop the whelks into the boiling stock and cook at a cheerful simmer for 8–10 minutes, then drain and leave to cool.

To make the salsa, combine all the ingredients in a bowl, adding the lime juice, fish sauce and salt to taste. Stir together thoroughly, then set aside to infuse for at least 1 hour.

Remove the cooked whelks from their shells with a fork, discarding the coarse cap from the front end and the dark digestive sac from the tail end. If any are still a little slimy, give them a wipe with a tea towel.

Toss the whelks thoroughly with the salsa. Leave to infuse for an hour or so, then toss again. Taste one whelk, adjust the seasoning with more lime juice or salt, if you like, taste another, then serve.

Fish thrift and standbys

Fish, like meat, is a particularly precious food – not least because a creature has been killed to provide it for us. Throwing away any of the edible parts of a carcass is quite an insult to that animal. So it's the duty of conscientious fish cooks to use their raw materials wisely and thriftily – which is where the last of our cookery chapters comes in.

However, this isn't just a 'branch' of fish cookery. The principle of maximising ingredients and minimising waste is very close to our hearts and, we hope, underpins this whole book. When we're cooking fish, we really try *never* to throw anything edible away – by which we mean anything except the scales, bones and guts (and even the guts, in the case of the red mullet, can be a bit of a treat – see page 315). The fact that we catch our own fish is significant here. It is particularly painful – almost shaming – to waste fish you've caught yourself (as you'll understand if you've ever done it). When it comes to ecological living, we're far from paragons, but when it comes to food generally, and fish in particular, we try to shop, cook and eat in the most sustainable way we can.

Duty aside for a moment, being thrifty with fish can and should be tremendous fun and very satisfying, presenting just as good an opportunity to express your creativity as cooking 'expansively' with unlimited fresh fish (although of course, in a wider sense, fish resources are *always* limited). Cunning and delicious recipes made with leftovers are one part of the thrift challenge, but the way you approach a fresh fish is important too. It may be the fillets you're really after, but could you not also eke out an extra – and surprisingly wonderful – meal from the heads, tails, even skin and bones?

You'll find recipes here that go beyond leftovers into really thorough-going thrift-with-fresh-fish – recipes where you are, essentially, stealing 'scraps' from the cat. Because, as with meat, it's at the thrifty margins of necessity that some of the most inventive and appealing fish dishes have been devised.

Fresh fish thrift

Your thrift radar must be allowed free rein from the moment you start thinking about acquiring some fresh fish. If you're going to the fishmonger's, might they have some lovely fresh heads and skeletons that could make a stock – the beginnings of some future fish soup or sauce? It's a far easier thing to prepare successfully (see pages 252–3) than a meat stock. But that is only the most obvious of many possibilities. Might one or two of those heads be substantial enough to stand up to a good roasting? If so, see page 380. (Or, in the case of salmon heads, a souping? If so, see page 378.)

Cultivate a good, discursive relationship with your fishmonger (or, more importantly, spend a bit of money in the shop) and you might find all sorts of treats coming your way. If you're splashing out on a princely sea bass or great slab of brill, then a couple of fistfuls of cockles or whelks might find their way into your bag, gratis, in the same spirit as your butcher will often let you have a pair of pig's trotters on the house when you're buying a Sunday roast.

Such casual generosity is often to be found when you buy fish straight from the boat, harbourside, as we love to do. The friendly fishermen at West Bay will make you a keen price, but not a silly one, when they sell you their sole. But it's hardly a Faustian pact when they also start offering you some of their bycatch – a couple of dabs or mackerel, or even a live crab 'for your tea'.

If you're catching your own fish, thrift should soon become second nature. As you're gutting the fish on the way back in, by all means throw the contents of your catch's stomachs to the gulls that mob and dive above the boat's wake. It's a time-honoured ritual. But if you get as far as filleting, then don't give in to their persuasive chatter, begging you to throw more. Stash the heads and neatly folded frames in the cold box, along with the fillets. They are all meals in waiting.

A tale of fishy thrift

Arguably our 'personal best' fishing-trip thrift (aside from regularly taking leftover fresh squid bait home to add to a stew of the day's catch) came on a spectacularly good bass fishing day out of Weymouth. The bass had been hitting the sprats – and our shiny lures designed to imitate them – hard. And from the jaws and stomachs of the bass we killed we managed to recover a number of the little silver fish in surprisingly good nick. They must have been snapped up only moments before our rubber imitations. So we took them home (the least digested half dozen or so) and fried them up as chef's perks.

Besides providing welcome sustenance (while we took our time in doing justice to the bass), it also felt like a good thing to do – almost as if the sprats hadn't died in vain. Not that it's a sprat's ambition to be gobbled by a bass – or indeed a human. But a bass would never waste a morsel of its prey fish; every scrap of it would go to nourish its powerful, predatory body. And so a dead sprat coughed up on the deck would somehow have failed to do its job, for the bass. Of course, we could have lobbed it to a passing gull. But somehow, by eating it ourselves, we were honouring the sea bass's own thrifty intentions. We kept the sprat on track, in line with the food chain that had already claimed it – the one that ended up on our plates.

Fish with rice and pasta

Of course, fish thrift is not only about what you do with the fish but also what else you put with it on the plate. Because everything you eat that isn't fish makes the fish go a bit further. To this end, the most obvious and versatile companion commodities are rice and pasta: the great bulkers, permanently on standby in the larders of every sane cook.

They are infinitely versatile with leftovers, as we'll see, but also, once in a while, brilliant with fresh fish that have been specially chosen to accompany them. Indeed, one or two of the recipes in this chapter depart somewhat from thrifty principles in that they call for fresh fish that may be far from cheap. But those dishes still don't use extravagant amounts of fish. Scallops with fennel risotto (page 397) springs to mind. It makes six juicy scallops feed four, and the frills from the scallops go into the stock for the risotto. The point about combining fish with rice or pasta is that, more often than not, it inverts the norm: the meat of the meal, so to speak, is the starch component. The fish is really the spice or, to recklessly mix metaphors (not to mention split infinitives), the icing on the cake. The point is that a little fish is made to go a long way.

In this context, it is perhaps worth remembering just how closely rice and pasta are related historically. Rice can also make noodles, of course, and in the

Herring roes on toast *serves 4 as a starter, 2 for tea*

One should always feel a little uneasy about eating roe. Try to source your herrings with care – choose MSC-certified fish where possible. If you catch or buy herrings that are full of roe (which can happen at various times of the year, see page 419), it would be a waste not to put it to good use.

You can, of course, buy the roes separately, though they will usually have been frozen, and you are unlikely to get any sourcing or sustainability information with them. Ideally, this dish uses both the firm roes of female herring and the softer roes (technically called milts) from males.

8 herring roes, or 4 roes and 4 milts
2 tablespoons plain flour, seasoned with
   salt and freshly ground black pepper
1 tablespoon olive or sunflower oil

Unsalted butter
4 slices of granary bread
1 tablespoon chopped parsley
2 lemons, halved

Lightly dust the roes in the seasoned flour. Heat the oil and a knob of butter in a large frying pan over a medium heat. Add the roes and let them sizzle gently for 5–6 minutes, until they develop a golden brown crust. Meanwhile, toast and butter your bread.

Serve one roe and one milt, piping hot from the pan, on each piece of toast. Sprinkle with chopped parsley and serve a lemon half on the side for squeezing to taste.

Salmon frame soup *serves 3–4*

Industrial-scale fishing involves the waste of hundreds of tonnes of fish frames – dumped off the back of the boat after the fish have been filleted, along with all the undersized and mangled fish from the day's trawl. There may be little we can do about this, but using up every scrap of fish that makes it into your kitchen feels like a gesture, at least, towards redressing the balance.

Moreover, creating something delicious out of what someone else might have thrown away – in this case, the head, tail and skeleton of a filleted salmon – is enormously satisfying. A decent-sized salmon carries a surprising amount of meat in and around its head, and if you combine it with a few inexpensive ingredients, it can be transformed into something hearty and filling. When you're filleting a salmon, if you know that you'll be making this soup, leave some flesh on the tail end section.

Also works with:
- Sea trout
- Trout
- Sea bass

The frame (head, tail and bones) of 1 large organic farmed (or self-caught wild) salmon (about 1kg total weight)
50g unsalted butter
1 tablespoon sunflower oil
1 large onion, sliced
1 leek, halved and finely sliced

200g new potatoes, scrubbed and quartered
6–8 dill stalks, plus 1 tablespoon chopped dill
6–8 parsley stalks
2 fresh bay leaves
100ml double cream
Salt and freshly ground black pepper

Place the salmon frame on a board and wipe it well with kitchen paper to remove any blood. Use a heavy knife to cut the head and tail from the skeleton, then chop the skeleton into 4–6 pieces.

Set a good-sized pan over a medium heat and add the butter and oil. Throw in the onion, leek and potatoes and let them soften for 5 minutes or so, without colouring. Add the salmon head, tail and bones to the pan, nestling them in among the vegetables. Add the dill and parsley stalks and the bay leaves and pour over a scant litre of cold water – just enough to cover the ingredients. Season with salt and bring up to the gentlest of simmers. Skim off any scum that rises to the top, then cook gently, scarcely simmering, for about 20 minutes, until the potatoes are tender. Remove from the heat.

Take the fish head and bones out of the pan and leave to cool for a couple of minutes. Remove and discard the herb stalks. Carefully pick the meat from the head of the fish, as well as any that is still clinging to the bones. You should really pull the head of the salmon apart, teasing out the various strangely textured bits around the eyes, cheeks and mouth. Anything that isn't a bone is meant to be eaten.

Return this 'meat' to the pan. Stir in the cream and chopped dill and adjust the seasoning with salt and black pepper. Serve straight away, in warmed bowls, with buttered bread.

Deep-fried fish skins *serves 4–6 as a snack*

There are many recipes in this book that ask you to skin your fish. If that skin is free of scales and in good condition then it will be, we have discovered, rather delicious lightly floured and deep fried. (Although we tend not to fry the skins of very oily fish such as mackerel.)

This simple snack, prepared in a truly holistic spirit and affectionately known as 'pollack scratchings', has proved a hit at River Cottage. Deeply savoury, crispy and salty, the little fried morsels are perfect for dipping. We like them with the citrus salsa that goes with the crab cakes on page 327, but they would also be good with tartare sauce (see page 324), a chilli-spiked tomato sauce (see page 340) or just some simple garlic mayonnaise (see page 332).

<u>Also works with:</u>
• Black bream
• Sea bass
• Salmon (organic farmed or self-caught wild)

Groundnut oil for frying
Skins from 2 large or 4 medium pollack fillets, scales removed

1 garlic clove, peeled
2 tablespoons plain flour
Flaky sea salt

Pour a 3–4cm depth of oil into a deep, heavy-based pan and place over a medium-high heat. Bring it up to 180°C, or until a cube of white bread dropped into the oil turns golden brown in about a minute.

Check your fish skins for scales and any bones that are still attached. The skins don't need to be completely devoid of flesh – in fact, it's good to have a very thin layer clinging to them. Bash the garlic clove with your palm to crush slightly and release its oils, then carefully rub it over the skins. Take care not to tear them.

Use a sharp knife to slice the skins widthways into strips, 1–2cm wide. Dip the pieces in the flour, shake off the excess, then drop them into the hot oil. Fry for 2–3 minutes, until golden and crisp. Remove from the oil and drain on kitchen paper. Sprinkle with flaky salt and serve immediately, with your preferred dip.

Spaghetti with cockles *serves 2*

This is our take on *spaghetti alle vongole* – *vongole* being the Italian name for various species of clam. Cockles, which are very similar bivalves, work just as well in this classic seafood pasta dish.

Also works with:
• Palourdes and other small clams

4 tablespoons good olive oil

2 tablespoons white wine

500g cockles, scrubbed (and purged if you think they may be very gritty – see page 580)

2 garlic cloves, sliced into paper-thin slivers

400g tin of chopped tomatoes, or 500g fresh tomatoes, skinned and chopped

A pinch of sugar

1 bay leaf

200g spaghetti or linguine

2 knobs of unsalted butter and a trickle of olive oil

1 tablespoon chopped flat-leaf parsley (optional)

Salt and freshly ground black pepper

Set a large saucepan over a medium heat and add 1 tablespoon of olive oil and the white wine. Throw in the cockles, cover the pan and give it a shake, then cook for 2–3 minutes, until all the cockles are open (discard any that steadfastly refuse to do so).

Tip the contents of the pan into a colander set over a bowl to collect the juices. Strain the juices through a fine sieve, or even a cloth, to get rid of any grit or shell fragments. Pick two-thirds of the cockles out of their shells, then set all the cockles, shell-on and shell-off, aside.

Heat the remaining olive oil in a large frying pan, add the garlic and fry until just beginning to colour. Quickly throw in the tomatoes, followed by the cockle cooking liquid, the sugar, bay leaf and some salt and pepper. Cook over a gentle heat, stirring from time to time, for 25–30 minutes, until you have a thick, pulpy sauce.

When the sauce is nearly done, bring a large pan of water to the boil. Salt it generously, then add the spaghetti or linguine and cook until *al dente*.

Add all the cockles to the tomato sauce with a small knob of butter and the parsley, if using, and toss over a medium heat for a minute, until they are piping hot. Drain the pasta and toss with the second knob of butter and a trickle of olive oil. Divide between two warmed dishes and ladle the cockle and tomato sauce over the top. Serve straight away – without Parmesan!

Crab linguine *serves 5–6*

This recipe is an old favourite (you may remember it from *The River Cottage Cookbook*) and a truly wonderful way to enjoy the luscious meat of the crab. It works brilliantly with spider crab, but brown crabs are very fine too.

White meat from 2 large spider crabs
 or brown crabs (see pages 89–93 for
 cooking and picking instructions)
500g linguine or other pasta
2 tablespoons olive oil
3 garlic cloves, chopped

1–2 small red chillies (according to heat),
 deseeded and finely sliced
1kg ripe tomatoes, skinned, deseeded and
 roughly chopped
1 tablespoon chopped chives
Salt and freshly ground black pepper

Make sure you retrieve all the white meat from the crabs, including the claws and legs. (Collect the brown meat too, to use for a fish soup or crab sandwiches.)

Bring a large pan of water to the boil, salt it well, then add the linguine and cook until *al dente*. Meanwhile, heat the olive oil in a pan, add the garlic and sweat until softened. Throw in the red chilli (check for heat and use sparingly). Before the garlic takes any colour, add the chopped tomatoes. Simmer for 5–6 minutes, until soft and pulpy, then add the white crabmeat and heat through. Season to taste, adding more chilli if you like, then add the chives.

Drain the pasta, return it to the pan and add the crab mixture. Toss lightly and serve straight away.

Crab pasta salad *serves 4 as a starter*

This salad is based on the same deliciously sweet set of flavours as our beloved Crab linguine (above).

150g shell-like pasta shapes, such as
 conchiglie or orecchiette
2 tablespoons olive oil
300–500g white meat from 2 large spider
 crabs or brown crabs (see pages 89–93
 for cooking and picking instructions)

½ hot red chilli, deseeded and finely
 chopped
250g sweet cherry tomatoes, such as
 Sungold, quartered
Juice of ½ lemon
A large handful of basil leaves
Salt and freshly ground black pepper

Cook the pasta in a large pan of boiling salted water until *al dente*, then drain, toss with the olive oil and leave to cool.

Meanwhile, put the white crab meat into a bowl. Add the chilli and cherry tomatoes, season well and toss together.

When the pasta is cool, toss it with the crab mixture and some lemon juice to taste. Shred the basil leaves finely, then toss them with the salad and serve straight away.

'Risoniotto' *serves 4*

In the Fearnley household, this is a much-loved teatime standby, devoured by young and old with equal enthusiasm. Basically 'leftovers with risoni pasta', it's never the same from one outing to the next – the spinach doesn't always get a look-in, for instance. But the principles don't change: garlicky, buttery onions meet flakes of leftover fish before joining a big pot of steaming pasta.

We favour risoni, which is pasta shaped like rice (or white mouse droppings, as Oscar has been known to point out). It gives the dish a particularly pleasing texture, not unlike a risotto. However, you could use other types of pasta, such as small macaroni, but nothing too big or too fancifully shaped. You want to keep that comforting texture, with everything mixed snugly together.

A small knob of unsalted butter
1 tablespoon olive oil
1 large onion (or a small bunch of spring onions), finely chopped
1 fat garlic clove, chopped
½ small red chilli, deseeded and finely chopped (optional)
100–200g blanched spinach or greens (optional), roughly chopped

250–400g cold cooked fish, broken into small flakes – e.g. tinned sardines, flakes of mackerel, chunks of white fish
Lemon juice
350g risoni pasta
Salt and freshly ground black pepper
Extra virgin olive oil, to serve

Heat the butter and olive oil in a frying pan over a medium heat and add the onion and garlic (and chilli, if you like). Cook gently for 10–15 minutes, until the onion is soft and translucent. Throw in the chopped spinach or greens, if using, and mix thoroughly with the buttery onions, then stir in the fish and a squeeze of lemon juice.

Cook the pasta in a large pan of boiling salted water until *al dente*, then drain and return it to the hot pan. Throw in the fish and onion mixture, add some seasoning and toss together well. Serve in warmed bowls, with a little extra virgin olive oil trickled over.

VARIATION
Risoni salad

Cold pasta is very often a terrible idea. However, this is simply a cooled-down version of the dish above, and works very well.

Cook the chopped garlic and chilli (no onions) in olive oil (no butter), before tossing them with the fish and the cooked pasta. Leave to cool. Throw in 1 small, finely sliced red onion, 1 tablespoon chopped flat-leaf parsley, some cooled, cooked petits pois (instead of greens), 1–2 tablespoons of crème fraîche or ricotta cheese and a good squeeze of lemon juice. Season well and serve.

Kedgeree *serves 4*

There are many variations on this classic Anglo-Indian dish. Some are complex, involving a plethora of different spices, a creamy sauce made separately and the addition of vegetables, while others are too baldly simple: fish, rice, eggs. We think this version is just about perfect, combining soft flakes of fish, lightly spiced oniony rice, a few herbs and the all-important hard (but not too hard) boiled eggs. The result is a soothing, perfectly complete dish.

300ml whole milk	2 teaspoons mild curry powder
300ml water	175g basmati rice, rinsed and drained
1 bay leaf	4 large eggs
400g smoked pollack or haddock fillet	2 tablespoons coarsely chopped coriander
1 tablespoon olive oil	1 tablespoon chopped lovage (optional)
2 good knobs of unsalted butter	Lemon wedges
1 large onion, finely sliced	Freshly ground black pepper

Put the milk and water in a pan with the bay leaf and smoked fish, cover and bring to a gentle simmer. By the time the liquid is simmering, the fish should be cooked through. If not, turn it over in the hot liquid and leave, off the heat, for 2–3 minutes to finish cooking. Remove the fish from the pan and set aside. Discard the bay leaf and reserve the poaching liquid. When the fish is cool enough to handle, break it into flakes, discarding the skin and picking out any bones.

Heat the olive oil and a large knob of butter in a pan over a medium heat. Add the onion and sweat for 5–10 minutes, until soft. Stir in the curry powder, then the rinsed rice. Stir the rice gently for a minute or two, then add 300ml of the fish poaching liquid. Bring to the boil, cover with a tight-fitting lid, turn the heat down as low as it will go and cook for 15 minutes. Turn off the heat, fluff up the rice with a fork, then put the lid back on until you are ready to assemble the dish.

Add the eggs to a pan of boiling water and simmer for 7 minutes. Drain, rinse under cold water to stop the cooking, then peel. Fold the smoked fish into the rice, along with half the chopped coriander and the second knob of butter. Cut the hard-boiled eggs in half – they should still be just a bit soft in the middle.

Spoon the spicy, fishy rice on to warmed plates or wide bowls, top with the egg halves and sprinkle with the remaining coriander – and the lovage, if using. Add a wedge of lemon and a good twist of black pepper, then serve.

VARIATION
Kedge-overs

Giving leftover cooked fish the kedgeree treatment – whether it be smoked haddock, mackerel, bream, bass, gurnard or even salmon – creates a tasty supper.

Fry the onion, then add the curry powder, a pinch of salt and the rinsed rice. Pour in 300ml water and cook as above. Meanwhile, flake the leftover fish – as little as 200g will do. When the rice is cooked, stir in a knob of butter, the fish and a handful of chopped herbs – coriander and lovage, or parsley or chives. Serve straight away, adding a couple of quartered hard-boiled eggs.

Anchovy and chilli dressing *makes about 200ml*

This is a truly fantastic way of putting a tin of anchovies to use, producing a piquant dressing of great versatility that can be served warm or cold. We love it with lightly cooked earthy greens, such as kale or broccoli, but it makes a great dip for crudités, or you can use it as a dressing for almost any other vegetable. Or, trickle it over any leftover fish tossed with pasta or Puy lentils, hot or cold.

50g tinned anchovy fillets with their oil
150ml olive oil
2 garlic cloves, roughly chopped
Leaves from 2 good sprigs of thyme
A few basil leaves (optional)
½ small red chilli, roughly chopped
   (or a pinch of dried chilli flakes)
1 teaspoon Dijon or English mustard

2 teaspoons wine vinegar or cider vinegar
A few twists of black pepper

TO SERVE:
500g curly kale or purple sprouting
   broccoli
A knob of unsalted butter

Put all the ingredients for the dressing in a blender and whiz until completely smooth and creamy. Pour into a jar or pot, for which you have the lid.

Bring a pan of lightly salted water to the boil, add the kale or broccoli and cook for 3–5 minutes, until just tender. Drain thoroughly and toss with the butter. Arrange the kale or broccoli on warmed plates and trickle or spoon over a generous amount of the dressing from the jar. Serve at once, with soft brown bread for mopping.

The leftover dressing will keep in the jar in the fridge for a couple of weeks. It can go a bit sludgy, as the olive oil partially solidifies when chilled. Take it out of the fridge an hour or two before using and, when the oil has liquefied again, shake the dressing vigorously in the sealed jar.

VARIATION
Warm bagna cauda dressing with crudités

You will need a selection of vegetables, such as fennel, carrots, baby lettuces, asparagus, courgettes, French beans and celery (tender stalks from near the heart). Lightly blanch the asparagus (unless very fresh) and the French beans. Cut the vegetables into thick sticks or other dippable portions.

Put the dressing in a small pan and warm it over a low heat, whisking in a knob of soft butter as it heats up. This should give you a nice, smooth emulsion but don't worry if it separates a bit. If it splits completely – into big lumps and a pool of oil – whiz it in a blender with a teaspoon of warm water and it should soon right itself.

Serve the sauce in a warmed bowl in the middle of a large plate, with the crudités arranged around it.

Puy lentil and mackerel salad *serves 4*

We cook a lot of mackerel and urge others to do likewise. Inevitably, we are sometimes faced with leftovers – the last few fish on the barbecue that no one could quite make room for. But mackerel's high oil content means that, even when cold, it retains its punchy flavour and moist texture, so any leftovers can be quickly transformed into a zesty and delicious standby meal. Almost all fish work well in this salad, though it is less good with delicate, soft white fish flesh.

Puy lentils are an essential storecupboard staple for anyone interested in thrifty cooking. They add protein, flavour and texture to a whole range of thrown-together, leftover-based dishes.

200g Puy lentils
Stock vegetables – e.g. 1 celery stick,
   cut into 2–3 pieces, 2 carrots, cut into
   2–3 pieces, 2 garlic cloves, unpeeled
   but roughly bruised, and ¼ onion
   (all optional)
A few parsley stalks (optional)
2–3 leftover cooked mackerel (baked or
   barbecued are perfect for this dish)

1 small onion, preferably red, or a few
   spring onions, finely sliced
3–4 anchovy fillets, finely chopped
1 tablespoon baby capers, rinsed and
   chopped
2 tablespoons chopped parsley
A glug of extra virgin olive oil
Juice of ½–1 lemon
Salt and freshly ground black pepper

Rinse the lentils under cold running water, then put them in a large saucepan – with the stock vegetables and parsley stalks, if you want to flavour them up a bit. Cover with fresh water, bring to a gentle simmer and skim off any scum that rises to the surface. Simmer for about 20 minutes, until the lentils are *al dente*, topping up the pan with fresh water if necessary. Strain the lentils, discarding the water and any flavouring vegetables you've used.

While the lentils are cooking, pick all the flesh from the mackerel, flake it and place in a bowl, making sure you discard any bones.

Toss the warm lentils with the mackerel. Add the red onion or spring onions, along with the chopped anchovies, capers and parsley. Stir in the olive oil, then season to taste with lemon juice, salt and pepper. Toss gently together and serve straight away.

3. British fish

Now here's a part of the book you might not have been expecting: our personal guide to the edible fish and shellfish resident in British coastal waters. Most of these we reckon to have handled (dead or alive) and eaten (raw or cooked) at some time in our rather fish-geeky lives. And those we haven't, we're very keen to hook up with…

We think of these species almost as a cast of characters in the great, sprawling story of our seas and rivers. Here are, if you like, their 'profiles', taking in a bit of history (natural or otherwise), several fishermen's tales (some taller than others), a fair few cooking tips – and, crucially, their current ecological status. They are biographies, not obituaries – though sadly one or two might be heading that way.

Why have we invested so many pages of a cookbook on such inedible (though not, we hope, indigestible) matters? Because we are convinced that the more you know and understand about your fish, the better equipped you will be to enjoy them at every level: the catching, the handling, the prep, the shopping, not to mention the cooking and eating. The list is by no means taxonomically complete, but we believe it covers all the mainstream food fish that are landed here in the British Isles and find their way on to the fishmonger's slab.

Of course there are anomalies, such as fish we don't eat much but should eat more of (garfish, pouting, velvet crabs and the like), and some freshwater fish that anglers might want to think about eating (perch, carp and zander spring to mind). There are also a couple of 'foreign' interlopers – several species of tuna

Sea fish

Herring family

Herring *Clupea harengus*

If ever a fish punched above its weight, it was the herring. For a small, rather insignificant-looking fish of barely half a pound, herring has had a major influence on our economic history. Two centuries ago it delivered unparalleled prosperity to a whole swathe of coastal Britain, at the same time underpinning the Scandinavian and Baltic economies to an even greater extent.

Like the cod – its only rival as a truly nation-shaping fish – the stocks of herring were once thought to be inexhaustible. In its heyday, the herring's potential to deliver prosperity to the communities well placed to exploit it was limited only by the fishermen's resourcefulness in removing it from the sea. In its way, the herring rush of the early nineteenth century was almost as sensational as the Californian gold rush. Remote Scottish settlements such as Wick and Peterhead became boomtowns on the back of herring fishing, and were said to harbour (as it were) some very wealthy individuals indeed.

One of the most notorious episodes in Scottish history contributed to this success story. The Highland clearances of the eighteenth century were a consequence of the booming wool trade – a mini gold rush in itself. Absentee English landlords and powerful Highland chiefs set about maximising the land available to farm sheep. Their henchmen 'encouraged' the resident tenants to move off the land (1792 became known, with bitter understatement, as the Year of the Sheep). Many of the displaced emigrated to North America (where they founded, among other places, Nova Scotia). Those who remained were accommodated in poor crofts in coastal areas where farming could barely sustain them. They had little choice but to take up fishing.

The lucky ones discovered huge summer shoals of herring. At first these merely provided vital subsistence. But as fishing techniques developed, the catches far exceeded what could be consumed locally. Herring, salted and stored in barrels, became an important commodity that could be traded. Some of the crofters were soon successful businessmen, building huge open-boat fleets to net the 'silver darlings', and trading their salted catch with brokers in the south. Here the salted fish were rinsed and dried, then smoked for several days to make a form of kipper – the original 'red herring'.

Salted and red herrings were all very well, but Londoners and other southern city folk also had a taste for fresh herrings from the short seasonal catches around the southeast coast. Clearly anyone who could feed this demand at other times of year would be on to a good thing. But fresh herring do not keep well. They are, like mackerel, very rich in oils – a plus for flavour but definitely a minus for shelf life. So shifting fresh herring from the ports to the cities had better be done quickly, or not at all.

And so the herring trade financed the infrastructure that was built in order to carry the fish from the ports that landed them to the cities that consumed

MCS RATING: 3 (1–5)

REC MINIMUM SIZE: 25cm

SEASON: N/A as spawning can occur throughout the year

RECIPES: pages 146, 147, 196, 304, 319, 357, 376, 400, 407

them. The uncompromisingly thorough reach of the British railway network in Scotland is directly attributable to the herring trade. By the end of the nineteenth century the network had penetrated to the furthest shores: Oban, Mallaig, Kyle of Lochalsh, Ullapool and Scourie in the west; Thurso, Wick, Helmsdale, Dornoch and Peterhead in the east. This engineering feat was undertaken not so much with the intent that men could reach these distant outposts, but so that fish could be transported to the great urban centres where they were in such demand.

Herring live in huge pelagic shoals, always on the move (herring means 'army' in Old Norse), following the clouds of zooplankton on which they feed. Mrs Beeton, in her *Book of Household Management* of 1859, pithily summarised the annual migration thus:

The herring tribe are found in the greatest abundance in the highest northern latitudes, where they find a quiet retreat, and security from their numerous enemies. Here they multiply beyond expression and, in shoals, come forth from their icy region to visit other portions of the great deep. In June they are found about Shetland, whence they proceed down to the Orkneys, where they divide, and surround the islands of Great Britain and Ireland.

In the north, herring were pursued for most of the year, while more southerly ports enjoyed them only as a brief seasonal catch. But even here in Dorset the summer catch was once economically significant enough to give its name to villages such as Langport Herring and Chaldon Herring.

It took two world wars to put a dent in the seemingly limitless herring stocks. The relationship between the national fishing fleet and the navy has always been symbiotic. In times of war, the skilled seamen and their vessels become vital to the navy. In times of peace, technology developed in the interests of national security – radar, echo-location and the like – is constructively redeployed within the fishing fleet. Yet while many commercial fishing boats were commandeered for service, the Scottish herring fleets continued to fish throughout both wars, as their contribution to the national diet was considered vital.

Throughout the first half of the twentieth century, the British government was particularly supportive of the herring industry, and awarded various grants to help build up the fleets. One key innovation was the introduction of 'herring buses'. These were huge motherships, into which the 'smacks' – smaller local herring boats – could transfer their catch. By the early 1950s, our herring fleet was huge and ruthlessly efficient. The Scandinavians and Dutch had made similar progress, in pursuit of what each regarded as *their* national fish. The unthinkable became the inevitable and between the early 1950s and mid-1960s the North Sea stocks fell by over 50 per cent.

The human greed that halved the herring stocks went beyond rampant culinary enthusiasm for the fish. It had become an industrial – and agricultural – commodity. By the mid-1960s, more herrings were being fed to animals and used as fertiliser than were being consumed by humans. After centuries of providing our nation (and others) with so much, our golden goose was cooked. From 1970, measures began to be taken, both internationally and locally, voluntarily and legislatively, to address the crashing population. Throughout Scotland, over 70 per cent of the fleet was either laid off by decree or simply gave up, because the fish just weren't there to be caught.

During the last twenty years, the fishery has shown a slow but encouraging recovery. There are now some recognised sustainable sources of herring in our waters, including the driftnet fisheries in the Thames, Blackwater and the eastern English Channel, as well as the North Sea and eastern English Channel autumn-spawning stock. Herring stocks in the Norwegian Sea (spring spawners), eastern Baltic and the Gulf of Riga are also assessed as being healthy and harvested sustainably. (Our own encounters with the herring hardly amount to scientific proof, but each summer we seem to see a few more of them – bigger shoals, staying for longer – in Lyme Bay; we even catch a few when feathering for mackerel.)

More than the decimated cod, the herring has shown signs that it may be capable of coming back from the brink. If it does, we can't take much credit. But we can endeavour not to make the same mistake twice. We must rely on our good judgement, not our good luck, to ensure a future for the herring, and the many irresistible forms in which we love to eat it.

Foremost of these are fillets of herring in some sort of cure or pickle. The Danish rollmop is a classic form – double herring fillets rolled up around sliced onions and pickled in vinegar. The quality varies hugely: at the cheaper end the 'vinegar' is industrially distilled acetic acid, a by-product of the brewing industry, which is so harsh as to obliterate the herrings' rich oily character. There are endless variations on the Scandinavian pickled herring but some of the best commercially produced examples we have come across are not from the fjords but from the Scottish islands. The Orkney Herring Company (see the Directory, page 591) has an excellent range that includes cures of sweet dill, juniper and sherry. Perhaps the only way to match these – or even improve on them – is to cure some herring fillets yourself. See page 146 for our own favoured procedure.

Kippers are the other great manifestation of the cured herring. These can range from the divine to the iniquitous. Those from Craster in Northumberland vie with Manx and Loch Fyne kippers for the title of most exalted. At the unforgivable end of the spectrum are any number of oversalted shoe-leather specimens and those unfeasibly red fillets that some fishmongers seem to get from God knows where. This unnatural colour is painted on to make them look more smoked than they really are.

Purists would advise favouring whole kippers, though we have noted that on occasion fillets can be excellent. The pale and interesting specimens from Isle of Skye Seafood's smokehouse (see the Directory, page 591) are exceptionally sweet and rewarding – and blissfully easy to eat (though Nick would argue quite vociferously that part of the joy of eating a whole kipper is to wrestle the flesh off the bone on your plate and nibble tasty morsels off the skeleton). Whether on or off the bone, a good kipper needs only to be grilled as it is, fried in a little butter or poached in a little milk. The only necessary accompaniments are toast (brown) and eggs (poached or scrambled).

There are other great regional riffs on the smoked herring, such as bloaters (which are big in Norfolk and Suffolk). These are not split like kippers but lightly smoked whole, traditionally with the guts still in, to give a lightly gamey tang. They may be eaten raw or grilled, or made into bloater paste. The buckling, of Baltic origin, is a subtle variation on the same theme. Also usually cured whole, sometimes guts in, sometimes out, and ideally with roes intact inside, they are hot smoked and traditionally eaten without further cooking.

Pickled and smoked herrings are endlessly diverting, but one shouldn't overlook the possibilities offered by a fresh specimen. For these, there is a Scottish recipe that is very hard to beat: herring rolled in oatmeal and fried gently in butter and/or bacon fat, rested for a few minutes and served warm (you can easily adapt the recipe for Fried mackerel in oatmeal with bacon on page 319). A fat lemon wedge is in order, and a dollop of homemade creamed horseradish never goes amiss.

Occasionally we've had the great good luck to prepare this dish with a herring we've caught ourselves – usually while looking for the early summer mackerel off Portland Bill. To eat a herring within hours of taking it from the sea feels very special indeed, and helps us understand just what a great fish this is.

The other unmissable treat from the herring is its tender, inimitably creamy roe. But how guilty should one feel about making a meal of a few hundred thousand unborn herrings? To be honest, not quite as wracked as one might about eating the eggs of other popular roe-yielding fish – cod, for example. Herring are fast-maturing fish that can often spawn within two or three years of their birth – and the timing of their spawning is, as we have said, unpredictable. So, in the management of herring stocks, the issue is less about avoiding the spawning season, more about not taking out too high a proportion of the fish in any given fishery. If your herrings come from a sustainable fishery, and they happen to contain roe, you should consider that a happy bonus, not a stick with which to beat yourself. Enjoy.

Sardine and pilchard *Sardina pilchardus*

What's the difference between a sardine and a pilchard? Answer: about one centimetre. From a biological perspective, sardines and pilchards are exactly the same fish. At 15cm they are still sardines, but by the time they have grown to 16cm they are officially pilchards. That's how the UK industry has traditionally made the distinction, though as we shall see, some are re-thinking the branding of this fish for the modern market.

From a British consumer's perspective, these fish have always been different. A pilchard is a fish that is only ever sold in a tin, made by companies like good old Glenryck, often preserved, headless but otherwise whole, in a thick, gloopy tomato sauce. They were traditionally served for tea on a Saturday (ideally circa 1972, just before *Dr Who*). Like the good Doctor himself, even as we were growing up, pilchards already felt somehow anachronistic.

Sardines, on the other hand, are sexy. Sure, they too are crammed into tins – rectangular ones with 'keys' taped to the side – but, compared to the pilchard, they have just a hint of added suburban chic. Take them out of their tins, though, and get them on the wet fish slab and they begin to drip with Mediterranean glamour. The tempting waft of sardines grilling over olivewood charcoal smacks of balmy summer evenings on a Greek island or in a Spanish fishing village.

Both these fish – the pre-Dalek snack and the Mediterranean appetiser – could well have been caught in exactly the same place: Cornwall. Around the Cornish coast there is a healthy, well-managed fishery that has been exporting *Sardina pilchardus* (yes, that really is its Latin name), packed and salted, to Italy since the middle of the sixteenth century. These fish have always been known as pilchards to the fishermen who caught and landed them, and sardines to the Italians who imported and ate them.

Sardines are a pelagic shoaling fish like herring and mackerel (see pages 416 and 444). They are nomadic wanderers who come and go with frustrating irregularity (if you're a fisherman), and feed on zooplankton as it rises and falls from a depth of 40 metres to the surface, depending on the light levels and time of day. The sardines caught around Cornwall mark the northern edge of the sardine range, and these fish, perhaps because food availability and water temperatures differ from those enjoyed by their more southerly cousins, grow slower but end up living longer and growing bigger. They can grow to 25cm and live to fifteen years of age.

Whatever you want to call it (and we'll always have a soft spot for pilchard), this is a lovely British fish, and one we'd encourage you to eat more of. Like mackerel, it's enormously rich in omega-3 fatty acids, known to be vital for maintaining coronary health, amongst other things. And currently, in a rare reversal of the modern trend, these Cornish sardines are not being overfished.

It's an unusual and cheering fishy success story, because in the past they were seriously over-exploited. Pilchards once underpinned a whole community in the Southwest with a modest export trade and a diverse range of products: oil for lamps, skimmings for soap makers, and dyes and lubricants for the leather-tanning trade. Then came the 'fishy gold rush' and, through greed, mismanagement and the forces of nature, the industry went into free-fall.

The problem was progress, specifically the completion of the Great Western Railway in the 1860s. The railway provided access to a previously untapped urban domestic market. In just a couple of decades, the number of pilchard

MCS RATING: 3 (2–4)

REC MINIMUM SIZE: 20cm

SEASON: best July–November

RECIPES: pages 146, 147, 148–9, 196, 218, 304, 316, 319, 357, 392, 400, 402, 403, 407, 408

fishing boats in the fleet rose from a couple of dozen to nearly 300. This extra pressure, combined with a natural change in pilchard migration habits, meant the fishery was practically exhausted by the time of the First World War.

Happily, the story isn't quite over: today, Cornwall is experiencing something of a sardine renaissance. Between the Wars, most pilchards were caught and canned in South Africa. All that was left of the Cornish fishery was the Pilchard Works in Newlyn, a business that exported a tiny quantity of barrel-salted whole fish to Italy, where they were known as *salacche inglesi* – the salted Englishman.

In the last few years, with some help from Marks & Spencer and Waitrose, the Pilchard Works has now re-branded its product as 'Cornish sardines'. And they can be bought fresh or tinned (though, sadly, no longer salted). The good news is that this time around, the fishing techniques are relatively gentle. The sardines are caught by small day boats, mostly skipper-owned and run, using old-fashioned ring-netting techniques that help prevent the accidental catching of other species. This is important not only to minimise the bycatch but also to prevent damage to the catch itself – a few dogfish, sharks or big bass thrashing around in the nets would wreak serious havoc on these delicate fish.

We always like to get our hands on a few boxes of fresh Cornish sardines (sorry, pilchards) at the height of the season (late summer and autumn) to grill on the barbecue or roast on a tray in the River Cottage pizza oven. About the only time we attempt anything more elaborate is when we make our favourite Sardine escabeche (pages 148–9). It may sound like a bit of a culture clash – but it's our culture clash and we love it.

Sprat *Sprattus sprattus*

Who'd want to be a sprat? Everywhere you look there's something – with wings, fins or a socking great net – that wants to eat you. Such is the heavy burden of being small, delicious and nutritious.

Understandably, being on everyone's menu makes sprats nervous. Standing out from the crowd is not their aim in life. In fact, losing themselves in the middle of it is the closest they get to feeling at ease. And so they travel around in massive shoals. Yet even when they're surrounded by their peers, packed tight into a protective school, sprats still show the jittery signs of being aware that they're someone's favourite lunch. Sprats are not hunters. Their 'prey', if you can call it that, is mere plankton. They're the hunted, and they know it.

Consequently a shoal of sprats is never still. They weave, twist and twitch with fraught anxiety. When they're not darting about trying to find their lunch, they're darting about trying to avoid being someone else's. And millions of them fail because when they migrate into our inshore waters, a sprat-killing frenzy begins.

Sprats are a seasonal migratory fish. When they arrive in late summer it's as if someone's flicked a switch and sent 5,000 volts zapping through the sea. Everything gets charged up, and the inshore waters start to boil and bubble. The mackerel, which may have been absent for a few weeks, are suddenly everywhere again, chasing shoals of sprats with ruthless abandon. Gulls, meanwhile, attack from the air. Harried from all sides, along the coast and into the surf, the shoals break up, exposing more individuals to snapping mouths and stabbing beaks.

MCS RATING: not rated
REC MINIMUM SIZE: 8cm
SEASON: Western Channel, avoid January–July (spawning); North Sea, avoid March–August (spawning)
RECIPE: page 245

Sometimes the assailants force splinter groups of sprats right on to the beach, leaving them flapping and flipping on the shingle, gasping their silvery last.

Near us, along Eype Beach, West Bay and Chesil Beach, these sprat beachings usually occur several times each autumn. It's not something you can plan for but, if you happen to be there when it occurs, it's tremendous fun. The dog walkers and sea gazers start running up and down the shingle, filling their wellies and pockets with the silver-sided freebies. In these days of mobile phones, friends are called in to share the loot, and it can turn into quite a party.

Like humans, gulls' eyes may be bigger than their stomachs. Swooping and plunging the surf, emerging from each dive with a silver snack across their beaks, they keep going, up and down, up and down, on auto-gorge. They can't go on forever, though, and eventually you'll see seagulls resting on the surface of the water, bloated and bobbing, looking as if they may never get airborne again.

These freebies are not only to be had from the beach. One year, over autumn half term, West Bay Harbour filled up with scared sprats taking shelter from the slaughter. This may have temporarily saved them from the jaws of some sea predators but it placed them within easy reach of hungry holidaymakers. Buckets were filled. Nets bulged. The revellers were walking back and forth to their cars, carrying plastic shopping bags that flipped and flapped as they went.

Being plankton eaters, these diminutive members of the herring family are hard to catch on rod and line. You might take the odd one or two on tiny micro-feathers but you'd struggle to muster enough for lunch. The only really effective way to catch them is with a net. We favour an American-style cast net. This circular throwing net is surrounded by weights, which can be dropped from the harbour wall over a shoal of fish.

All kinds of nets can be used – and some are almost too effective. Last year we watched a man dragging a small draft net behind a tiny rowing boat. He caught so many sprats that he couldn't pull the net out of the water. It was a biblical moment as he struggled to heave it on to the stone steps of the harbour. But he saw sense and let most of his huge haul escape back into the water.

Further out to sea, big boats are doing the same thing with bigger nets, working long hours to cash in on a seasonal bonanza that lasts just a few weeks. Sprats don't yield high profits but they are easy to sell – who can resist these juicy little shards of silver? The good news is that, as a short-lived, fast-growing species, they have what's known as 'a high resilience to fishing'. That means that the sprats we catch are quickly and easily replaced by next season's youngsters. Their stocks are currently healthy. To help them remain so, avoid fish caught using the pair-trawling technique, where two boats sling a huge net between them and scoop up whole shoals. It's better to buy fish caught with seine or trawl nets because some will be left behind to perform their function as one of the crucial links in the marine food chain.

Sprats are easy to cook as well as to catch. When they're super-fresh, you don't even have to bother removing the guts. Frazzle them in a hot pan, or under a fierce grill, then all they need is salt, pepper and a squeeze of lemon. You can munch them up, heads and all. But if you're feeling (a bit) more dainty, you can nibble or suck the flesh off the bones. Either way, knives and forks aren't needed.

During the sprat rush, we gorge ourselves on them. We grill or fry them, obviously. Then we devil them, mush them on toast, salt them to make phony anchovies, and smoke them in their dozens. If they continue to make themselves available, we even freeze some in small bags as pike bait. And then, one day, it's over. The sprats are gone. We'll just have to wait again till next year.

Whitebait

The Italians enjoy a famous dish called *fritto misto*, which is a cunning ruse to make a lot of undersized fish edible. They deep fry a random collection of small whole fish – little red mullet, tiny soles, juvenile bream – in batter or lightly dusted with flour, and serve them piping hot with garlic mayonnaise and salad. The Spanish and French also have a long tradition of eating all manner of small fish whole, including heads, fins, bones and tails. Ecologically, as we'll see, it's a highly questionable practice – but gastronomically it's hard to resist.

In Britain, we rarely eat whole small fish, except for whitebait. In a country where most diners go all wobbly and weird if you so much as serve a fish with its head still attached, it seems strange that whitebait have managed to remain so popular. But you'll often find them served as a starter, even on an otherwise uninspired pub menu (though they're almost certain to have been

MCS RATING: N/A as whitebait is not a specific species, but the advice is to avoid eating them

frozen and imported). The critical point is that whitebait are so tiny they're hardly recognisable as whole fish at all. Their bones, fins, heads and tails barely register – so they bypass British squeamishness altogether.

The first record of whitebait appearing on an English menu dates back to 1612, but it wasn't until the 1780s that they became the smart thing to eat in London's riverside taverns. Back then, the fishermen and chefs who championed whitebait believed – with some support from contemporary biologists – that it was a separate and distinct kind of fish. The French naturalist Valenciennes even instituted a new genus, *Rogenia*, to accommodate the new 'species'. The truth, though, is that whitebait is simply a collective term for the fry of Clupeoid fish – members of the herring and sprat family. This is why whitebait doesn't have a Latin name – although you could call it *Clupeas varias*.

So when you sit down to a plate of 'whitebait', you're actually eating a plate of immature herrings and sprats – and probably quite a few more species besides. In 1903, Dr James Murie, in his 'Report on the Sea Fisheries and Fishing Industries of the Thames Estuary', conducted studies on the contents of boxes of whitebait being sold from Billingsgate to the Thames-side pub market. He discovered that some boxes of whitebait contained up to twenty-three species of immature fish, including the fry of eel, plaice, whiting, herring, sprat and bass. For good measure, there were also shrimps, crabs, octopus and even jellyfish.

It seems the whitebait craze of the late eighteenth century was started by an entrepreneurial fisherman, Richard Cannon of Blackwall. In 1780 he persuaded local tavern keepers to serve this crispy, salty, fish fry-up to their thirsty punters.

The season ran from February to August and at its height there were daily races between Thames water taxis to see who could carry MPs from the Houses of Parliament to Greenwich, the centre of whitebait consumption, the quickest. Like schoolboys racing to the tuck shop at the playtime bell, politicians would pour out of Parliament, grab their favourite water taxi and see who could be first to sup a pint and crunch a whopping great basket of crispy whitebait.

The unfettered consumption of whitebait, which was caught in purse nets all around the Thames estuary, caused the river authorities to attempt a ban on whitebait fishing. Surprisingly conservation minded for the time, they rightly believed that whitebait were immature herrings and sprats. But Cannon and a few tame scientists kept on claiming that whitebait were a separate and distinct species and so no harm would come to the precious herring stocks. They had the Lord Mayor of London on their side, and the fishing continued unchecked.

By the 1890s, whitebait was still the toast of the Thames, but the famous Greenwich taverns, such as the Trafalgar and the Crown and Sceptre, were now serving whitebait that had been caught way downstream in the Thames estuary, beyond Gravesend, or else in the River Medway. At Greenwich, whitebait fishing was completely spent. The huge shoals of whitebait that had annually turned the river silver from Tower Bridge to Greenwich Docks had vanished.

Overfishing wasn't the sole cause of the destruction. Much of the damage was done by toxic pollution pouring downstream, as a result of all the new industrial development along the river. Old tanneries and new factories pumped industrial effluent into the Thames, which, along with the sewage of London, combined to turn the river into a kind of noxious liquor.

We've cleaned up our act considerably since those dark days. Now the Thames is one of the cleanest major rivers in Europe, and vast shoals of whitebait are returning to the capital. There's even been talk of starting up the fishery again and persuading some of the Thames-side publicans to spark up their deep-fat fryers (at least for something other than breaded scampi – see page 544). Who knows, we might once again see politicians scuttling down Parliament steps to launch themselves into a high-speed race to an early lunch of whitebait.

It's a tempting and romantic idea – but surely a mad one. Given that whitebait consists of the immature fry of herrings, sprats, sardines, mackerel, bass, plaice and many others, it simply makes no sense to harvest from this valuable fish nursery. By removing these fish at a juvenile stage, before they've had a chance to grow much bigger than a stickleback, we'd be decimating future stock – adult fish that could be either eaten or left to breed.

There is still plenty of imported frozen whitebait for sale in fishmongers and supermarkets. Those bags you see nestling in the bottom of the freezer cabinets may seem insignificant – a fishy surplus that might as well be enjoyed. In reality they are much more insidious than that. They come from various far-flung parts of the world, and may consist of all kinds of rare and threatened species. Once they're smeared in batter, it's impossible to tell. Ignorance is bliss – there's no regulation, because the contents, be they from home or abroad, are unknown.

This is one of those occasions when the conscience wrestles with temptation. Because properly prepared, freshly fried, lightly floured whitebait – crunchy and sweet, with a wedge of lemon of course – is absolutely delicious. We could never bring ourselves to order it. But should some wickedly mischievous publican place a bowl of it in front of us, could we honestly say that we'd push it back at him? It might be a struggle, but we like to think we'd make the right choice.

Cod family

Cod *Gadus morhua*

For a fish that has changed the world, the cod is a little unremarkable. It's greedy and rather dim, and certainly no athlete. On the contrary, it will seek out the least taxing location in which to exist – along with a few thousand of its brethren. Somewhere out of the strong currents, where it won't have to put in much effort to hold position and where the food will mostly come to it. Usually it'll dine on shoaling baitfish, such as sand eels and sprats – provided it doesn't have to work too hard. But it'll happily scavenge too, with the widest possible interpretation of what constitutes a meal. All manner of debris, from boots to bottles, has been recovered from the bellies of cod.

Perhaps the only predators hunting at sea who are greedier than the cod are humans. And it's cod's misfortune to be our favourite fish supper. This is the fish that the whole world wants to eat, for no better or worse reason than that it's easy to catch, and people like it. Not love it – their passions are reserved for soles and mullets, and even eels. But cod will always do. It has 'done' so well that in the thirty years from the 1960s to the 1990s, we managed to reduce the cod population of the North Sea by over 90 per cent. We also managed to drive a fish that was so plentiful as to defy calculation, and vital to the economies of several nations, to the brink of extinction.

In our 'codmania', we made and destroyed communities and collapsed entire ecosystems. In fisheries such as the Grand Banks, off the coast of Nova Scotia, where there once massed biblical shoals of cod, there are now only crabs, shrimps and a few small sharks. In towns that were built on the backs of the cod, towns like Fortune, Grand Bank, Trepassey and Marystown, communities are decimated.

MCS RATING: 4 (2–5)

REC MINIMUM SIZE: 50cm

SEASON: avoid February–April (spawning)

RECIPES: pages 150–1, 178–9, 179, 180, 331, 380–1, 403

Despite the cod crash, we're still fishing for them, squabbling over the few that are left. It continues because, for commercial fishermen, catching cod, where they are still to be found, is not hard. Only the weather stands in their way. The fish themselves do everything to make things easy, shoaling where there is little current, relying on their ample swim bladders to keep them weightless in the water. Trawling in such seas, where there is little current to drag on the net and the fish are reluctant to abandon their easy holding pattern, is a relative cinch.

Its torpor is in many ways the cod's undoing. Besides making it an easy catch, it also enhances our desire to eat it. Because basically, the lazier a fish is, the whiter its flesh will be (see page 21). And we all love white fish, don't we? Yes please, the whiter the better... If we haven't obsessed to the same degree over the cod's cousins, the coley and the pollack, it's surely not because of how they taste. They taste great. But it may be because there is a subtle greyish tinge to their flesh. The fillets don't scrub up quite so shiny white on the slab. What lethal prejudice.

It's clear that a series of social upheavals in the UK have also played their part in the cod's fatal story. The two World Wars had far-reaching effects on the nation's choice of food, and changed forever the technology we used to produce or provide it. During both wars, fishing boats were requisitioned by the Royal Navy and fishermen were conscripted, so many of the traditional fishing grounds went unmolested for the duration. After the Second World War, fish stocks were in better shape than they had been for decades. Inevitably there was a rush to plunder them; pure white cod flesh was just the kind of treat with which to loosen the belt of wartime rationing.

In the UK, and other maritime nations, huge resources were directed at reviving the fishing fleet. It wasn't just about claiming our share of those plentiful cod; it was also about the defence of the realm. Governments had been reminded – all too forcefully – of the benefits of an experienced navy in time of war. Our Second World War fleet had been built upon the backs of our fishermen – so it made perfect sense to develop a big fishing fleet that could form the backbone of another navy in the event of future conflict.

In this era of new technology, the rules of engagement with the cod were changing fast. During the war, naval engineers worked feverishly on sonar equipment, radar, navigation aids, echo depth sounders, and faster, more efficient marine engines. All of these were incorporated into the fishermen's armoury after the war was over. (In the US and Canada even spotter planes were handed over to fishing fleets to help track down the biggest shoals.)

Food fashion was changing too, and people wanted a bright new diet to go with their bright new kitchen appliances. The fish that had continued to feed people during wartime were those that could be caught relatively easily in the inshore fishery – such as herring, pilchards, sprats and mackerel. But these fiddly, bony, oily species were suddenly old hat. They had become not only overfamiliar but overfished – whereas the cod, with its big, white, boneless curds of flaky flesh, seemed somehow new and exciting. Amongst the modern appliances that housewives welcomed into their brave new kitchens were fridges with ice compartments that could conserve frozen food for months. These piled greater pressure on the cod stocks, as innovative frozen food companies such as Birds Eye and Findus created irresistible new lines, including the redoubtable fish finger, launched in 1955. With the benefit of hindsight, it's easy to see that from that moment, the cod was in serious trouble.

Pollack _Pollachius pollachius_

'Oi wouldn't give pollack to me cat,' said Padraig, a salmon ghillie we fished with in County Mayo. 'Pollack is rubbish. Not fit for human consumption. Any man in Ireland who could even be bothered to bring pollack back home would only be after using it to fertilise their veg patch.'

Sadly this is not merely the ranting of an obsessive riverman who has made salmon his life's work. Badmouthing pollack as an eating fish is practically a national sport among anglers – even those who like to catch these handsome, green-gold lovelies. These days, cod stocks are crippled and haddock's taken a serious knocking too; yet few cooks and anglers stop to reassess the potential of the other members of the cod family – coley and pouting, as well as pollack. They take the rotten reputation on trust, and pass it on as a 'well-known fact'.

The anti-pollack brigade are the fishy equivalent of flat earthists, and it's time they were stopped. We eat a lot of pollack (more, perhaps, in the last couple of years than any other fish with the exception of mackerel), and we think it is delicious. We fillet and flour them for the frying pan, batter them for that chip-shop experience, smoke them, salt them, put them in pies, even eat them raw as pollack carpaccio or sashimi.

The simple fact is that anything you can do with a cod, you can do with a pollack. It may be a touch less pearly white in colour and, if not stored well, prone to becoming a bit soft, but in terms of taste and texture, fresh, well-iced pollack is very hard to distinguish from fresh, well-iced cod. We'd go further, and say that if history and habits were reversed and the cod was the pollack and vice versa, we are utterly convinced that it would be the cod that would be disparaged as cat food, and the pollack worshipped as the great white fish that changed the world. Do we make ourselves clear?

We have a theory about how this terrible reputation, so at odds with the plain facts, has come about. Because of its habits and lifestyle (of which more shortly) the pollack just happens to be a rather hard fish to target commercially. But it's a relatively easy one to catch on rod and line – one of the mainstays, in fact, of British coastal wreck and reef fishing trips for angling clubs and happy amateurs up and down the land. Now, at the risk of offending a lot of people, we say this: sea anglers have generally been more concerned with sport than food, and for the most part have been rubbish at looking after the fish they catch with a view to its end use in the kitchen. Okay, okay, things _are_ improving. But until recently, hardly any charter boats bothered to take ice chests out with them, even in the summer. When it came to protecting their catch from the glare of the summer sun, a stinky old fish box with a wet rag draped over it was as far as most went. No wonder the poor pollack and pouting were barely fit for pot bait by the end of the afternoon.

When pollack is treated with the same respect that a cod gets when it hits the deck of an Icelandic trawler (i.e. gutted, washed, wiped and packed in ice within minutes) it actually stands some comparison with that revered fish. And that, of course, is what we do when we go pollack fishing. We stun the fish as they come on board, cut their gills to bleed them for a few minutes in a holding box, give them a wash and a wipe, then put them in the ice chest. On the way back into port, we gut and descale them and remove the gills, maybe fillet a few of the biggest fish, and then put this lovingly prepped fish back on ice until we get it home – where it goes straight into the fridge.

MCS RATING: **2 EAT MORE!**

REC MINIMUM SIZE: **50cm**

SEASON: avoid January–April (spawning)

RECIPES: pages 130–2, 133, 134–5, 150–1, 170, 176, 177, 178–9, 179, 180, 182–3, 236, 238, 258, 260–1, 261, 262, 331, 338, 380–1, 382, 393 et al.

Happily, pollack is common all around the coast of Britain and Ireland. It looks superficially similar to cod, with a large head and big eyes. But it's really far more handsome. Its back is a darker, greeny-brown colour and its flanks are often bright bronze or gold. It doesn't have the cod's green measles or pot belly either, which can only be a plus. Like cod, however, it does have a very distinctive lateral line. This runs the length of its body, like a cod's, but just behind the head it curves sharply downwards in a very stylish-looking 'hip' – just like the rear end of a 1950s Italian sports car.

Pollack can be caught from beaches, boats, rocky headlands and even piers, but most are caught by anglers on charter boats on offshore wreck marks. We catch them on wrecks between 30 and 75 metres deep, where they've often become resident and territorial. They make a living by hunting small fish, worms and crustaceans that use the wreck for shelter. They have big eyes and big mouths, and they're not too fussy what they wrap their laughing gear around. A pollack bite is powerful, especially in a strong tide. They nail a bait firmly, and once they realise they're hooked, they fight with impressive runs and reel-straining dives.

The best pollack fishing around Dorset is among the copious collection of First and Second World War wrecks that litter the Channel from Weymouth to Cherbourg. Our favourite way to fish these wrecks is by drifting over them using rubber jelly worms, red gill lures, storm lures, or even a string of baited mackerel feathers. We drift, preferably during a strong tide, with the lures bumping across the seabed and then we reel up a few turns to bring our tackle clear of the wreck structure. Depending on the force and direction of the tide, the fish will have taken up residence either in front, behind or on top of the wreck. They'll be facing into the current, waiting for prey fish (or preferably our baits) to be swept past on the tide.

Rod and line wrecking trips are a great way to catch pollack and have much less of an impact than trawling or wreck netting. Nonetheless, it is still important to keep stock conservation in mind. Pollack that have been reeled up from a depth of over 50 metres rarely survive being released. Their gas-filled swim bladders expand as they ascend and they're unable to deflate them to descend again, so if they're released at the surface these fish will perish. That means that pollack caught at this depth are destined for the fish box from the moment they're hooked. As a consequence, any charter skipper or commercial rod and line fisherman needs to self-regulate how many fish they take from a wreck. They also need to be aware of the spawning season (January to April), and if female fish are caught full of ripening eggs, then it makes long-term sense to take very few fish during this period.

Although we love, *absolutely* love, pollack roe (salted, smoked and made into taramasalata or squished on squares of wholemeal toast with lemon juice), to take too many breeding fish before they've had the chance to spawn is madness. If we kill a fish that turns out to be full of roe, we'll use it. But once we've landed a couple of roe-laden females, we'll move on elsewhere and fish for another species.

Most commercially caught pollack are netted from wrecks using tangle nets, or taken as bycatch by conventional cod and haddock trawlers. Trawled pollack suffers the fate of most trawled fish, in that it gets unduly crushed in the net. It's unlikely to get much attention until after the more valuable fish have been stacked and stowed, so the best pollack to buy is rod and line caught (Cornwall is a good place to find it), or caught by static inshore nets.

There are encouraging signs that pollack is finally beginning to shrug off its image as cod's poor relation, and it does now appear on the menus of enlightened chefs and the slabs of more forward-thinking fishmongers. It's used more and more in commercially produced ready meals too, such as fish pies and fish fingers, as an alternative to cod.

That's exactly how we should all regard pollack: not as a poor substitute for cod but as a genuine and worthwhile alternative. And also, perhaps, as the fish that might just do its cousin, the cod, with whom it's been so insultingly compared, a massive favour – by giving it a break.

Coley *Pollachius virens*

This is one of those fish that has somehow, over time, slipped from our consciousness. Only a couple of hundred years ago, it was so important to the British diet that we had over fifty different regional names for it, including blockan, coalfish, cuithe, gilpin, greylord, piltock, saithe, sillack and sillock. Now, most of us wouldn't recognise a coley if it moved in next door.

Coley looks very similar to pollack (if that helps you) – its closest relation in the cod family. Perhaps the easiest way to tell them apart is by looking at their tails: a pollack's is shovel-shaped, a coley's forked. Coley also have dark,

MCS RATING: 2 (2–4)

REC MINIMUM SIZE: 60cm

SEASON: avoid January–March (spawning)

RECIPES: pages 144, 270, 321, 380–1

blue-brown, almost black colouring along their backs, as opposed to the green-gold of the pollack, and a salmon-like silver to their flanks. And if pollack is underrated as an eating fish, then coley is doubly so.

Like pollack, coley can be caught on wrecks, but large specimens are usually only found on deep wrecks, over 50 metres. We don't see much of them here in the Southwest, as they don't come into the inshore rocky headlands or kelp beds in the way that pollack do. But in northern England and Scotland they congregate closer to the coast, particularly when young, and half-pounders (cuddies, as they're known) are a not uncommon catch when you're out mackerel fishing.

In many areas, including the waters around the British Isles, stocks of coley are very healthy and look likely to remain so, thanks to sustainable fishing methods. Indeed, several fisheries in the North Sea and off Norway are currently being assessed for MSC certification (see pages 33–4). There are areas where overfishing of this species is a danger – notably Iceland and the Faeroes – so avoid fish from there. As with any species, line-caught fish are the most sustainable option.

Like most cod family members, coley will eat just about anything. But they're hunters rather than scavengers – opportunistic fish with big eyes and big mouths. They'll hide in the lee of a wreck or rock and gobble up smaller fish that swim by. Generally they live in dark, deep sea where little light penetrates. At 60 metres down, visibility is minimal, so they have to rely on vibrations, smell and instinct to find their food.

It's in Scotland that the economic contribution of coley (or saithe, as they're best known there) has been most critical in times past. For the rugged island dwellers of Orkney, they provided not only essential protein but also, by way of a bonus, illumination. The traditional way to prepare coley was to split them, salt them and slowly smoke them over a smouldering peat hearth for a few days. As the coley dried out, they began to emit a phosphorescent glow. Orkney folk claim that when the catch had been good, the abundance of hanging coleys would produce enough light to read by.

Mackerel family

Mackerel *Scomber scombrus*

For a fish that is often barely given a second glance, the mackerel is stunningly beautiful, and a just-caught specimen is always worth a long, appreciative appraisal. In France, they may consider his sartorial style a little *de trop*: the French name, *maquereau*, also means pimp. But to us, the mackerel's blue-black-green tiger-striped back and flanks and disco-shimmering silver belly are always an inspiring, and indeed mouthwatering, sight.

Here in Dorset, you know winter has finally been kicked into touch when the first mackerel are caught from Chesil Beach, often in early April. It's best to avoid them so early in the year as they may still be spawning, but as the water hots up, so will the fishing. Mackerel are the harbingers of plenty, running ahead of the summer migration of bass, black bream, sole, garfish and smoothhound.

They are full of promise and full of fight and, truth be told, empty of sense. A shoal of mackerel will snap at anything. You can catch them on a simple strip of foil wrapped round a hook, and sometimes even bare hooks are enough. But the classic tackle that has been luring these kamikaze fish to their doom for generations is a string of 'mackerel feathers' – six hooks, each with a coloured feather tied to its shank. When a mackerel shoal is passing, it's not unusual to catch a 'full house' of six wriggling specimens.

Mackerel are so co-operative with even the most inexperienced angler, that many people remember them fondly as the first fish they ever caught – usually on a round-the-bay mackerel trip at some seaside resort. And for many once-a-year holiday anglers, mackerel will remain the only fish they ever catch.

Because of its obliging nature, you could say that, economically speaking, the mackerel works harder than any other fish in the sea – twice as hard, really. It provides both a steady catch of quality food fish for inshore commercial fishermen and a very welcome boost to the tourist economy in small harbour towns all over Britain. The mackerel provides a great example of how the economic value of fish should not be measured purely in terms of the cash generated at the fish market. It's a lesson that could and should be applied to a number of other popular sporting species: notably bass, bream and pollack.

Related as they are to the mighty tuna, mackerel are designed for speed and distance. Being true pelagic fish (see page 21), they roam the seas searching for food, burning up calories and maintaining a permanently taut muscle tone. They have a classic streamlined torpedo profile: deeply forked tails, fins that fold back into recessed slots like the wings on an F-16 jet fighter, a mouth that hermetically seals, and eye sockets flush to the head – all of which minimise water resistance and maximise speed. They are tireless hunters who feed at any depth from the seabed to the surface, on anything from ragworms to sprats, sand eels to plankton.

Their healthy lifestyle makes them a great source of nutrients – much appreciated by seabirds, seals and all kinds of predatory fish (our beloved bass

MCS RATING: 3 (2–4)

REC MINIMUM SIZE: 30cm

SEASON: avoid March–July (spawning)

RECIPES: pages 130–2, 133, 134–5, 137, 142–3, 147, 148–9, 175, 182, 194, 218, 222, 286, 304, 316, 319, 326, 357, 392, 393, 400, 403 et al.

is that rays breed like their cousins the sharks (see page 452), and depend on a high survival rate and few problems from predators to maintain a steady population. The smaller species, such as the spotted, starry and cuckoo rays, aren't in such bad shape because they grow faster and reach sexual maturity younger than the larger rays.

The tradition of cutting and skinning skate wings on board the boats that catch them presents an increasing dilemma for the ethical fish shopper. It makes it impossible to accurately identify the species of origin. Even wholesalers and supermarket fish buyers cannot always tell which species they're buying and then offering for sale. This has been the case for decades, but is only just being addressed by the major players in the food industry. In 2006 Sainsbury's, the biggest retailer of fresh fish in the UK, made a bold and laudable decision, based on consultations with the Marine Conservation Society, to stop selling skate wings altogether. (Subsequently, Marks & Spencer, Waitrose, Tesco, Asda and Morrisons have also restricted their range to just a few of the smaller ray species.)

However, even when wholesalers can identify the species they're dealing in, it doesn't necessarily solve the problem. Rays don't hang around in species-specific groups. If a trawler is dragging for flatfish (which tend to inhabit the same kind of ground), it could easily catch several different species of skates and rays in the same haul. On the other hand, skates and rays are some of the few species able to survive relatively well after being trawled, so there is an opportunity to return the more vulnerable species alive. The key is to educate fishermen in order to ensure they can identify the most threatened skates and rays, so they can be released to breed another day. Just recently, real progress has been made in this area. A joint partnership between the Sea Fish Industry Authority, the Shark Trust and MCS has produced skate and ray identification guides for fishermen and an online database so they can check what they land.

As sea anglers, we catch the occasional ray, usually when bottom fishing for bream, gurnard and plaice on the shingly banks off Portland Bill. This allows us to identify the species – usually with a little help from our skipper – so the 'wrong' rays can always be returned unharmed and the 'right' ones theoretically kept for the pot. A few years ago we might indeed have killed and eaten a cuckoo or a spotted ray, whereas a thornback, undulate or blonde ray would always be released to fight another day. Now they all go back. They are such intriguing fish to encounter that returning one, and watching it flap those aptly named wings as it heads back to the bottom, is no great hardship.

We must admit that we still buy the occasional pair of wings directly from one of the day boats in Weymouth or West Bay. They're usually cut but not yet skinned, so we can see what type we're buying. But we acknowledge that it's a flawed ecological gesture to choose a pair of cuckoo ray wings when those of a good-sized blonde ray, taken in the same net, are clearly visible in the fish box.

It's the sheer joy of eating this fish that has made occasional hypocrites of us. A skate wing gently fried in foaming *beurre noir* (perhaps the only dish for which the cook is actively encouraged to burn the butter), then finished with a scattering of capers and a squeeze of lemon, is and always will be one of the best fish suppers there is. The flesh is easily pulled from the cartilage in immensely satisfying long, flaky strips. Like piscatorial tagliatelle, they curl neatly around the capers, and soak up just the right amount of buttery juice. All that remains of those alarming odours is the merest hint of gaminess.

It is, very sadly, a pleasure we are now resolving to forego. If only some enlightened fishery could get together with a credible conservation body, do whatever it takes to manage and certify the right species of ray, and restore it to our menus with the promise of a clean conscience... but, if there's to be such a ray of hope in our lifetime, they'll have to get their skates on.

Flatfish

Turbot *Psetta maxima*

The French Revolution was a bloody affair: a violent uprising of the masses, ending with a flurry of decapitations of the rich and famous. Heads rolled. Hearts stopped. The streets ran red with blue blood.

None of this had much impact on the great chef Grimod de la Reynière, however, whose only diary entry relating to the entire Revolution stated: 'Disaster. Not a single turbot for sale in the market for weeks.'

Amongst the gourmets and gourmands of Europe, turbot has always been held in high esteem. Turbot is fish royalty. The Victorians were particularly enamoured of the thick curds of flesh and the rich, almost gamey flavour, which gained it the reputation of being the 'pheasant of the sea'. It was luxurious food for grand occasions. Served out of a turbot-shaped fish kettle (a *turbotière*, no less), steamed with its white underside upwards, it was often slathered in a pink lobster sauce.

Turbot are the largest of the most important flatfish family – important because it also includes plaice, brill and flounder. And, like their cousins, they have a remarkable natural history. Turbot eggs have a droplet of oil attached to their egg sac, which makes them buoyant. As a result, instead of the eggs lying on the seabed, where a catalogue of scavenging bottom-feeders would eat them, they float to the upper layers of the water column and comparative safety.

Like all flatfish, turbot don't start life flat. After the eggs hatch, the young fry swim around for their first six months or so in a conventional 'upright' manner, eyes on top of their heads and belly below. They feed on plankton, and as they grow they tip over sideways and gradually metamorphose into flatfish. They develop their characteristic 'squashed head' appearance as their right eye slowly migrates around their head towards the left. The wandering eye ends up cheek by jowl (so to speak) with the left eye, giving the turbot its typical cross-eyed visage. This eye migration happens as the juvenile fish itself is leaving its mid-water nursery and migrating downwards to the seabed. When it gets there, it'll give up plankton sucking and start to earn its keep amongst the other bottom-feeding crew.

Turbot are highly successful predators who grow to be big, powerful fish. This is perhaps largely due to their economy of energy. They might actively hunt at the start and end of each tide run, but mostly they like to lie buried in the sand and wait until something dumb or dead just happens to drift by on the tide. Like most flatfish, their chief weapons are stealth and camouflage.

Being flat makes hiding in plain sight easy. A flatfish only has to worry about the top elevation of its body, because its belly is always going to be hidden snug against the seabed – which is why all flatfish have white bellies and seabed-imitating backs. Instead of scales, turbot have a thickish skin covering their backs with a few bumpy, bony lumps called tubercles. These give the fish a

MCS RATING: 4 (3–5)

REC MINIMUM SIZE: 30cm

SEASON: avoid April–August (spawning)

RECIPES: pages 141, 222, 231, 283, 290, 318–19

degree of protection, as well as adding a bit of texture to their camouflage. A few flicks of their fins half-buries them in the sand, and the whole 'I'm-just-a-patch-of-seabed' deal is complete.

Turbot have enormous, gaping, articulated mouths, which can open to suck in a vast array of food – and the generous baits offered to them by keen turbot anglers. They are enthusiastic omnivores. Biggish fish like them will hunt the slower, bottom-dwelling fish such as poor cod and pout, they'll crunch up crabs, mussels and all manner of crustaceans, and they'll eat their share of any carrion drifting about on the seabed. However what they really love is sand eels, which at dusk need to dig themselves into the sand to hide from predators. It's while the eels are digging their holes for the night that they're at their most vulnerable: too busy working on their overnight quarters to notice the large turbot creeping up on them.

Most turbot are caught from boats and are rarely targeted from the shore. But Chesil Beach is famous for producing some stunning shore-caught specimens, especially when fished with big mackerel and squid baits close behind the surf after a gale. Bass anglers who lob out big, hopeful bait occasionally hook turbot by accident – a very happy accident.

When we're in search of turbot from a boat, we normally drag fresh bait (a mackerel fillet, lightly hooked through the end of the tail) along the sandy undulations of the Shambles Bank. The boat drifts broadside across the bank, and fishing's best at the quieter ends of the ebb or flood tides. Even slack water can be productive. Lazy turbot don't feed when the tide is racing. They'll move away from big currents to find somewhere calmer to hide out.

Such is the premium price for this fish that it is inevitably targeted by commercial fishermen as well as anglers. Heavy bottom-trawling gear is what will find turbot and other flatfish, and such equipment is no friend to the sea floor. It's not that it couldn't recover from it – given time. But it can't take a beating week after week, year after year. So the conservation issues here are not merely to do with turbot numbers, but also the preservation of a fragile ecosystem that supports a vast range of interdependent species. As with scallop dredging, the common-sense answer to this problem is the zoning of the fishery, with zones left to 'rest' in rotation for ecologically meaningful periods of time.

Until such conservation measures are in place, it is perhaps best to uphold the tradition of turbot as a special-occasion fish – an annual treat, perhaps. Turbot from the North Sea fishery should certainly be avoided, as these stocks have already taken a hammering and, in all cases, line caught or static net caught is far preferable to trawled.

Catch a good one yourself (anything over 2 kilos is a keeper in our book), however, and you should feel more than entitled to take it back to the kitchen. Not only have you pulled off a mean feat of angling, you've picked that fish cleanly off the sea floor with your baited hook, barely troubling the fauna – micro and macro – with which it shares its habitat. Putting a smaller one back is hard, but when your hunger pangs have been assuaged by the cheese sandwich in your lunchbox you'll realise it was the right thing to do.

The quality, firmness and succulence of the turbot's flesh is such that it will stand up to most cooking techniques: frying, grilling, baking, steaming, poaching and even barbecuing – though in all cases, it would be a heinous crime to overcook it. Turbot is so tasty that minimal accompaniments are required – a trickle of butter and a squeeze of lemon or lime will do the job. At the same time, it's robust enough to withstand more elaborate saucing – hollandaise is the classic accompaniment (see our cheaty version on pages 281–2), salsa verde (see page 316) makes a pleasingly piquant modern alternative, especially to a barbecued tranche (see page 72). Traditionally, one should never remove the fins of a turbot before cooking – they're meant to be saved as a tasty treat for the most honoured guest. Pulled gently from the cooked fish, they come away with some shards of particularly juicy flesh attached.

A final tip: if you are ever lucky enough to catch a turbot yourself, or happen to buy a just-caught fish direct from a boat, it would be a mistake to eat it on the day it was caught. Curious as this may sound, a turbot can actually be too fresh to eat (a characteristic it shares with skates, rays and Dover sole, among others). It requires at least 24, ideally 48 hours – on ice of course – for the flesh to settle and become tender and palatable. Prior to that, you might find your turbot rubbery and curiously bland, and may well end up wondering what all the fuss is about.

Halibut *Hippoglossus hippoglossus*

Our friend Dave Holt, with whom we fish on the west coast of Scotland, was once birdwatching high on the cliffs at Duncansby Head near John O'Groats, where the fulmar colony was in the full hue and cry of nesting.

Looking down from the birds to the water below, he saw a massive, green-brown shape just below the surface, which at first he took to be a huge raft of floating kelp. 'But I could see it was a bit too tidy for that,' says Dave, 'and it was moving. I saw it heading for a dead fulmar chick that was floating in the water. It came up and sucked it off the surface, like a trout taking a dry fly. I watched it for a couple of minutes, and it took two or three more chicks. It must have been 12 feet long, and at least 4 feet wide, and well over 400lb. I knew exactly what it was, but I still couldn't quite believe it. It was simply one of the most awe-inspiring things I've ever seen.' As the shape slipped back down into the slate-blue water and disappeared, Dave was sure he had seen not a shark or a seal, or even a dolphin. He had just seen a halibut.

Fish witnesses don't come much more credible than Dave Holt. Apart from birdwatching, fishing is his great passion and, for over ten years now, he has been catching giant skate in the Sound of Mull, tagging and releasing them as part of a programme run by the Glasgow Museum's Science Department. He knows how to estimate the size and weight of a huge fish.

Nor is he the first man to have been profoundly moved by an encounter with a halibut. On 26 April 1784 William Cowper wrote his heartfelt ode, 'To the Immortal Memory of the Halibut on which I Dined This Day'. It wasn't the quality of its flesh that inspired him. Rather, not unlike Dave, he was full of admiration for the fish as a physical specimen, and a totem of maritime adventure:

> Indebted to no magnet and no chart,
> Nor under guidance of the polar fire,
> Thou wast a warrior on many coasts,
> Grazing at large in meadows submarine.

MCS RATINGS: wild 5 DON'T EAT!; farmed 4

REC MINIMUM SIZE: N/A

SEASON: N/A

At the time halibut was a reasonably common eating fish but by no means a fashionable one. It was reckoned to be rather coarse and dry – a big, cheap, chewy fish that poor people were forced to eat. Some disdainfully called it 'workhouse turbot'. And, for all the passion of his ode, Cowper does not at any point seek to redress popular culinary opinion of the fish.

By the late nineteenth century, halibut had garnered a few fans, but its 'workhouse' reputation was always going to be a hard one to shake off. *Cassell's Dictionary* of 1880 put it in a nutshell: 'This excellent fish is not as prized as it ought to be, probably on account of its cheapness.' Well, it's not cheap any more. Today even farmed halibut costs at least £20 per kilo, while a wild-caught Alaskan halibut can fetch double that, putting it right up there in the UK's 'Top Ten Most Expensive Fish'.

Halibut went through the transformation from food zero to culinary hero within a generation. Post-war, it gained ground as the price of other 'smart' fish, such as turbot and Dover sole, went up. In the 1950s it was a regular on the menu at Wheeler's restaurant in Old Compton Street, Soho. The artist Francis Bacon, who dined there regularly, was said to be a fan. As Wheelers expanded into a chain in the 1960s and 1970s, halibut caught on as a restaurant-menu kind of fish that was chef-friendly – it made a lovely square fillet portion in the centre of a big round plate, and took a sauce well. The consensus among chefs was that halibut was no longer a fish to be denigrated but one to serve up with buttered spinach, hollandaise sauce and a hefty price tag.

However, being so slow growing, halibut offer very little resistance to commercial fishing pressure. By 1983, wild stocks of Atlantic halibut had been so overfished that the Seafish Industry Authority's Marine Farming Unit in Argyll began attempting to farm them. There were many teething problems, principally the high mortality rate of the tiny, larval fish in the first year of life. These have now been overcome, and the farming of halibut is a growing area of aquaculture, both in northern British waters and in the fjords of Scandinavia.

One would hesitate, however, to call halibut farming a success story: it is subject to many of the same environmental criticisms as the farming of salmon (see page 508). Particularly problematic are the huge amounts of food – usually meal made from wild-caught 'industrial' species, such as sand eel and blue whiting (see page 504) – required to fatten these slow-growing fish. Progress is being made on more sustainable halibut farming in Scotland but there is still some way to go.

Halibut is a true flatfish, and the unrivalled giant of the family. It prefers colder, deeper water than most of its relatives and, as a result, grows slower but much, much bigger. The largest recorded halibut ever caught in a net was landed in Norway and tipped the scales at a massive 282kg. Fishing for wild halibut, by trawl and also with deep long lines carrying baited hooks, has always been at the tough end of a tough business, not only because of cold waters and rough seas but also because this huge fish has something of an attitude. Halibut seem to deeply resent being caught. If you drag a 25–50kg halibut on to the deck of your boat, the chances are it is going to use every steel-hard muscle in its powerful body to try to smash nine kinds of crap out of you and your vessel.

Broken bones and seriously damaged boats used to be commonplace, until fishermen decided to swing the odds somewhat back in their favour. Most hand-lining commercial halibut boats (and even, in Canada, some halibut angling boats) now carry a handgun or captive bolt gun (the kind used for slaughtering cattle) in the wheelhouse, in order to shoot the hooked halibut in the head when it comes alongside the boat. (There is hardly any recreational halibut angling in British waters. Apart from the distances and dangerous seas involved, our strict gun laws continue to stack the odds in favour of the fish.)

We almost never eat halibut. We'd hesitate to malign it as an eating fish – it's good, but not *that* good. Having a tendency to dryness, it needs careful cooking and a good sauce to help it slip down. We couldn't square choosing a portion of wild halibut, from either the fishmonger's slab or a restaurant menu, with the very serious concerns about its stocks (wild halibut scores a 5 in the MCS list and is considered endangered by the World Conservation Union). As to farmed – not only, for the reasons mentioned above, is halibut a questionable choice of fish for aquaculture in the first place but the end product is another rung or two down the ladder of eating quality. So halibut, in any form, is currently too expensive, too unsustainable and, frankly, too replaceable to justify a purchase. There are many better options, farmed and wild, for both the palate and the conscience (check out our lists on page 49).

But to see one in the wild, as Dave did – now that we'd pay good money for. Is anyone out there offering halibut safaris?

flatfish, plaice love sand, mud and gravel because they can hide in it, or stir it up with their wing-like fins and snouty mouths to expose crabs and other goodies. They migrate to the huge seed mussel beds to the west of Portland Bill in spring and early summer. Their tough, bony mouths allow them to tear off these tiny mussels and swallow them whole, digesting their sweet orange flesh. Often they are so fixated by the mussels that they won't eat anything else – certainly nothing as mundane as a regular angler's bait. Hence the plaice-obsessive's fancy rigs, a desperate bid to distract their quarry from the business of gorging mussels. The culture of rig and tackle adornment began with the humble plaice spoon: a dessertspoon with the handle chopped off and a hole drilled in one end. A ring was clipped to the spoon and attached to the line a few inches behind the hook bait. The purpose of the spoon was to kick up sand and sediment during the boat's drift, suggesting a lively alternative to the mussel menu for the plaice to come and investigate. Over the years, the spoons have become more elaborate, and are now fully accessorised with coloured beads and rattling balls.

The bait and its presentation generate almost as much discussion as the rigs on which it is presented. 'Plaice like a long bait,' says Pat. 'Long, fat, with lots of movement. Two hooks, one above the other and then alternate ragworm and squid strips until the whole bait's about eight inches long.' But big baits don't mean big bites. Plaice bites are tender, twitchy, teasing little affairs that leave anglers unsure and insecure. They don't know whether to lift slowly, to strike hard or just wait and hope – hence the furrowed brows.

A plaice's brow is a curious thing too. Like most flatfish, they start life as normal upright, side-on fish. But as they grow, they tip over to one side and one eye migrates around the head, to sit squashed up against the other. Plaice are pleuronectidae, or right-eyed flatfish (most are left), with both eyes ending up together on the right side of the 'face'.

What makes them stand out most obviously from the flatfish crowd are the bright orange spots and splodges sprinkled across their greeny-brown backs. No other flatfish sports spots like these. Underneath, the bottom-hugging side of the plaice is, like most other flatfish, pure milky white.

Plaice skin is thick and tough and relatively easy to peel off in whole, unbroken sides. This makes it one of the few species suitable for tanning into leather. In the Second World War, when the Nazis invaded Denmark, they requisitioned all 'leather' (as conventionally made from mammal hides) for military use. The resilient Danes responded by making their leather from cod, salmon and plaice skin. In its heyday, it was known as 'Neptune's suede'. Even Queen Ingrid of Denmark put her best foot forward in a pair of evening sandals made from purple-dyed plaice skin. (If you want to see a pair of fish leather slingbacks in the flesh, or rather skin, then make your way to Northampton, where you will find a pair on permanent display in the Central Museum.)

Plaice have always been a popular eating fish and are easy to find on fishmongers' slabs all over Britain. But, sadly, they are victims of their own success. They have been subject to intense fishing pressure in many areas, and the Irish Sea is the only definite sustainable European source at the time of writing. Ask your fishmonger exactly where his or her plaice comes from and, if it's not Irish, it's best not to buy it. Choose otter-trawl-caught fish, if available: most plaice are caught by the beam-trawl method, which damages the seabed and also results in a very high bycatch of juvenile fish. The speed at which plaice grow, and the age at which they breed, varies hugely according to the depth and

MCS RATING: 4 (3–5)

REC MINIMUM SIZE: 30cm

SEASON: avoid spring (spawning)

RECIPES: pages 216, 222, 231, 246, 290, 306, 321, 324, 381

temperature of the water where they live and the availability of food. But they are generally slow maturing, and it takes between three and six years for a female to grow to spawning size.

The flesh of plaice is exceptionally fine and delicate. At its best, it's as white as a Hollywood Christmas and melts to velvet on the tongue. But this unusual tenderness and fragility may translate to 'mushy and watery' if a fish is out of condition, a day older than perhaps it should be, or has been cooked for a few minutes too long. Rather surprisingly, given its subtlety, plaice has survived for many years as a chip-shop fish. It's not the ideal fish flesh to batter, because the fillet is never that thick, so the batter–fish ratio will always be high. No doubt that appeals to some. But the delicate meat won't stand much squirting with industrial-strength malt vinegar.

Plaice are relatively easy and satisfying to fillet (see pages 68–9), and plaice fillets rolled up and stuffed (for example, with orange zest and breadcrumbs) were rather a popular conceit in the 1980s. But it all seems a bit fussy for a fish of such simple charms. Our favourite way to eat plaice is whole and on the bone. The skin, though substantial, is a definite asset and, if treated right, should end up nice and crispy (so not like shoe leather at all). If you've got a big pan, plaice can be fried in oil and butter or, better still, grilled under a hot, even, overhead grill. Bigger fish can be baked whole in a piping-hot oven (page 216). When you get it right, it's rather dreamy: the skin crispy-but-sticky and the melting, moist flesh gently clinging to the bone frame. Eat one side, flip it over and eat the other. Pick any cheeks or shoulder flesh from the head end and nibble the crispy tail. Then, when all the obvious bits have gone, just pick up that frame and suck every shard and flake of flesh out of the skeleton.

Oddly enough, the really obsessive plaice anglers, those who like to dream up new rigs with beads and rattling balls, rarely cook or consume their catch. They mostly want to photograph them, record their weight, the weather, water temperature and climatic conditions. Bizarre as it may seem, the true plaice fanatic may *only* be interested in catching them. In which case, nutty or not, he might be a good friend to cultivate.

Flounder *Platichthys flesus*

Dab *Limanda limanda*

If turbot and sole are the aristocrats of the flatfish dynasty, and plaice and brill the respectable middle classes, then dabs and flounders are, in the eyes of the trade at least, little more than snot-nosed street urchins. But we feel they are worthy of higher regard.

Although both dabs and flounders can be easily caught close inshore around most of the British Isles, there's no targeted fishery for them. Any flounder or dab that finds its way into a fish market gets there by accident – a casualty of bycatch from a vessel targeting top-end flatfish. (It's better, by the way, to buy fish caught by seine-netting rather than the more damaging demersal trawl method.)

There's no doubt that these two are hiding their light under a bushel. They're drab-looking fish with plain, rough skin and no elaborate markings or exotic

MCS RATINGS: both 2 EAT MORE!

REC MINIMUM SIZE: flounder, 25cm; dab, 20cm

SEASON: flounder, avoid January–April (spawning); dab, avoid April–June (spawning)

RECIPES: pages 216, 231, 246, 290, 306, 318, 321, 324

dab

flounder

coloration. They're also much smaller than the fancier flatfish, with the average dab weighing in at about 250g. Flounders can grow bigger, but it's unusual to see one much over 500g. And when it comes to preparation, small means fiddly. None of these characteristics exactly endears dabs and flounders to the British fish consumer – but they do ensure that they are usually offered at a very keen price.

The further good news is that dabs and flounders are plentiful around the British Isles and easy to catch on rod and line: from beach, estuary, pier, harbourside or breakwater. Summer is the best time to catch them – and harbour dabs are popular with fair-weather holiday anglers. They have small mouths, so small hooks are essential, but they will eat just about any bait, including lug worms, rag worms, mussels, crabs, fish strips or shrimp. It doesn't have to be fresh bait, either, since dabs and flounders won't turn their noses up at bait that has grown a bit old and stinky.

Most serious sea anglers tend to target these species in estuaries. Neither shows any aversion to living and feeding in brackish water (where fresh river water mixes with the sea). Flounders particularly seem to revel in the reduced salination. Although they're sea fish, they can often be caught many miles upstream in a river where there is almost zero salinity. In Holland flounders have even been successfully fattened up in freshwater pools.

The flounder's love of shallow, muddy estuaries led to an unusual style of fishing, which evolved long before the invention of static nets or rod and line. This is known as 'flounder tramping' and involves locating flounders at low tide as they hide just beneath the wet mud, using your bare feet. Once a flounder is felt, one foot is kept on top of it to pin it down, until it can be hand-speared or grabbed and placed in a wet sack.

This method of fishing was revived in the nineteenth century in Dumfriesshire, and has now become an annual sporting event – the Palnackie Flounder Tramping Championships – held on the estuary of Urr Water. Every

August, over 300 contestants compete to see who can tramp and hand catch the most – and biggest – flounders. In some ways, the indignity of this fate speaks volumes, but we are assured by those involved that all the flounders end up being put to good use in local kitchens. So, to put a positive spin on it, you could say it goes to show that there is, somewhere, some affection and appreciation for the flounder – and so there should be.

Disparaging comments about their texture and flavour – they've variously been accused of being 'watery', 'poor eating' and a 'wet flannel' – are wholly unfounded. We believe this short-sighted, uneducated propaganda is being circulated by a vicious gang of turbot-supremacists. They must be stopped!

Because flounder is lovely. A whole one simply grilled and served with a generous trickle of melted butter, flaky sea salt and chopped fresh parsley can make a grown man cry fat tears of joy. And dab meat is some of the sweetest, softest fish flesh ever to grace a fork. A pair of dab fillets served in a crusty bun, smeared with homemade tartare sauce, is almost a religious experience.

As is so often the case, our national prejudice against dabs and flounders is not shared by the rest of Europe. In Galicia, on the Atlantic coast of Spain, the flounder is considered a great delicacy and is served fried, steamed or filleted, often with a light, creamy saffron sauce. In Belgium, flounder is smoked and served with lemon and soured cream. In Denmark, dabs are salted and dried; they are the celebrated regional speciality of the Jutland peninsula.

So, we'd like to invite you to join our new group, SPUDF (Society for the Promotion and Understanding of Dabs and Flounders). There's no subscription, and no monthly newsletter. All you have to do is shop positively. Whenever you see dabs and flounders on the fishmonger's slab – and you certainly will from time to time – snap them up quick, and tell him you'll be back for more.

Dover sole *Solea solea*

Dover sole doesn't actually come from Dover – but you probably didn't think it did. It acquired the name because Dover was the most reliable port from which to source sole for the thriving London market. These days, most Dover sole for the British table is bought and sold at Brixham market in Devon, though it's caught all around the British coast, and its wider distribution stretches right across the North Atlantic, from the fjords of Norway to Senegal. However, the plump soles that are landed in British ports are considered the best, and are in demand all over Europe. They have been for a couple of centuries.

Throughout the nineteenth and early twentieth centuries, sole was the most prized of all sea fish, rivalled only by turbot. The size of the sole you served reflected your level of success on the social ladder. The upper echelons, and those aspiring to buy their way into them, ate the bigger soles, while the next social tier had to make do with smaller soles called 'slips' or 'tongues'. So revered was the flesh of the Dover sole that it sent classical chefs into a frenzy of fiddly excess. Chef Louis Saulnier's massive tome of 1914, *Le Répertoire de la Cuisine*, listed no fewer than 340 different ways of presenting sole fillets. Maybe he was cocking a snook at his former master, Auguste Escoffier, who could only manage to muster a paltry 180 sole recipes in *Le Guide Culinaire* of 1903.

MCS RATING: **4 (1–5)**
REC MINIMUM SIZE: **28cm**
SEASON: avoid April–June (spawning)
RECIPES: pages **231, 290**

Historically we have been spoiled by the ready availability of the most distinguished sole – the Dover (see page 471). This flatfish has always enjoyed the limelight, and consequently the lion's share of the UK sole market. While the flavour and texture of its flesh are indisputably fine, its tidy shape and dapper good looks certainly help make it popular (and increasingly unsustainable).

Beauty may be in the eye of the beholder, but it's doubtful that anyone would describe either witch or megrim as much of a looker. Compared to the Dover, with its rich, nut-brown top skin, both are rather anaemic-looking soles, almost transparent in fact – as you'll see if you hold one up to the light. But aside from their strange appearance and spooky names, witch and megrim are excellent eating fish. Pale, maybe, but definitely interesting. They really are a canny choice. Just consider the price difference: in today's market, a kilo of Dover sole costs anywhere from £15 to £20, while megrim and witch usually sell for between £4 and £5 a kilo.

All three of these soles share a similar lifestyle. They like to inhabit a muddy/sandy/shingly seabed, where they efficiently prey on crustaceans, worms and small fish. Their habitats overlap but megrim and witch tend to be caught in deeper water and further out to sea than Dovers.

Current stocks of megrim and witch are generally in better shape than those of Dover sole. So, is this a fish to eat with a clear conscience? Almost – but there's a catch. Most British hauls of these species are currently taken by beam trawlers targeting cod, haddock, plaice, monkfish and other deep-dwelling demersals. Several of these species are under grievous threat – even if the megrim/witch bycatch is not. Furthermore, beam trawling can cause deep structural damage to the seabed (see page 29). 'Otter-trawled' soles are a better choice, if you can find them, because the way in which they are fished has less impact. There is currently much constructive discussion amongst the West Country fisheries and the many trade outlets they serve about improving both the environmental impact of the beam trawl fishery generally (see pages 41–2) and the public image of the megrim in particular.

It's a tough call, but on balance we'd say choosing megrim and witch is a positive move, even if you don't know how they've been caught. It helps establish a market for species that *could* be targeted more sustainably in the very near future. No authority will bother to regulate or certify these fish for the UK market if no one wants to buy them.

So what can be done to stimulate demand for these very worthwhile species? Those in fish retail are convinced that what's required is 'rebranding'. And if that's what it takes, let's get on board. It's not exactly a makeover – nothing can be done to change the appearance of these insipid-looking soles. But the prevailing feeling seems to be that, from a retail perspective, they'd both benefit from a name change. We think megrim is a rather charming name but, according to the branding gurus, it has too many negative connotations. First of all there's the 'grim' bit. Secondly, the whole word sounds a bit like a 'migraine'. Ouch. Fair enough, megrim is a rubbish name.

A few years ago, Waitrose decided to market megrim as… megrim. They didn't shift. No matter how chunky and fresh the fillets on the slab, shoppers just couldn't see past the unappetising name. The latest plan, supported by Waitrose and other retailers, is to relaunch megrim as 'Cornish sole'. The model for this exercise was the successful relaunch of passé 'pilchards' as sexy 'Cornish sardines'. Maybe the same will work for megrim. We'd buy a Cornish sole.

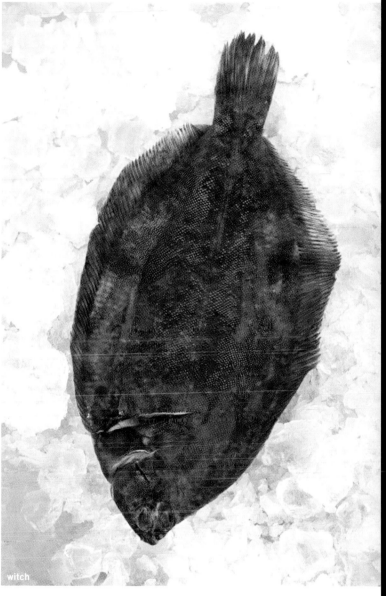

megrim witch

Unsurprisingly, the 'witch' moniker is also up for a rethink. With the help of food marketing consultants, the Irish Sea Fisheries Board came up with the name 'Rockall sole' – after the famous fishing grounds. But there's competition, as Marks & Spencer has recently agreed with the Trading Standards Agency to sell witch under the name of 'Torbay sole', after the Devon fishery where many are caught. Surely only one brand can prevail. Our vote goes to Rockall sole – it's just more catchy. Not everyone wants to see witch rebranded, however. The readers of *Pentacle*, the 'UK's leading independent Pagan magazine', regard the ditching of 'witch' as proof of a widespread prejudice against weavers of spells.

In the kitchen, you'd cook megrim and witch in exactly the same way as any sole or plaice. The flesh of both species is slightly more delicate than Dover sole, slightly more robust than plaice, and they will happily stand in for either. A whole fish, well seasoned, started in a frying pan and finished in an oven (see page 296) is an excellent default treatment. A trickle of herb or garlic butter over the finished fish is all you need to make these soles soar.

the fish to feed. This is basically a sloppy mix of bread, fish guts and fish oils, which is spooned into the water little and often. It creates an underwater scent trail to lure the garfish to the bait (and their fate). Many anglers have their own secret ingredients with which they customise their chervy. These may include Thai fish sauce, anchovy oil, malt extract and even ox or pig's blood. Obviously they're not *that* secret – that's fishermen for you.

Hooking a **garfish** on light tackle is a thrilling experience. They are often described as 'miniature marlin', on account of the aerial acrobatics they can perform in their attempt to escape. A hooked garfish will leap right out of the water, 'walk' on its tail, or dive deep in a vigorous attempt to shake the hook.

The perfect garfish to cook is over 40cm long and around 500g in weight. This size is easy to gut and can even be filleted (if you want to remove the green bones). It'll feed two people as a hearty main course or four as a starter. From an ecological perspective, at 40cm long a garfish has reached sexual maturity and will have already had the opportunity to spawn. In fish-boffin speak, garfish are said to have 'medium resilience to fishing'. In other words, they grow fast and mature early, so the population can fairly readily replace the fish it loses. Nevertheless, it's still best to opt for garfish caught by the least intensive methods – i.e. fish you've landed yourself or those taken as a bycatch.

Once you've come to terms with the visual oddities of this fish (which are mere tricks to stop you eating it), you can set about enjoying its excellent flesh. The classic French method for cooking garfish is to poach or fry bite-sized chunks and serve them with a sorrel sauce. The Channel Islanders prefer to grill them and serve them up with mushy peas and mashed potato. The Danes like their *hornfisk* fillets pickled, smoked or lightly cured. All of which is testament to the surprising versatility of this fish.

The Japanese go one better – they like to eat the bones as well as the flesh. Once the cooked flesh has been taken from the bones, they dust the skeleton in spicy flour and deep fry it in hot oil. Needless to say we had to try this – with some we caught during a fishing trip to Guernsey. See page 374 for the verdict...

Conger eel *Conger conger*

Every sea fisherman has a conger story to tell; some twisty tale of a huge, snapping eel with a head the size of a boiled ham, teeth so sharp they could fell a pylon, and the attitude of a Jack Russell with a wasp up its nose.

We love the story of the Dorset crab potter who found a five-footer curled up in one of his hauled pots. He shook the felon on to the deck, only to have the conger respond with a tantrum so malevolent and violent that the fisherman dived into the wheelhouse for safety and locked the door. According to local legend, he stayed there, peering out of the window, for the next six hours, while the conger ran amok on the deck. It smashed everything of value while thrashing round the boat, until eventually escaping out of one of the scuppers.

Another favourite conger-revenge tale is of an angler who lost control of a big, fat wriggler he'd just hauled out of the sea on to a low pier wall. He put his foot on the conger's neck to 'pacify' him and in the next blink the conger twisted around and bit through his welly boot, top and bottom, sinking his fangs

MCS RATING: 5 DON'T EAT!
REC MINIMUM SIZE: N/A
SEASON: N/A
RECIPE: pages 229–31

Freshwater fish

simultaneously through the sole and upper. The howling fisherman kicked so hard he broke two of the eel's lower teeth. The tips of them are still buried in the arch of his foot to this day.

Congers are great fable fodder because, let's face it, there aren't many British fish likely to give you a serious fright. No one's going to be traumatised by a surprise encounter with a roach. Nobody ever went to A and E after a mauling from a whiting. Congers have been called 'legless pit bulls with scales' – which is apt except not only do they lack legs, they also lack scales. They are quite uncannily smooth skinned. Even freshwater eels have scales on their skin – practically undetectable by the naked eye, but they're there nonetheless. A conger, on the other hand, has not a speck of a scale on it from fang to tail. It does have a thick layer of slime, though, that helps to ease it in and out of tight hidey-holes.

Conger eels love to hang out among deep shadows. They slither around undersea wrecks and reefs, lurking in holes and caves, from where they ambush

their prey with surprising speed and agility, given their size. During the rush of tide, congers like to keep themselves tucked away from the current in the sanctuary of wreck or reef. But when the tide slackens, small- to medium-sized eels (up to 10kg) will venture on to open ground, ranging the bottom in search of a feed. They're not fussy – almost any fish or crustacean will do, dead or alive.

Anglers who target conger eels tend to position themselves near reefs and wrecks, and to sit at anchor on slack water, when there's little or no tide. They use big baits, such as half a mackerel or a chunky fish head, on large, strong hooks. These are attached to the reel line by either a steel wire trace or an extra-thick (60kg) nylon leader, to offer resistance against the conger's teeth.

The sensible way to tame a big eel is to steer it straight from the landing net into a coarse hessian sack, cutting the line so the hook stays in the conger's mouth until it has calmed down somewhat. Then it is a two-person job: let only the head out of the sack, one person gripping it firmly through the hessian just behind the gills, while the other goes for the hook with a pair of pliers held in heavily gloved hands. Unhooking should *never* be attempted solo by a conger novice. It would be better to cut the line and return the conger with the hook still in. The facial piercing may or may not impress its friends but it will rust away soon enough.

Bagging a conger for the pot is something we do only once in a blue moon – this is not a species we should be yanking out of the sea at every opportunity. Congers only breed once in their lifetime (and they swim to the waters off Portugal to do it), so there's every chance that the conger you haul in will not yet have had a chance to reproduce. They also take a long time to reach sexual maturity – up to fifteen years. They are not under serious commercial fishing pressure but 'specimen-hunting' anglers have taken their toll on certain heavily fished wrecks and reefs over the years. Since the conger is primarily an angler's fish, we think those who do battle with them should return them to the sea unharmed – and this is increasingly the practice among conger enthusiasts. The only conger you kill and eat, we feel, should be the one you've had to kill because it has swallowed your hook deep, and cannot be unhooked without causing serious damage.

If you do choose to kill a deeply hooked conger, prepare for something of an ordeal. Again, the hessian sack comes in handy. When the conger is fairly still and steady, you should deliver several very hard blows just behind the eyes with a very heavy priest. If this seems to make things worse rather than better, back off for a moment and then try again. Once the conger is stunned and subdued, you need to finish the job by stabbing it between the eyes with a stout knife and/ or severing the spinal column with a deep cut behind the head. Don't be alarmed if some twisting and writhing goes on after this operation has been carried out – the conger's nervous system continues to operate, sometimes for an hour or more, even after the fish is dead.

And what should you do with this reluctantly acquired carcass? Take some trouble over turning it into dinner, surely. In Britain generally, conger has a reputation for being bony, rubbery, grey and unpalatable. But that judgement is unduly harsh. Cornish fishing communities used to eat a lot of conger eel, stewed and served up with a garnish of fresh marigold petals (we like to imagine the sheer chagrin of the mighty conger thus prettified). And among Cornwall's cultural kin in Brittany, the conger is still highly rated – so esteemed in fact that it's been nicknamed *boeuf bellilois*, to celebrate its meaty prime-rib qualities. On the coast of Morocco the conger eel thrives in the harsh rocky crevices and reefs that are pounded by the Atlantic, and in the fishing port of Essaouira, *tagine de congre* is a speciality, served with couscous. The vital elements of the recipe are hotly debated by local chefs and fishwives – rather like the bouillabaisse of Marseille.

We've enjoyed experimenting with the occasional conger we've killed in the last few years. We've beer-battered and deep-fried trimmed fillets, chip-shop style. We've road-tested the British Conger Club's classic of conger poached in cider. We've smoked a whole 'side' of conger and used it to make kedgeree. We've dropped little scallops of conger 'loin fillet' into our Fish and chorizo soup (pages 260–1). We've even stuffed and roasted a thick hunk of conger 'saddle' as if it was a meat joint (see pages 229–31). All these dishes have been successful. They work because conger meat is white, firm and ready to take on any number of flavours.

The tail section – final third, if you like – is the only piece that doesn't yield good meat. It's just too tough, bony and fibrous. But it does make a fine addition, along with the head, to a good fish stock.

In Britain the conger is unlikely to become the fish cook's favourite – and nor should it, when you take its biology into account. But if you find yourself in possession of one, it's well worth investing some time in getting to grips with its substantial carcass. Otherwise, once you've had your adrenalin rush, return your conger alive to the sea so it can give another angler an even bigger fright.

Sand eel *Ammodytes tobianus*

A sand eel doesn't command much public attention or affection because, at least in the UK, as a food fish, it's considered worthless. However, as an intermediary in the fish-to-human food chain, it plays a crucial role. You may never have eaten sand eel but you are sure to have eaten a fish that has. We love them, because they are by far the most effective bait to catch sea bass, one of the fish we most love to eat. But they also play a major part in the economics of commercial fishing – as a much-abused 'industrial' species, caught in vast numbers to be processed into fishmeal.

To anglers, the best sand eel is a live one – freshly scooped from an aerated bait bucket, ready for a size 3/0 long-shank hook to be inserted through its top lip. Live sand eels are a deadly bait, and we have to admit we have skewered hundreds of them over the years, then dropped them on a weighted line to the seabed, in the hope of hooking a sea bass. As bass anglers, we require our sand eels to be full of vim and vigour. The more lively they are on the hook, the more likely they are to tempt a passing bass (or pollack or ling) to suck them in and gulp them down in an underwater dine-and-dash. Then we will have our sport and, with a bit of luck, a fine dinner to show for it.

However, sand eels are often reluctant to play ball. Frail creatures, they like nothing better than to curl up and die. Once they've been caught, either with a small trawl net dragged behind a boat, or by fishing a string of tiny feathered hooks (like mackerel feathers, only smaller), keeping them alive and wriggling is a tricky business. Good charter angling boats will have a live bait 'well' – some kind of tank in which freshly drawn seawater is aerated by a pump, in order

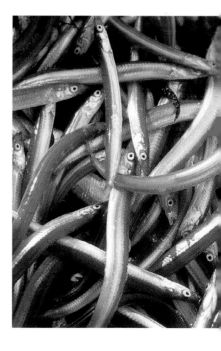

MCS RATING: not rated
SIZE AT MATURITY: 8cm
SEASON: avoid February–April and September–November (spawning)

to keep the moody sand eels hanging on in there. Charter skippers know the value of keeping a catch of sand eels lively all day, because to some extent their reputation depends on it. On his amazing new boat, *Channel Chieftain*, our friend Pat Carlin has installed a rather ancient blue plastic barrel for a bait well, which is connected to a pump circulating seawater. 'You've got to keep sand eels in something *round*,' says Pat. 'If you do that, they'll swim in circles, which keeps them happier, so they stay alive. I've known boats with smart purpose-built tanks that are rectangular. They look great, but all the sand eels just huddle up in one corner and die.'

Few anglers have the patience to catch their own sand eels. Instead they buy them. Through the bass season (summer and autumn) in busy sea-angling ports, sand eels are gold dust. The charter skippers in Weymouth, for example, collectively employ a local fisherman to trawl for sand eels and provide a constant supply for visiting anglers. But, even so, the supply can still be erratic. Certain stages of the tide cycle make it impossible to trawl for sand eels and as soon as the cold weather starts, the eels move out into deeper water. Frozen dead sand eels can be bought all year round. On a good day when the bass are on a voracious feed, dead eels will work just as well. But on a tough day, when the fish need to be enticed, only a live eel will do the business.

You may or may not approve of using live fish as bait for other fish. We do it regularly, so it would be hypocritical to suggest it troubles us greatly. Perhaps it should trouble us more, and perhaps, as we get older, it will. But it's hard to argue against the economics of this enterprise. On a local level, trawling for sand eels, to sell live or frozen as bass bait, makes perfect sense. It's often said, if not economically proved, that the Weymouth bass are worth more alive, to visiting anglers and the tourist economy that they support, than they are dead to the local fish trade. Sand eels play a vital role in that, and the relatively modest harvest required to supply the charter boats is perfectly sustainable.

What isn't sustainable, though – nothing like it – is the way sand eels are plundered further offshore. In parts of the North Sea and northeast Atlantic, vast shoals of sand eels are removed by 'industrial fishing'. They congregate so tightly, and can be targeted so clinically, that 'removed' really is the correct word. Sometimes sand eel trawlers fill their massive holds on just a single trawl, and have to head back to port at top speed before returning for their next enormous scoop of the shoal. At the end of the 1990s, sand eels accounted for around half of all the fish taken from the North Sea, with up to a million tonnes a year being hauled in. Catches have dropped significantly in recent years but are still in the hundreds of thousands of tonnes.

Sand eels – along with capelin, blue whiting and scad (page 481) – are classed as an 'industrial' species. This grim epithet describes fish destined not for direct human consumption but for processing – into fishmeal and fish oil – and thence into pellet food for farmed fish and poultry, and even into fertiliser. The wisdom of taking vast quantities of fish for such purposes is highly questionable, since we are effectively stealing from the mouths of valued eating species, such as cod, salmon and bass, all of whom thrive on wild sand eels. It's inefficient, too – 3 kilos of wild fish, for example, are required to make the pellets to produce 1 kilo of farmed salmon flesh. But one particular use of sand eels seems to us sheer ecological insanity: in the 1980s and early 1990s the Danish government found themselves with so much surplus sand eel oil that they used to burn it in their power stations.

It seems almost self-evidently wrong to use fish to fuel a furnace. But it wasn't until 1996 that public outrage, harnessed by environmental campaigning groups including Greenpeace, brought an end to the practice of turning fish into electricity.

The long-term implications of taking such vast quantities of bait fish out of the food chain are impossible to measure. When assessing falling cod stocks, for example, how do you distinguish between the effect of catching fish by the thousands of tonnes and the effect of catching their lunch in even greater masses? You can't – but clearly there will be an effect.

Until recently, there was scant public awareness about the plight of sand eels and its ecological significance. The PR breakthrough came not from concerns about fish (a familiar tale this – see dolphins and tuna, page 451) but from concerns about another group of animals. Around 1995 the plummeting sand eel numbers were believed to be affecting the seabird population, especially around the east coast of Scotland. Certain colonies of kittiwakes and puffins seemed to be struggling to find food to raise their young; the RSPB, one of the most powerful charities in the world, was on the case in a flash. Questions were asked in the House of Lords, which subsequently led to significant areas of the sand eel fishery being closed altogether in 2000. It would be nice to think that the local cod population drew some benefit. But if they did, it was never intended. We're all for the conservation of seabirds – watching them fish more successfully than us is one of the pleasures of sea angling. But we absolutely do not see why their protection counts for more than the management of our fish stocks. Surely the conservation of species we like to eat is at least as important as the conservation of those we like to look at?

We say 'like to eat' but, as we have implied above, sand eel cuisine is not, in our view, the gastronomic heights. In French fish markets you'll often see a modest pile of dead sand eels offered alongside other small species as *fritures*, to be fried up like whitebait. Having tried this on sand eels, big and small – tossed in seasoned flour and fried in hot fat – we cannot get evangelical about them. They are soft and mushy, and surprisingly bony for their size. Getting them to crisp up, whitebait-style, is something of a struggle. In our view the best final resting place for a sand eel is not a human stomach, and certainly not the belching belly of a power station, but rather that of a cod, bass, pollack or salmon.

Freshwater fish

Salmon family

Salmon *Salmo salar*

The extraordinary and complex life cycle of the wild Atlantic salmon makes it an immensely impressive fish – but also a vulnerable one. Even as we have admired its greatness, we have inadvertently plotted its downfall. In fact, if we'd openly declared war on the fish, we could hardly have done a more thorough job – first almost annihilating wild stocks, then corralling fish into huge concentration camps – or fish farms, as they are known.

This may sound a tad melodramatic – but the history of salmon evokes passion. Here in northern Europe, the war against this fish has been waged for a century and a half. The industrial pollution of its river habitat and systematic harvesting of wild fish from the sea, estuary and river have taken a massive toll. Salmon stocks are now thought to be at a quarter of their pre-industrial abundance.

A new front opened up in the latter part of the twentieth century, as the farming of salmon became a major economic enterprise. At the time, it was vehemently argued that this could only benefit wild stocks of fish. It hasn't. Fish farming has led directly to the spread of sea lice, and to fungal infections that have killed wild fish in their tens of thousands. The farmed fish are inoculated against such problems (through additives in their feed); wild stocks, obviously, are not. And the pollution of sea lochs, by rotting fish food, fish excrement and fish-farming chemicals, has had a devastating effect on local ecosystems.

To cap it all, escaped farmed fish (up to half a million a year in Scotland alone) have crossbred with wild fish, leading to the dilution of 'river specific' stocks of salmon. Ever since the retreat of the ice sheets, wild salmon have been subtly adapting to the individual rivers in which they are born, and to which they return. Adding farmed-fish DNA to the mix is messing with 10,000 years of fish evolution. It's still not clear what the effect of these maladapted, crossbred fish will be on the future of salmon stocks.

The natural life cycle of the wild salmon places enough obstacles in the path of its survival. Faced with such man-made meddling on top, you might think it's a wonder there's a salmon left anywhere on the planet. But salmon are epic survivors, and their future doesn't look entirely gloom-laden. Their resilience comes from the extraordinary journey that is the story of every salmon's life.

The curse of the wild salmon is that it can successfully spawn only right up in the tiny, clean, bubbling, oxygen-rich streams at the head of their river, where shallow gravel beds provide the cool, aerated environment essential for eggs to grow. They'll hatch from eggs laid in these tiny tributaries, move down into larger tributaries that feed into fatter rivers, such as the Blackwater in Ireland, the Tweed in Scotland, the Wye in Wales and the Exe down here in the West Country. They hatch from their eggs in spring and live off their nutritious egg sac for a few weeks before starting to forage on their own. It takes this tiny newborn (called

MCS RATINGS: wild 5 DON'T EAT!; conventionally farmed 4; organically farmed 2 EAT MORE!

REC MINIMUM SIZE: 70cm

CLOSED SEASON: generally November–January in England and Northern Ireland, mid-October to mid-March in Wales, and December in Scotland

RECIPES: pages 133, 134–5, 138, 143, 281–2, 340–1, 355, 378, 387, 393, 403 et al.

an 'alevin') about three years of feeding on tiny aquatic insects to develop into a 'smolt': a hand-sized silver fish with black spots on its back and sides.

They grow so slowly because food is limited in British rivers, especially through the winter months when aquatic insect life is in short supply. In order to pack on the pounds and become hefty great fish, these puny smolts have to undergo a life-threatening transformation – because the food that will make real salmon of them is out at sea. Sand eels, herring, capelin, prawns, squid and crabs are the high-protein foods that can transform 20cm runts into fish that weigh up to 30 kilos and stand as tall as a man. So the smolts will swim downstream, in the river that has been their home since birth, into the estuary – the threshold to their impending greatness. But before the would-be salmon can reach the seafood banquet, it has to make the transition from fresh, sweet river water to harsh, salty seawater. It is one of an elite group of fish that are 'anadramous' – able to pass from one aquatic atmosphere to another. The change is severe: the salts in seawater attack the tissues, eyesight and gills, leaving the tiny fish weak and disorientated at the most crucial moment of its life. The mortality rate is correspondingly massive: from every 5,000 eggs laid, only fifty smolts will make it to the sea.

The lucky ones – or perhaps the brilliant ones – will have survived the journey downriver, past pike, eels, otters, mink, herons, cormorants and everything else keen to dine on fresh smolt. It will have resisted the trauma of salt water. And it will be ready to attempt the journey of several hundred miles to the salmon feeding grounds just west of Greenland or in the North Norwegian Sea.

After one to three (or even sometimes four) years of dining on sand eels, squid and prawns, fully-fledged adult salmon may weigh anything from 3 to 30 kilos. They'd better be fully fit, because they now have to embark upon an even more strenuous journey, from the deep northern sea all the way back to the same tiny tributary in which they were born. And this time they're travelling upstream.

The miracle – or madness – of a salmon's life cycle is that this fish, having experienced the death-defying danger of escaping its river environment to take its chances at sea, now has to make precisely the same journey – in reverse. Only now it's not 20cm long, running downstream with the flow, it's 60–120cm long, struggling over rocks, against the current, up rapids and even waterfalls. But it *has* to go back, or it will never reproduce.

How a salmon manages to navigate across an open ocean to the same estuary mouth that it left several years before is still a mystery. It's widely believed that they possess some incredibly accurate receptors that can sense tiny differences in the earth's magnetic field, and perhaps also in water quality, and that they use these as a homing device. But the honest truth is, nobody really knows.

Its size gives it the strength and stamina it needs but makes it no less vulnerable to predators. On the contrary, it's now the king of edible fish, the best pack of protein in the sea, and it's worth the most strenuous efforts of the sea's finest predators – seals, sharks, whales, dolphins, otters and even eagles – to try to catch one. But the most vigorous and deadly efforts come from humankind, to whom a fresh wild salmon is currently worth around £30 per kilo – or maybe five times that, served up in a fancy restaurant.

Trawl nets, drift nets, gill nets, haaf nets, ring nets and poacher's fish traps… these are just some of the death-dealing obstacles that have been put in the path of the salmon as they home in on the mouths of the rivers of their birth. At best, only five of the fifty smolts that originally survived (from the 5,000 eggs laid) will ever return to the river – which is where their problems *really* begin. They return in the spring and summer when river levels are often at their lowest. But these huge fish require a reasonable depth of water to swim in. Often they are kept waiting for weeks, stuck in shallow, stagnating pools, for rain to come and fill the river before they can continue on their way. Dams, weirs, lock gates and pumping stations will also obstruct their passage. As a result of continued pressure by salmon preservation groups, salmon 'ladders' and even cage-like lift devices have been installed to transport them upstream. But such 'luxuries' merely transform their journey from the impossible to the miraculous.

Like all great missions, there's a deadline. Salmon have to get all the way up to these streams before autumn turns to winter. To make matters worse, they stop eating as soon as they enter fresh water. Even if it takes months of waiting for rains to swell the river to make it navigable, they won't eat a morsel for sustenance. Their quest requires total focus; hunting or feeding would simply waste time and energy. The salmon will even begin to digest its own muscle tissue and bones; every nutrient is directed towards the development of the all-important eggs or sperm. As they ripen, the salmon withers. And yet still it's capable of leaping waterfalls, climbing rapids and scurrying through stony shallows no more than a couple of inches deep – just to reach the very same spot where its mother laid the egg from which it hatched. Then it has to find a mate.

By the time they arrive they are wasted, covered in fungus and scars, and very weak. Once they have laid their eggs or delivered their sperm, most will die. Only an average of 5 per cent will ever make it back to the sea, for a slim chance of healing themselves and growing strong again. An infinitesimally small elite may even breed again. The rest will do so only once, before succumbing to predators, disease or exhaustion.

Now for the promised good news: our unwitting war on the salmon is finally abating – it seems we may be capable of calling a truce. In Britain, a century and a half of industrial poisoning of our river courses is gradually being reversed. Those who for generations have set coastal salmon nets in the North Atlantic have finally responded to the radical new policy of 'buying out' (or perhaps 'selling off'?) their rights to fish. Through the actions of various fishery boards and international bodies such as the North Atlantic Salmon Conservation Organisation, they are now being paid not to catch salmon – giving migrating fish a better chance of re-entering the rivers and breeding.

The last three years on the Tweed have been the best on record, with rod catches around the 14,000 mark, of which over half are now returned as part of the conservation effort. The Tyne is currently the most productive salmon river in England – whereas in the 1970s its salmon stock was almost extinct. Salmon stocks are recovering in the Clyde, the Severn and the Thames, and in many previously industrialised streams all over Britain. Given a chance, they will recover and perform.

Yet despite these signs of hope, the wild salmon population is, at best, fragile in most European rivers. Eating wild salmon is a contentious act. Even the most fanatical salmon anglers – in fact, especially the most fanatical anglers – return almost all the fish they catch to the river alive. Their prize may be the occasional cock fish – the logic being that any gravid hen (pregnant female ready to spawn) who gets as far as a viable redd (spawning place) is unlikely to be short of male companions ready to offer their sperm. As with many threatened species, conservation of breeding females takes precedence.

You could argue (and we would) that the only people entitled to eat a wild salmon are those who are actively engaged in their conservation. If you want to join their ranks, either as an angler or simply as a concerned conservationist, you should contact the Association of Rivers Trusts (ART) in England and Wales or the Rivers and Fisheries Trusts of Scotland (RAFTS) – see the Directory, page 592. Then, once in a while, you may feel entitled, through the knowledge you've acquired and the commitment you've made, to kill, buy or eat a wild salmon.

Dare we put ourselves in this category? Perhaps writing this book has earned us a portion or two. We love to fish for salmon, and grab any chance we get. But success is rare. Through the sheer enthusiasm with which we regularly fail to catch them, I think we're entitled to call ourselves salmon conservationists.

The obvious alternative is farmed salmon, of course. It's a whole different subject and, as we've touched on above, a controversial one. It's also a whole different – and lesser – eating experience. Since it is such a key part of the fish economy, and such a critical issue in the environmental impact of fish production, we've already said plenty about it in our discussions on fish farming (see pages 35–9). But we'll summarise here, for reasons outlined there: if you're going to buy farmed salmon, make it organic.

In the kitchen, you'd be ill advised to do anything too elaborate with a wild (or organically farmed) salmon. A fillet with the scaled skin on, fried until that seasoned skin is crispy, then turned to the flesh side for just a minute (so verging on rare in the middle), is perhaps the best way to enjoy the flesh cooked. Poached and then served cold (page 355), with mayonnaise, appeals to traditionalists. If you've managed to build a cold smoker at home (see pages 161–6) and you rate its performance, then at least once in your smoking lifetime you'll want to put it to the ultimate test: smoking a whole side from a fresh wild salmon, just in from the sea. And, if your smoker comes up trumps, you may well enjoy one of the most exquisite treats of your fish-eating career.

Sea trout *Salmo trutta*

Here's an enigma. Sea trout look just like salmon; even experienced anglers find it hard to distinguish between the two. And they behave like salmon, migrating between fresh water and the sea. Yet sea trout are a quite distinct species – distant cousins only of the salmon (with which they are incapable, for example, of interbreeding).

Here's another enigma. Sea trout look nothing like the river-dwelling brown trout, which are bronze rather than silver, covered with a sprinkling of ruby-red spots, and usually much smaller. Yet a sea trout, taxonomically, actually *is* a brown trout. In fact, all sea trout and all brown trout start their lives as the same thing: *Salmo trutta* eggs. After hatching, some will remain in fresh water as brown trout, while others head out to sea and a quite different destiny – which is why we have two entries for the same species (see also pages 515–18).

You'd think it might be timing or geography that determines the future life story of any given *Salmo trutta*, but it's subtler than that. Two trout eggs laid side by side from the same mother at the same moment, in the spawning beds of the same river, may be destined for totally different futures. The eggs hatch, they mature into fry, and become 'parr', all at exactly the same time. But then, within a year or two of birth, one parr might be behaving brown troutishly, living and feeding inland, in fresh water, while its sibling, though it still looks like a brown trout, begins to change into a sea trout. There are many factors that determine which direction a little *Salmo trutta* will take – environment, the amount of food available, and an element of genetic predisposition. But to the casual observer, it's an unpredictable and mysterious toss-up.

Before it even leaves the river and heads to the ocean, the soon-to-be sea trout will start to 'silver up' – an ingot of bronze dashed with rubies becoming a bar of polished platinum subtly speckled with black. Then, when it enters the estuary and meets salt water for the first time, the trout has to perform the complicated biological somersault of all anadromous fish (those born in fresh water who migrate to sea to feed and then return to fresh water to spawn). It grows salt glands in its gills to cope with the increased salinity that would otherwise quickly kill it. And it starts to hanker after seafood.

Two or three years later, those two siblings are living very different lives. The brown trout, having not moved more than a mile from where it was born, weighs anywhere from 100–600g. The sea trout, which by now tips the scales

MCS RATINGS: line-caught 3; organically farmed 2

REC MINIMUM SIZE: 40cm (but check local regulations)

CLOSED SEASON: generally November–March

RECIPES: pages 172, 220, 281–2, 308–9, 355 et al.

at anywhere up to 9kg, is meanwhile many miles away, searching the wide
ocean for protein-packed prawns, crabs, small fish and squid. The sea trout will
continue to grow at a rate of one or two kilos a year, while the stay-at-home
brownie, who has a more frugal diet of tiny aquatic insects, may remain
a stunted sprat all his life.

One thing we do know about these two siblings is that the adventurous sea-
faring one is much more likely to be female. The seafood diet is good for growth
and fecundity, and the most successful females eventually grow into magnificent
sleek silver torpedoes of anything up to 10kg. Meanwhile the males, waiting for
another drowned fly and reluctant to move even as far as the next downstream
pool, are lucky to put on 50g a year. But oddly enough, female sea trout and male
brownies may yet come together to breed. Since a disproportionate amount of sea
trout are female, they inevitably accept as their mates small brown trout who
have never gone to sea – in other words, the fit female supermodels are content
to be served by the runty little males. Which is somehow consoling.

Generally, sea trout don't venture nearly so far as salmon in their maritime
mission to gain weight and become healthy breeders. British-born salmon will
range several hundred miles to the seas off Greenland (see page 508), whereas
the latest research suggests that most sea trout stay within a radius of fifty or so
miles from the estuary of their river of birth. All but a tiny fraction of the salmon
who migrate to Greenland only ever do the journey and the re-entry to fresh
water once. Most of them die after spawning. Sea trout, on the other hand, by
staying local are able to shuttle back and forth from river to sea quite regularly.
And so they can spawn several times – in some cases over a dozen.

In many ways, sea trout should be the more plentiful of the two species. They don't submit themselves to the same levels of stress and danger and they are, in theory, more adaptable to anadromous change, simply because they 'practise' it more often. Yet in recent years the sea trout populations around our coast have been falling at an alarming rate.

One of the identified causes of sea trout decline is the salmon. Not wild, but farmed. One drawback to farming salmon (there are quite a few – see page 508) is the vast number of sea lice a concentration of caged salmon will attract. Migrating sea trout increasingly have to run the gauntlet of nearby salmon farms, and the resident lice love to hitch a ride on a passing sea trout. These parasites do rapid damage to their host fish, sucking nutrients through its skin, leaving it weakened and covered in sores. Already weak from the stress of moving from salt to fresh water, sea trout succumb easily. Fatalities in some areas are reckoned to be in the thousands – and most, of course, are females who were looking to get back to the river and breed.

When not under pressure from sea lice and the like, sea/brown trout can breed and spread extremely successfully. In Argentina, Chile and New Zealand, where British brown trout eggs were seeded in the late nineteenth century (see page 516), they have flourished and, by virtue of their double life as sea trout, successfully populated other rivers adjacent to the ones into which they were introduced. Unlike salmon, sea trout are quite broadminded about the fresh water they return to in order to breed in. Since they have several chances at spawning, tactically it makes sense to ring the changes, spreading their genes through different rivers in the same area. Southern hemisphere sea trout have grown huge – the record in Argentina stands at over 15 kilos – and even the landlocked brownies, whose food supply tends to be far richer than that of their European cousins, can reach 10 kilos and more (in Britain, only farmed and ferox brownies ever get close to this kind of size).

One thing that can be said of all sea trout is that they are truly delicious. They are not as rich and oily as a salmon fresh in from the sea; they have lighter, paler flesh with a more delicate flavour and finer texture. They are more 'sea fresh', though, than brown or rainbow trout, without a trace of muddiness. When we have a plump sea trout of over a kilo in our hands, there aren't many fish we'd swap it for. Whether fried (pages 308–9) or baked (page 220), very lightly cured (page 172) or even completely raw (page 134), it will be a matchless treat.

You could argue that a species under pressure should not be caught and eaten at all. At the same time, as with salmon, those who love to catch and cook these wild fish are often those working hardest to protect them. It seems harsh to begrudge them the occasional fish for the table. We have a good relationship with the Axe Valley Fly Fishers' Association, which is working hard to improve spawning conditions in the lower reaches of the Axe, Yarty and other local rivers. They are looking at the streams on our land at River Cottage HQ to see if they might make a suitable site for hatching boxes (artificial shelters that improve the survival rate of the newly hatched fish). In return, we get the odd evening's fishing – though neither of us has yet managed to land an Axe sea trout.

Fresh wild sea trout isn't easy to buy and, given current anxieties about stocks, nor should it be. In the West Country we see them occasionally in fishmongers during the summer months. The returning fish are usually caught in gill nets as they enter the estuaries. They are often outstanding value: a fraction of the price of wild salmon and every bit as good. We'd sympathise if you felt unable to resist buying the odd one. Line-caught fish, if you can find them, would be preferable. Should you feel the need to appease your conscience after such a treat, you could always make a donation to the Atlantic Salmon Trust (atlanticsalmontrust.org), since their conservation work encompasses sea trout as well as wild salmon.

Farmed sea trout are increasingly coming on to the market. Some argue that they are better suited to life in a sea cage than salmon are. Others who champion the wild sea trout emphatically disagree. As with any type of fish farming, it's the source and content of the feed, the location of the farm and the quality of the water that determines how environmentally friendly (and indeed how tasty) that fish will be. With farmed fish, you really should find out what you are buying before you hand over your money (see page 38).

But the best sea trout you'll ever eat – and arguably the only one you *should* eat – is the fish you have caught yourself. Most sea trout are caught in rivers by fly-fishing. They're not easy to catch (although often easier than sulky salmon) and it's best to fish for them at and after nightfall, as they're easily spooked during the day. Casting a fly rod at night in a river surrounded by trees is often fraught with pain, grief and fairly profane swearing. But should you actually manage to catch, cook and eat a sea trout, you'll remember all that misery and suffering as some of the best fun you've ever had fishing.

Brown trout *Salmo trutta*

While Queen Victoria sat on the throne, her armed forces were on the march, painting the map of the world pink. For good or ill, they carried with them the values of colonialism – and some big boxes of brown trout eggs.

Back home in Britain, the noble sport of fly-fishing for trout was in its infancy. Hitherto, catching trout and other freshwater fish by rod and line had involved the use of natural bait. A worm, a maggot, a slug or a grasshopper threaded on to a hook would, of course, tempt a fish, because these are the things a fish likes to eat. But in the mind of a gentleman, this was so obvious and easy as to be unsporting. Surely a fairer challenge would be to fashion something by hand that *looked* like a trout's lunch. For example, to tie together scraps of fur and feather to imitate a daddy longlegs with such accuracy that a brown trout was duped into swallowing it – now *that* would require skill and intellect.

To master this new art, the budding fly fisherman would need a grasp of entomology and an understanding of trout feeding habits, as well as some insight into light levels and water quality. He would need to study books, to keep journals and to have enough expendable income to afford state-of-the-art fly tackle, which was at that time in limited supply and very labour-intensive to manufacture. Using the latest rods made of bamboo canes that had been split, whittled and reassembled, fly lines made out of pure woven silk and clear tippet lines made from catgut, the aspiring fly-angler would present his hand-tied artificial lure to the fish.

Naturally many such gentlemen were serving officers in Her Majesty's Army, charged with the vital work of defending and extending the Empire. But the prospect of being posted to some far-off land where their beloved trout didn't exist filled them with dismay. So why not take the brown trout with them?

MCS RATINGS: line-caught 3; organically farmed 2

REC MINIMUM SIZE: 25cm (but check local regulations)

CLOSED SEASON: generally 1 October to 14 March

RECIPES: pages 134–5, 200, 244, 403 et al.

The plan was to introduce them to likely looking rivers and lakes around the colonies. But it soon became clear that the fragile fish would not travel well; their eggs, on the other hand, were a different matter. Refrigerated transport and electric circulation pumps – vital tools of modern fish farming and live egg transportation – were as yet uninvented. But what this madcap scheme had on its side was the full logistical resources of the British Civil Service, coupled to the determination of some deeply competitive individuals. The race – to find a method that would keep the eggs alive during sea voyages of several months – was on.

Scottish trout from Loch Leven were chosen because they were known to be a hardy breed that could survive cold winters and scant food. Their fertilised eggs, gathered from the spawning burns that fed the loch, were gently packed between layers of damp, living moss for the long journey. The moss was stacked in custom-built wooden crates with drainage holes top and bottom, into which fresh water, filtered through charcoal, was poured daily. The living eggs were developing into tiny trout even as they crossed the world.

The first successful acclimatisation took place in India in 1863, followed by Tasmania in 1864, elsewhere in Australia and New Zealand in 1867. South Africa and Canada, Chile and Argentina were soon colonised too. Within twenty years, the small, ruby-spotted Scottish strain of wild brown trout had spread to every continent of the world bar Antarctica. And the European sea trout had hitched a ride too – being, genetically, the same species, how could it not?

In truth, some of these trout actually preferred their new homes. They thrived in waters that, though similarly cool and clear, were far more abundant in food than the dour Scottish lakes and rivers from whence they came. They also often benefited from an absence of predators and disease. In the Southern hemisphere there were no salmonid competitors – just a variety of rather placid bottom-feeders that posed little threat to the arrivistes. In Scotland, to catch a brown trout of even 5lb was (and still is) exceptional. But in New Zealand, within a dozen years of introduction, fish of 20lb and more were being recorded. In British waters, until recently, only the ferox strain of brown trout ever attained anything like that kind of size – a 10 to 15lb fish being the catch of a lifetime. These ferox trout are wild fish that have grown large enough to take on other small fish as prey, and so achieve the potential to grow much larger. Mostly they cannibalise their own kin – smaller brown trout, which are sometimes the only other fish in the water they inhabit. Today, farmed brownies can also be reared to this kind of size, simply by fattening them up on pelleted fish food. They are released into commercial fisheries, often along with similarly bloated rainbows, where anglers will pay for the chance to catch a double-figure fish. But it's not what a Victorian gentleman would have called sport.

As brown trout thrived around the world, they started to struggle at home. The Industrial Revolution brought terrible pollution to our inland waterways – and brown trout are particularly sensitive. They need clean, well-oxygenated water in order to survive. In many ways they are the canary in the watery coal mine – if brown trout turn belly up, then other species will soon follow suit.

The good news is that, after suffering over a century of pollution, our native wild brown trout are on the up again. De-industrialisation and strict legislative action against polluters mean that our waterways are now the cleanest they have been for over 150 years. Once again, brown trout are populating rivers where they hadn't been caught in over a century. They can do this because of their double life as sea trout – fish that leave one river to feed at sea may return to spawn in another (see page 514). Some of the resulting progeny will become the river's resident brownies, and may never go out to sea. Sea trout have recently been caught in the Thames in central London – and wild brownies found a hundred or more miles upstream in places like Lechlade.

It is the larger, female sea trout, returning to the river systems, that will be the most successful breeders, and their eggs may well be fertilised by 'local' male brownies who have never left the river (of the resulting progeny, only a few, mostly females, will go out to sea). However, amongst landlocked populations of brown trout, such as those in Scottish hill lochs, even fairly tiny females (of no more than half a pound) will develop and lay eggs.

Those brown trout that have settled for the freshwater life are pretty fiercely territorial. In rivers, they compete to take possession of a specific 'lie' – a strategic position in the current, in the lee of a rock or bend perhaps, to provide them with maximum security and maximum feeding potential. Once a fish has found a good 'lie', it will hold it for days, or even weeks, until it is forced away by a bigger fish or a predator. It will position itself with its head facing upstream, gills flaring to extract oxygen from the running water. Trout don't so much 'hunt' for their food as station themselves in the spot where an insect lunch is most likely to be served up on the passing current. They'd rather not move more than a few feet to grab it (and their eye sockets can swivel upwards to spot any food being carried past in the current). This all adds to the art of catching them. First you need to spot your fish. You may need to stalk it, to get within casting range. You then have to choose a convincing-looking fly and cast it to land in a natural manner within the feeding zone of your chosen fish. You can perhaps sense the thrill of this kind of fishing – it is, after all, the reason that brown trout have spread all over the world.

We love catching wild brown trout and we love eating them. But in many truly wild fisheries, particularly among the chalk streams here in the Southwest (such as the Piddle, the Puddle and the Stour), most fish are returned to the water alive in the interests of conservation. Taking one or two good fish for the pot per season is an honoured convention in many club-run fisheries. The mayfly hatch is the most exciting time to fish. For several weeks in late May and early June, these ephemeral insects, with their errant wings and fat, long bodies, emerge in such numbers that the trout lose all sense of caution and are moved to a feeding frenzy. The trout can still be heart-stoppingly hard to hook, though. Such is the generosity of the natural banquet that the artificial imitations have to look, and land, just right if they're going to persuade.

We probably get to catch more brownies on Scottish holidays than in Dorset downtime. It's particularly good fun fishing with imitation daddy longlegs on wild Scottish hill lochs. Here the fish are often small but plentiful – they breed successfully, but lack the food supply to maintain a weight much over half a pound. There is generally quite a relaxed take on killing these fish for the kitchen.

The brown trout that you find on sale (at fishmongers, supermarkets and by mail order) will invariably have been farmed. Truly wild brown trout are generally too small (and too difficult to catch) to find their way on to a wet fish counter; even at 3 to 5 years old, a wild brown trout will often weigh well under a pound. But farmed brownies can be delicious, especially if they've been reared in a location where they can feed on some natural aquatic insect life as well as their processed pellets (which is much more likely to be the scenario in an organic trout farm). There is no real difference in eating quality between a farmed brown and a farmed rainbow trout – in both cases it's the quality of the farming practice that counts (see below).

A genuinely wild brown trout is an even better prospect in the kitchen. Its taste will reflect the quality of the water from which it has been taken – clean as flint if it comes from a Dorset chalk stream; lightly peaty if it comes from a Highland burn or hill loch. Those that have been feeding on freshwater shrimps (mainly summer fish caught in the south of England) have a distinctive pink-orange flesh and are the tastiest of all.

They're easy to cook – by pan, barbecue, or wrapped in foil and baked in the oven. Bigger isn't always better either. If you're lucky enough to get a chance to fish on one of those Scottish hill lochs we mentioned, then treat yourself to a pair of little brownies. Rolled in oatmeal, then fried in butter or bacon fat, there's no better angler's breakfast.

The only trout that'll top a wild brownie for taste is a wild sea trout. As it happens to be exactly the same species, biologically speaking, perhaps that's no surprise. See pages 512–15 for more on what happens when a brown trout embarks on this extraordinary biological adventure.

Rainbow trout *Oncorhynchus mykiss*

While brown trout are seen as a noble, honourable member of the salmonid family – a fabulous British colonial gift to the world (see pages 515–16) – rainbow trout are not always spoken of with such admiration, either by anglers or by chefs. To many they are flashy, garish American invaders who give trout a bad name: they're oversexed, oversized and over here. And the fact that they often taste muddy doesn't help their cause.

But in truth, any problems we have with them are largely of our own making. They are only here because of the trout angler's lack of patience with our native brown trout, which, for all their pedigree, can be moody, awkward little buggers. When conditions don't suit them, they will sulk in deep water, eating nothing and avoiding eye contact with even the most artfully tied fly. In contrast, rainbow trout are usually enthusiastic and obliging, ready to snap at almost anything.

Consequently, almost all commercial trout fisheries – where fly fishermen pay to come and fish for stocked, rather than wild, trout – will keep some rainbows as well as browns. So when it's too hot, too cold or too something-you-can't-quite-put-your-finger-on for the brownies to bite, the rainbows, with a bit of luck, will still come out to play.

This mix-and-match approach to stocking our lakes and rivers began in the mid-nineteenth century. At the same time as Britain was exporting brown trout to the far corners of the Empire, it was also importing rainbow trout from their native west coast of America. In 1854 the first boxes of rainbow trout eggs were brought to Britain by steamships and seeded in lakes and rivers. They survived, but never really thrived. It soon became apparent that rainbow trout would struggle to breed naturally in Britain, mainly because our average water temperatures are too cold. Whilst rainbows will feed, grow and stay healthy in relatively cold water, for breeding they like it a bit warmer than we can

MCS RATINGS: line-caught 3; organically farmed 2; farmed 3

REC MINIMUM SIZE: 25cm (only relevant for wild fish)

CLOSED SEASON: no compulsory UK closed season (but check local regulations); avoid October–December (spawning)

RECIPES: pages 134–5, 200, 220, 244, 403 et al.

generally muster. And so, apart from a few rare resident breeding populations (for example, in the Derbyshire Wye and the Erfon in Wales), every single rainbow trout in Britain has been artificially bred.

Initially rainbows were bred purely for sporting purposes. The first commercial fish farm in the UK, breeding plate-sized rainbows for the 'table market', was started in 1950. Now there are over 350 trout farms nationwide, producing rainbows for food as well as for stocking and restocking our sporting fisheries.

The market for farmed rainbow trout for eating has seen a steady increase over the decades. But the quality of such fish varies hugely, depending, as you might expect, on the way in which they are farmed. Freshwater fish will always taste of the water in which they live. So when rainbows are crammed into small, muddy ponds, which soon become polluted with their own excrement and uneaten food that sinks to the bottom, it's no great surprise that they'll end up tasting mucky. In contrast, spring-fed, gravel-bottomed ponds, where the water is constantly changed and naturally filtered, will produce far sweeter-tasting fish, provided they are not overstocked.

The Soil Association now certifies organically farmed rainbows. It stipulates strict limits on stocking densities and the use of chemicals and insists on additive-free, sustainably sourced fish feed. One excellent trout farm in Wiltshire, Purely Organic (see the Directory, page 591), from which we regularly buy fish, has holding ponds downstream from an organic watercress farm. So, apart from the pellet feed they receive, the trout also have freshwater shrimps, snails and insects washed downstream to them from the watercress beds. The farm's owner, Tony Free, reckons that well over half their feed comes from this natural source. This kind of mutual back-scratching, fish-and-food-farming relationship is exactly the kind of aquaculture that makes sense to us. More power to you, Mr Free.

If you're going to dine on rainbow trout (and we'd recommend you do), we think you should find out where your fish was farmed and what it was fed on. Unfortunately, farmed fish provenance is generally invisible. It requires good labelling, or a knowledgeable fishmonger, to tell you the story of the fish you're thinking of buying. Such guidance is not always easy to come by – particularly in a supermarket. You should always press for it, but if you can't get it you can at least look hard at your trout...

There are some visible clues that will tell you what sort of a farm life your trout lived. Check the fins and tail. If the fins are worn and split, or bloody, then the fish have been cramped and badly handled. Tails should have sharp edges. If the tail or fins are rounded and stubby, they've been worn away by frequent rubbing against net mesh – in other words, the fish have been kept in a very confined space. Any lumps or fungus in the gills or sores on the head or flanks are also a sign of poor water quality and/or overstocking.

Meanwhile, the fly fisherman's appetite for the feisty rainbow is now on the decline and so, correspondingly, are stocking rates in our fisheries. This is due to a sort of sporting snobbery, borne of a desire to turn the clock back to a time when only pure, native trout roamed our rivers. It's a bit like the current trend for chopping down all the Norwegian pine forests that were planted in the 1970s and replacing them with broad-leaf, indigenous trees. One can understand these purist sentiments. And perhaps it's right to phase out the stocking of these American-spawned salmonid in some of our more historic rivers, such as the Test and the Itchen. But a shift in conservation sensibilities doesn't make a spruce a 'bad' tree, or a rainbow trout a 'bad' fish.

On the contrary, rainbows are a great fish. We should be producing them to the highest possible quality, enjoying the sport they offer in our lakes and reservoirs and eating them with pleasure. They could hardly be more kitchen-friendly. Plate-sized rainbows are easy to cook by any of the obvious methods: baked in foil with butter, a splash of wine and a few herbs (page 220); fried to get the skin crispy (page 296); or barbecued. Bigger rainbows smoke and cure beautifully too: gravad trout and cold-smoked rainbows are two of our favourite ways of honouring any fish we catch that tip the scales at over 2 kilos.

So, let's call a truce and stop the rainbow bashing. On the end of our lines or in our kitchens, a well-fed rainbow from good, sweet water is always welcome – no matter which side of the Atlantic its forefathers came from.

Grayling *Thymallus thymallus*

There's a saying amongst purist, old-school trout anglers and river keepers: 'The only good grayling is a dead grayling.' There was a time, a couple of decades ago, when any grayling caught in the chalk-stream rivers of southern England was unceremoniously knocked on the head and, quite probably, tossed over the hedge. What a senseless waste of a fine sporting fish and its surprisingly palatable flesh.

From a trout-centric point of view, it's easy to see why grayling might have been unloved. For starters, they were aliens – at least to our southern chalk streams – having been introduced from northern English rivers. The Ouse system of East Yorkshire originally acquired its grayling via the Danube basin, courtesy of the last Ice Age. These grayling have been present in our northern rivers for many thousands of years; those in the south for just a couple of hundred.

Grayling breed like aquatic rabbits and lay up to three times as many eggs as trout. They also compete with trout for food but, being better equipped, they win. Grayling have a down-slung mouth and downward-swivelling eyes, so they can feed from the river bed as easily as from the surface. Trout have beady eyes too, and lightning reactions, but they aren't made to feed from the river bed. So, in a harsh winter, grayling will survive whilst trout go hungry or die. And among the things grayling will eat during lean times are trout eggs. To the fly fishermen, a fish that snacks upon the unborn progeny of the hallowed trout is just too evil. Because of this, the closed season for trout was traditionally open season for grayling. River keepers would net them and electro-fish for them (along with the equally loathed pike), in the hope of giving the trout an easier ride, come spring.

However, this wasn't just river management, this was snobbery, fuelled by the fact that, as well as being alien to southern rivers, grayling were also classified (erroneously, as it later turned out) as a 'coarse' fish in the 1878 Freshwater Act. Technically, coarse fish are generally non-migratory fish such as perch, roach, pike or carp that spawn in the spring, whereas game fish are the salmonid species – trout, salmon and the char of the Lake District – that spawn in the autumn and, given the opportunity, migrate to the sea. But in truth, the distinction is a human one. In practical terms, coarse fish are freshwater fish that ordinary rod-and-line anglers like to catch, using simple, natural baits, such as live worms or maggots. Game fish, on the other hand, can – or rather should – be caught on a 'fly', which is a man-made confection of fur and feather that

MCS RATING: not rated
REC MINIMUM SIZE: 30cm
CLOSED SEASON: generally 15 March to 15 June
RECIPES: pages 200, 289, 330

imitates an aquatic creature. Once fly-fishing had been invented, coarse fishing was deemed crude and unsporting – suitable only for the working classes.

Grayling drew the wrath of the fly-fishing elite simply because it swam so happily in the same rivers as the trout. The fact that it would take a fly as readily as any trout did not seem to let it off the hook (so to speak) at least for a couple of centuries. It was the plebeian impostor, and was duly punished.

As if a class divide was not enough, the grayling also reflected the geographical one between north and south. Up north on the rivers of Yorkshire, Lancashire and Derbyshire, grayling enjoyed a more honourable reputation, even among the gentry. This was no doubt partly because they are meant to be there. Northern coarse and fly anglers on rivers such as the Wharfe, Ure and Swale were content to catch them, each by their own methods, and they loved and respected grayling, calling it 'the lady of the stream'. They still do to this day.

In the last twenty years or so, the southern attitude towards grayling has softened. The bad habit of culling them by all available means has been reassessed. Indeed, grayling has been reclassified since the original Freshwater Act, and now enjoys the distinction of being 'the fourth game fish' (after salmon, sea trout and trout). Apart from being ready to take a fly, all game fish have to display an adipose fin – a small, nub-like bump, located between the dorsal fin and the tail. Happily the grayling does. It is now officially a member of the sacred Salmonidae family. And it's been welcomed into polite society.

It's certainly dressed for social elevation. The outstanding feature of the grayling is its stunning sail-like, rainbow-speckled dorsal fin. It's not just for show, though, it's highly functional. It helps a fish hold station in a fast-flowing stream; it can 'bristle' an alarm to the rest of the shoal; and it can tenderly wrap over the back of a mate during spawning, to maximise fertilisation potential.

Whenever we fish for grayling, simply seeing one in the water, sail flaring as you try to bring it to the bank, is a great part of the pleasure of the day. And so is taking one or two home for supper. They can be cooked as you'd cook trout. We've smoked them, both hot and cold; we've baked, grilled and poached them too. We've had them hot topped with butter and toasted almonds, and cold with herby mayonnaise (see page 355). But perhaps the best grayling we ever shared was an early-spring fish from the River Wylie in Wiltshire. We sizzled it on the riverbank in a pan still greasy with sausage and bacon fat from our breakfast fry-up, then ate it scattered with just-picked, roughly chopped wild garlic leaves.

Other freshwater fish

Perch *Perca fluviatilis*

Perch are cheeky and gregarious fish, ducking and diving, bobbing and weaving, scheming and teaming up with their mates to traumatise the neighbourhood minnows. We're rather fond of perch – but not half as fond of them as they seem to be of themselves.

In their freshwater habitat of rivers, lakes and reservoirs, they are pretty much top dog. They know it, and have the uniform to show it: bright scarlet fins, black, warrior-like stripes down both flanks and an array of flesh-piercing spikes fanned through their fins. Only a pike, or a bigger perch, is likely to see them off (or have them for lunch).

If you watch the surface of a lake on a balmy summer's evening, you'll often see a frantic scattering of tiny, fry-sized fish leaping out of the water. These are juveniles (of any number of different species) being hunted by packs of omnivorous perch. These bullies corral the jittery juniors into cowering bunches and take it in turns to charge them with their gaping jaws and bristling spikes. Perch are, in their spiky, strutting way, very much the freshwater equivalent of their sea bass cousins. And they love doing to minnows exactly what bass do to sprats. So it should be no great surprise that, like bass, perch are really rather good to eat.

The Victorians loved to eat perch, which they ranked as high as any other freshwater fish. Favourite recipes of the day included Mrs Beeton's perch stewed with wine, and boiled perch with Dutch sauce. This fondness for perch may in part have been due to a perceived glut of salmon. Before the Industrial Revolution polluted our major rivers, salmon – hulking and plentiful – was considered a poor man's meal. Perch – small and colourful, with firm, pearly white flesh – was posh.

In fact, the Victorians held the perch in such esteem that it was the only fish, apart from their beloved brown trout, chosen to colonise the fresh waters of the expanding Empire (see pages 515–16). Cleverly transported as unhatched eggs in barrels of living wet moss, trout and perch were transplanted to the furthest corners of the globe.

The perch weren't always welcome. For example, in Australia, where they were introduced in 1860 as a sport and table fish, they ran amok. Within ten years the Inland Fisheries Service had declared them a 'noxious fish pest', because they had depleted, and in some cases eradicated, indigenous species. To this day, *Perca fluviatilis* is still near the top of Australia's most-hated-pest list. Huge populations of perch, stunted through overbreeding, now dominate waters that were once home to a diverse range of species.

Perch's gradual demise as an eating fish – in the face of ever-increasing competition from sea fish – was sealed by the Second World War. The best-known perch fishery, on Lake Windermere, had been trapping tons of fish each year,

MCS RATING: not rated

REC MINIMUM SIZE: 25cm

SEASON: avoid April–July (spawning)

RECIPES: pages 200, 289, 330

both for food and fertiliser. As the wartime scarcity of protein took hold, perch meat became commonplace. It was even tinned and re-branded as 'Windermere perchines', an austerity substitute for tinned sardines. But, as with so many of these make-do-and-pretend wartime foods, people came to resent them. Perch never recovered its former posh image – while our enthusiasm for cod was becoming a blinkered obsession. To cap it all, in the 1950s perch went on to suffer from a terrible plague that left the big Lake District populations reduced to a fraction of their previous size.

Perch today are in fine fettle again, with huge numbers in rivers, lakes and reservoirs all around Britain. Yet, like so many 'Great British Fish', actually buying a fresh perch to eat in this country is not easy. Markets such as Billingsgate do sell perch that has been netted from the Lake District or Ireland, but nearly all of it is exported to Europe. In Britain it's easier to buy a Nile perch, imported from Egypt, than it is to buy one of our own natives. By contrast, in northern European countries such as Finland and Sweden, native wild perch are still at the top of the locals' fish wish-list, prized even above trout and salmon. In Scandinavia, perch farming is a thriving form of aquaculture. It's worth noting that we have just the right conditions to do it here. Where are you, perch entrepreneurs?

Until we get a response to that rhetorical question, if you want to eat a perch, you'll just have to go and fish one out yourself. Patrolling their waters, as they do, in an ever-hungry rabble, they're not difficult to catch – at least until they grow big, solitary and wary. Three-quarter pounders, which make fabulous eating, can often be caught in good numbers, one after the other, if you find a good shoal and have the right bait.

Nearly every freshwater angler has caught a perch at some stage. Like mackerel, they are often the first fish a novice will catch. They're a classic 'bamboo-and-string-with-bent-pin-and-garden-worm' fish. They will eagerly attack a worm or maggot bait, and always put up a good fight, often coming reluctantly to the landing net with colours blazing and spikes flared indignantly. The best perch bait of all is minnow, either dead or alive. Minnows can be caught in simple traps made out of empty bottles that have been baited with bread. Fish them with a small treble hook under a float, or simply lying dead on the bottom, and await the attention of a hungry perch.

To cook your catch bankside, collect some wood and make a fire. As it burns down to hot embers, wrap each fish in a couple of pages of newspaper (two broadsheet, three tabloid) and dip them in the stream till the paper is thoroughly soaked. Place them on a grill and steam-bake over the fire (see page 200). When the paper is all but burned away, remove from the heat and cool for a minute or two. Then peel off the perch skin with the paper and season with a spot or two of butter, plus some salt and pepper. Get to it with fork or fingers and you'll soon see what the Victorians were excited about. And please call us when you've started your own perch farm.

Pike *Esox lucius*

Like so many predators that hang around at the top of the food chain, pike are bone idle. They may be hunters, but they're thrifty with their fuel. They want to avoid the vicious circle of constant hunting to replace the calories they just burned in the last hunt. And so, with their tiger-like green and gold camouflage, they are lurk-and-pounce merchants. They hang out among weeds and underwater obstacles, waiting for lunch to practically deliver itself.

The biggest and baddest pike are female. They live longer than males (to over thirty years, as opposed to the males' fifteen to twenty) and they grow much larger too. There's another reason male pike may well be cut off in their prime: mating. It's a risky business for him because when his job of fertilising the female's eggs is done, he stops looking like a potential father to her children and starts looking like a very tempting post-coital snack. From her point of view, it would be foolish to waste him.

Pike inhabit most forms of fresh water: rivers, gravel pits, lakes, reservoirs and ponds. They aren't fussy – they don't care if the water is clear or murky. Anglers like to say of pike that they 'thrive on neglect'. Before he saw the light and moved to Dorset, Nick regularly fished the ancient network of London canals and pulled out some deeply impressive pike (well in excess of 9 kilos) from amongst the shopping trolleys and joy-ridden scooters.

The biggest pike are the ones with easy access to the best food. In the last twenty years, increasing numbers of huge pike (13 kilos-plus) have been caught from large reservoirs that have been stocked with trout for angling. Providing a hungry pike with a constant diet of pellet-fed trout is a bit like feeding a sumo wrestler with fresh piglets on demand.

The angler's relationship with pike has changed over the centuries. Up until Victorian times the pike was regarded as a formidable sporting fish, being hard fighting yet co-operative: ready to attack a bait or lure in almost all weathers. Real fish baits – from small live roach to dead sprats or herrings – have always tempted pike. But the increasing sophistication of artificial lures, such as spinners, spoons and plugs, extended the culture of pike fishing into a wily art. It was also a culinary endeavour, since the flesh of the pike was highly rated as food. Pike was a noble fish pursued by both gentleman and yeoman.

MCS RATING: not rated
REC MINIMUM SIZE: N/A
CLOSED SEASON: generally 15 March to 15 June
RECIPES: pages 220, 281–2, 289, 330

Then the Victorians — at least the upper echelons — were seduced by a new development in angling: the art of dry fly-fishing for trout (for more, see page 515). The gentry turned its focus to managing rivers and chalk streams so that the wild brown trout could breed and grow with maximum mollycoddling and minimal molestation. As the principal trout killers, pike became *persona non grata*. In the hallowed fly-fishing rivers, such as the Test, Frome and Itchen, the pike culling began.

For most of the next century, trout fishermen were at war with the pike. They (or their river keepers) would net, gaffe, trap and catch them on night lines baited with minnows and the like. And instead of eating or selling them, they would usually throw them away with disdain. In any case, with the boom time in commercial fishing for species such as cod, herring and Dover sole, the public appetite was now for sea fish.

By the mid-twentieth century, even coarse anglers (who theoretically welcome all comers) had begun to persecute pike because they were known to devour roach, bream and all other freshwater fish. Coarse fishing was booming as a leisure activity. Gravel pits and reservoirs all over the country were increasingly run as coarse fisheries — a nice little earner, as they could charge anglers for day and season tickets. By the 1970s, up to four million people in Britain were regular anglers — more went coarse fishing on a Saturday than went to watch the football. But a rampant pike or two could easily ruin a fishery (or so it was widely believed at the time). Consequently, most anglers would kill any pike they caught by chance. Some fisheries turned to the relatively new techniques of electric fishing, by which all fish in a given strip of water are stunned with an electric current, so the less desirable species can be netted and removed. Soon some waters were even able to declare themselves completely pike-free.

Eel *Anguilla anguilla*

On moonless autumn nights, in streams, ponds and ditches throughout the land, an almighty slithering begins. In the Fenland drains and the Somerset Levels, in Highland burns and Welsh ditches, the shortening days are the trigger for big, dirty-yellow eels, with black eyes and nicotine-stained bellies, to up sticks. They leave their home water, slithering across wet grass if necessary, and slide into the nearest rain-swollen river, to embark upon a journey that seems implausible – even impossible.

All over Europe, the eels are mobilising. From the Rhine, the Loire, the Ebro and the Danube they are heading, at the same time, to the same place: a fabled body of water to the east of Bermuda, known as the Sargasso Sea.

The Sargasso is a sea within a sea, bounded by ocean currents: to the west by the Gulf Stream, to the north by the North Atlantic drift, to the east by the Canary current, and to the south by the North Atlantic equatorial current. It has its own counter-clockwise vortex, known as the Central Gyre, which can hold millions of tons of floating seaweed called sargassum, and other marine debris. Boats have often fallen foul of its strange forces. Spanish sailors travelling to and from the New World called these the 'Horse Latitudes', as those who got the worst of them were trapped in the vortex for weeks on end, and would slaughter their horses to conserve water and extend their rations. And it is to this place that every European eel heads, on a journey of thousands of miles, to find a mate and to perpetuate a species that is now in desperate decline.

What we know about eel spawning in the western Atlantic has only been understood for a matter of decades. Before then, our understanding of the sex life of the eel was largely conjecture (and fantasy) until the 1920s, when final proof, in the shape of minute, new-born eel larvae, was extracted from the depths of the Sargasso Sea. It's a complex tale and, if you fancy unravelling it some time, it's compellingly told in *The Book of Eels* by Tom Fort (HarperCollins, 2003).

Before the 'Sargasso proof', some bizarre theories about the origins of eels had circulated over the centuries: they were produced from the entrails of the earth; they grew from a mixture of horse's hair and river water; they condensed from dew drops; they sprung spontaneously from decaying mud; they even grew from the hair of dead sailors lost at sea.

The truth – only marginally less mysterious – is that an eel's life cycle is an epic round trip, from mighty ocean to muddy ditch and back, like that of a salmon in reverse (see page 508). A salmon is anadromous – it's born in fresh water and migrates to the sea, only to return to the river where it was born, as a mature, spawning adult. Whereas eels are catadromous – they are hatched out at sea, move to fresh water to feed and mature, then migrate back to sea in order to spawn.

As these fat, greeny-yellow river eels prepare to slither back towards the sea, a transformation begins. They turn silver and their eyes grow big and develop blue-sensitive eye pigments, required to see in salt water. Migrating silver eels, in their single-minded journey downstream, in the company of hundreds if not thousands of their fellows, also become easier to trap – and, according to those who trade in them, tastier to eat.

Once they reach the estuary mouth, it's believed (though not proved) that the eels then use the Earth's magnetic field as a navigational aid to guide them to the Sargasso Sea. Their mating – which is assumed to take place at great depth

MCS RATING: 5 DON'T EAT!
REC MINIMUM SIZE: N/A
SEASON: N/A
RECIPE: page 175

– has never been observed, though it seems certain that once they've spawned the adult eels die. The eel eggs then hatch into flat, leaf-shaped larvae no bigger than your smallest fingernail. Within a few months they will have grown to about an inch in length, but retaining their larval form. These larvae have no fins, tail, wings or method of propulsion. They are effectively little underwater 'sails', relying totally on the transatlantic currents to carry them away from the churning Sargasso, back towards Europe. This journey will take about a year.

As the swarms of larvae approach the European coastline, they change shape, transforming into tiny, transparent baby eels, about the thickness of a matchstick and the length of two. These are known as glass eels, or elvers. They seek fresh water and swim up tidal rivers en masse, moving with the high incoming tides, mostly under the cloak of darkness to avoid predators. These little elvers have an adhesive quality that allows them to climb weirs and waterfalls against the flow. They wriggle upstream in their tens of thousands, seeking new, safe waters to inhabit.

They might choose to stay in a mighty river, or settle in some drab little ditch, drain or pond. Here they'll feed, first on small aquatic invertebrates, later on frogs and fish, until they too grow to sexual maturity, which will usually take between eight and fifteen years. Then the Sargasso pilgrimage begins again.

This heroic life cycle makes the eel a natural wonder – but it may also prove its undoing, now that consumers have exerted such pressure on stocks. Eels are in great demand in all parts of the world, especially in Japan, where thousands

an evening, reliably hook half a dozen or so (using worms for bait). We'd keep the best two or three, salt them with their skin on, then cold smoke them for a few hours before finally cooking them through with a blast of hot smoke (see page 158). We'd eat them hot from the smoker, with buttered brown bread and homemade horseradish. Happy days.

Today the case of the slippery eel offers an apt example of the kind of grappling-with-guilt that we, as fish lovers, can hardly avoid. In truth, we are now wavering about the ecological soundness of our only-eat-what-we-catch approach to the eel. Of course, if everyone ate only eels that they'd caught themselves, the wild eel population would be in a lot less trouble. At the same time, by catching and killing even just a few eels, we are clearly adding to, not subtracting from, the problem. Should we settle instead for buying the odd one that's been commercially caught, or a delicious whole smoked eel from our friends at Brown and Forrest (see the Directory, page 590)? Or should we, if climate change is going to take the matter out of our hands, simply gorge ourselves on as much eel as we can, while we still can? Or perhaps – barely thinkable, this – simply never eat an eel again?

Such are the battles currently raging between our consciences and our appetites. And sometimes, but rarely these days, our appetites still win.

Carp *Cyprinus carpio*

Not everyone is grateful for what the Romans brought to Britain. We both have small boys who deeply resent the introduction of the bath. But neither of them – nor anyone else we know – has a problem with another Roman introduction: the carp. Indeed, *Cyprinus carpio* has been so wholeheartedly adopted in Britain that it is assumed by most to be a native of our waters. Mrs Beeton refers to it as the 'queen of the river' – a slight misnomer, since most British carp have been settled in still waters.

Originally from around Turkestan and the Black and Caspian Seas, for centuries carp were cultivated by the Romans as an eating fish in man-made ponds – these were early fish farms. For its generous contribution to the Roman table, carp was honoured by association with Venus, the goddess of fertility (a female carp is so fecund that she can produce up to a third of her body weight in eggs). As their Empire expanded through Europe, Roman armies took with them supplies of live carp, stored in bundles of wet moss. By the time of their retreat, carp was a valued food fish throughout northern Europe.

The Britons particularly took to carp. They are easy to breed, can be kept alive for years – even in fairly stagnant 'stew' ponds – and will eat practically anything. For many households, they came to serve almost as aquatic pigs – mooching around in a pond out the back, ready to grow fat on any scraps that came their way. They were (and still are) good eating – the flesh rich and robust, and easily removed from the uncomplicated skeleton. The only downside might have been a distinct earthy flavour – derived from the often rather grubby water they lived in and their mud-sifting feeding habits. But unless you lived near the coast and were spoilt with fresh sea fish with which to compare them, carp's silty tang would be unlikely to bother you.

MCS RATING: not rated
REC MINIMUM SIZE: 25cm
CLOSED SEASON: generally 15 March to 15 June
RECIPES: pages 175, 220, 223, 281–2

In medieval times, carp served the Church and its ecclesiastical communities exceedingly well. Monasteries kept carp ponds, where the fish would be fed on corn and potatoes. Every Friday, a day of abstinence from meat, one of the monks would hoick out a couple of fat ones to feed the brothers. At various times over the centuries, during periods of heightened fervour, such 'fish days' were extended to two and even three times a week. This inevitably led to the digging of further ponds and the stocking of yet more carp. Hence the fish's remarkably thorough distribution throughout the British Isles.

However, the carp's ancient and traditional pond life, settled for almost two millennia, has changed massively in the last few decades. It has ceased to be a food fish and has been claimed almost aggressively by modern anglers, who never eat them. In fact, the British carp angler would rather swallow his maggots, or shave off his beard, than harm a carp. There are hundreds of thousands of carp anglers who are all, in varying degrees, obsessed with this fish (some save their passion for the weekends; others think about carp more than most men think about sex). And as there is no longer a compulsory closed season on stillwater carp lakes or canals, most can pursue their 'hobby' 365 days a year. But though they might well stop for a portion of cod and chips on their way home from yet another 48-hour marathon carpathon bivouak, most would blow a fuse at the thought of one of their beloved fish in a crisp beer batter.

To people who have recently arrived from Eastern Europe, where carp is still valued as a food fish, this is all very confusing. Over the last couple of years there have been a number of incidents of carp club members reporting Polish carp anglers to the police for having the temerity to take a fish home to cook. Admittedly, their 'angling' methods are not always conventional. Just last summer, police in Hertfordshire questioned four Eastern Europeans about an incident at the local carp lake involving snorkels and a spear gun. You can see why this might have been inflammatory, but you have to admire their determination. Or their appetite.

Maybe this is our problem, however, not the Poles'. Maybe we should be a little less uptight over a fish that was brought here to feed us in the first place, is in plentiful supply, and could take pressure off other threatened species. We'd like to see coarse anglers adopt a more 'holistic' approach to their fishing. By all means enjoy a day's sport, and take all the photos you want to impress your friends. But if you want to impress your family – which is not a bad plan, given that you are in the habit of deserting them for days at a time – why not take 'one for the pot' and bake them a carp when you get home?

At the same time, let's be even-handed. We understand how an angler would feel if a thirty-pound fish he'd known by name (yes, carp anglers recognise and name individual fish) was plucked from his local gravel pit and turned into Christmas lunch for a bunch of foreigners. But how about a bit of give and take? We'd like to see Polish anglers invited to carp clubs to learn a little British fishing etiquette – perhaps in exchange for revealing the secrets of a good stuffed carp.

So what happened in this country to turn carp from dinner into deity? Progress? Certainly, from the late nineteenth century, with the development of bigger and better trawlers and the rapid expansion of the rail and road network, fresh sea fish became much more readily available. Coarse freshwater fish, including carp, roach and perch, simply faded from the cook's consciousness as herrings, haddock and the mighty cod took over the kitchen.

In 1952 the fishing writer Richard Walker captured a mirror carp on Redmire Pool, near Hereford, weighing 44lb. He smashed the British rod-caught record and his catch became a national news story. From that moment, serious carp fishing took off in Britain. The fish was christened Clarissa and she took up residence in the aquarium at London Zoo. Clarissa became the inspiration for a new generation of carp anglers, many of whom made a pilgrimage to visit their living goddess. Carp became big business: angling clubs bought specimen fish to lure carp hunters to their waters. Ultra-modern tackle – brand new carbon-fibre rods and invisible monofilament lines – were developed to aid carpists in their quest for behemoth fish. The mother of all British carp had spawned a new brotherhood of British carp anglers (it wasn't until 1981 that Clarissa lost top billing to 'the Bishop', a 51lb 8oz monster, again bagged at Redmire).

The carp's large eyes and sensitive hearing make it a wily prey. And the older and larger it grows, the more canny it becomes. For British anglers, these huge, hard-fighting carp, previously considered almost uncatchable, presented a brand new sporting challenge. And they still do: a fish of over 20lb gives you unofficial entry into the brotherhood – you can dare to speak to your fellows. Catch a 'Thirty' and you will be invited to pass the pictures round, and may even get a slap on the back. Land a fish of over 40lb and you can reasonably expect other carp anglers to genuflect as you pass. But the obsession to catch such a specimen can grow so strong that it can rule an angler's life – even ruin it. True 'carpoholics' hunt their prey for days and nights on end, 'bivvying up' by the waterside, boiling up strong coffee and Pot Noodles to stave off sleep and hunger, lest they miss a bite. We've heard it said that in Essex, carp fishing is the number-two reason cited by wives in divorce cases. (In legal terms, we imagine it covers both 'unreasonable behaviour' and 'desertion'.)

Carp have a good memory – all that 'goldfish have a memory span of four seconds' stuff is nonsense – and they are savvy enough to avoid eating the bait that caught them out last time. So anglers have to dream up novel foods to tempt the suspicious specimen fish. Luckily carp seem to have adventurous appetites: bread, cheese, curry paste, custard powder, dog food, honey, luncheon meat, Marmite, pasta, pepperoni, pilchards, potatoes, strawberries and sweetcorn are just a tiny selection of the ingredients with which people have persuaded carp to take their hook.

If only they would apply such culinary creativity to the carp itself. There's undoubtedly tremendous potential for reviving the culture of eating carp in this country. A couple of millennia's worth of British and European cooks are not wrong about this fish. We've both eaten and enjoyed it: the rich, meaty flesh is not unlike salmon in its texture. Yes, it can taste a little muddy – but, as with trout, this is a reflection of the water it has taken in, not an intrinsic quality of the flesh itself.

So, we are delighted to hear of one Jimmie Hepburn, who has just started the country's first organic carp farm, not far from us in Somerset. Quite apart from the thrill of seeing this great fish back on our menus, there is another reason to be excited about this venture. Carp farming is potentially more sustainable than any other kind of freshwater aquaculture. Carp will thrive on an entirely vegetarian diet, so there is no need to bring in food made from processed wild fish (see page 37). The combination of organic standards and sweet Somerset water could prove a winner, and we can hardly wait to sample the first fish from Jimmie's spring-fed ponds – due to be ready in late 2008.

When it arrives, we will honour it with a classic recipe from Hannah Glasse's *The Art of Cookery*, published in 1747. We'll stuff it with onions, herbs and anchovies, spiced with mace, cloves and nutmeg, and bake it with half a bottle of white wine. And we'll rustle the cooking liquor into a sauce by whisking in butter and a little flour. It may be 260 years old, but that recipe looks very sound to us.

And after that initiation, we may well turn to carp to see how it holds up in various recipes in this book. With that in mind, and in anticipation of the great carp revival, we've already sprinkled the fish around the 'also works with' lists alongside the recipes. For the time being, that may seem eccentric. Ten years from now, we hope it'll just look like good sense.

Zander *Stizostedion lucioperca*

The zander is the dangerous stranger of our inland waterways – hunting mostly in the dark, peering out of spooky, killer eyes and then biting its unsuspecting victims on the neck with its stiletto-sharp fangs. Everything about this Eastern European infiltrator is murky and mysterious. And how it first arrived in England is a tale cloaked in intrigue.

Francis Russell, the ninth Duke of Bedford, was a naturalist, animal collector and all-round eccentric nobleman. On his travels to Germany he became so enamoured of the local freshwater predator, the zander, that he decided he just had to have one – or rather a couple of dozen. So in 1878 a deal was struck with the German Fisheries Association of Schleswig-Holstein and, after a hazardous

MCS RATING: not rated
REC MINIMUM SIZE: 30cm
CLOSED SEASON: generally 15 March to 15 June
RECIPES: pages 198, 226–7, 281–2, 283, 289, 330

journey involving a stormy Channel crossing and a dash from London by horse and cart, twenty-three fish arrived at Woburn Park. They were released into the lake by lantern light, in the dead of night.

The Duke was President of the Royal Agricultural Society, whose motto, 'Practise with Science', he interpreted in a rather gung-ho manner. Introducing alien species was his somewhat reckless hobby and many of them, having slipped beyond the walls of Woburn, are still with us today. The Chinese water deer and the muntjac are notable among them. They shouldn't really be here, but at least they have in their favour the fact that they are singularly good eating. And exactly the same is true of the zander.

For eighty-five years, like a time bomb slowly ticking, the zander stayed put, doing little harm at Woburn except eating the local roach and producing numerous little zander. Then, in 1963, ninety-seven of these were scooped from the lake and released into the wide, open waters of the Great Ouse Relief Channel in East Anglia. The Fenland River Board, having observed their apparent good behaviour over the years, introduced them in a well-meaning attempt to increase the variety of fish available to local anglers. Guess what? It went horribly wrong. Cut loose from the confines of a small still water, the zander went on a killing spree, wreaking havoc amongst the huge shoals of bleak and dace that swarmed through the Fens. The zander's perfect night vision meant the slaughter was relentless. They could hunt all day and all night. Within three years the local populations of shoal fish had been decimated.

The angling press went wild. 'Kill them all!' screamed the headlines. Throughout the 1970s, fishery managers and environmental agencies did just that. The zander were netted, electro-fished and persecuted wherever they cropped up. And they were cropping up in all sorts of places, with a little help from a few human allies – mainly misguided zander anglers. Whether out of curiosity, overenthusiasm or malice, they caught zander in the Fens and hoicked them off to different parts of the country. The most successful populations have been established in the canals of Birmingham and Coventry, and in the River Severn and its Gloucestershire tributaries. (These zander anglers, like the fish they pursued, became pariahs of the fishing fraternity. They would not be welcome in the bars of many fishing clubs.)

The spread of the zander struck fear into the heart of dedicated coarse and match anglers – the kind whose stock in trade is catching roach and bream by the hundredweight every Saturday and Sunday of their lives. Until this point they'd reserved their worst expletives for the pike. But, being a native, it at least earned some grudging respect. The foreign zander tapped into a different level of anxiety and bigotry, and some truly wild accusations were made. Anglers spoke of the zander's psychotic habit of killing purely for killing's sake. They insisted that, like a fox, zander would kill and kill again, taking out whole shoals of fish without even bothering to eat their prey.

It was all nonsense, of course. Their piercing vision makes zander at home in murky water but, as predators go, they're actually quite finicky feeders. They may have impressive fangs but they don't like too big a mouthful. They prey on small shoal fish, rarely taking on the kind of adult breeding fish that a big pike would relish. For all the talk of their thuggery, a hooked zander actually puts up a very limp fight. Some of the best zander we've caught, of 2.5–3.5kg, have come to the net displaying all the savage indignation of a damp rag. Nor have zander, as a species, fulfilled the paranoid predictions of the piscatorial doomsayers.

They have a sporadic distribution and, like other predators, survive or thrive only in proportion to the available bait fish. In the middle of the Fens, where all the turmoil began, you'd now struggle to catch a zander even if you set out specifically to get one. Nature is a powerful leveller. This imposter, having taken the locals by surprise, may have briefly held sway at the top of the food chain but order and balance have been restored. It scratches a predatory living, along with the resident perch and pike, but dominates no longer.

If you've never eaten zander, you really should. In parts of Eastern Europe, where zander are native, they are the top-selling freshwater fish, more popular even than trout. Mostly this table zander is farmed, although wild zander are available too. As in any comparison between wild and farmed fish of the same species, the wild ones are firmer of flesh (they work harder for a living) and sweeter of taste (they eat a more natural diet).

Here in the UK, zander does appear on some adventurous restaurant menus from time to time. And farmed zander, mainly imported from Holland, are just starting to appear on wet fish slabs too. We're betting that, sooner or later, one of the supermarkets will champion it.

If you do get hold of some, you'll be impressed. Its flesh looks like cod: nice big curds of milk-white flakes interspersed by easily removable bones. If anything, it's even firmer than cod. It fillets easily and, once scaled, its thick skin fries up satisfyingly crisply in the pan. It's one of those versatile fish, ready for baking and battering, frying and grilling and even cold smoking – after which you could happily use it in any recipe that called for smoked haddock or pollack.

A fresh wild zander is worth making a fuss of in the kitchen – particularly as acquiring one is no mean feat. Realistically, you'll need to befriend a zander angler. Or become one.

Shellfish

Crustaceans

Brown shrimp *Crangon crangon*

Afternoon tea. Cucumber sandwiches, scones with jam, coffee and walnut cake if you're lucky, Dundee cake if you're not. All washed down with a pot of Earl Grey. And, if you're striving for out-and-out perfection, something salty and fishy on toast – bloater paste, perhaps, or the Gentleman's Relish. But if you really want the best, you should make it potted shrimps.

The finest potted shrimps are still made from brown shrimps caught on the vast tidal sands of places such as north Norfolk and Morecambe Bay (where James Baxter became the first shrimp processor in 1799). They're still unbelievably good. If you think of shrimps as somehow inferior to prawns, then perhaps you haven't tasted them for a while. Or you may have fallen victim to the curious modern phenomenon of 'crustacean inflation', whereby the sheer size of prawns is peddled as a mark of quality. It's not. And we'd rather have a solitary Morecambe Bay shrimp on our plate than a swollen half-pound tiger prawn from some dodgy Malaysian prawn farm (see pages 542–3 for more on the shortcomings of prawn farming).

In the wild, the modest brown shrimp spends most of the daylight hours buried in sand or mud, with only its eyes and antennae poking out. Being such a scrumptious morsel makes life precarious. Most things in the sea would love to eat a shrimp. So a wise shrimp only comes out at night, when it'll go hunting for its own menu of even more minute invertebrates or juvenile fish.

Wide, silty estuary mouths are the habitat brown shrimps love best: the Severn and the Wash have had their boom times, but Morecambe Bay remains the mother lode of the British brown shrimp. Harvesting Morecambe Bay shrimps began centuries ago with simple hand nets, progressed through horse-drawn nets and those pulled by small sailing tubs called nobbies, and was eventually mechanised in the early twentieth century with the use of beach-going tractors and motor boats. Whether pushed by hand or pulled by a boat or tractor, all shrimp nets operate on the same principle: a pole, bar or board is dragged through the sand, forcing the shrimps out of it so they can be scooped up by the net that comes behind. Traditionally the shrimps are then boiled in seawater – sometimes in special shrimp kettles on board the boats.

Shelling or 'picking' Morecambe brown shrimps was until quite recently literally a cottage industry, with hundreds of local women processing them at their kitchen tables and then taking them on to the potting plant. Predictably, after two hundred years of providing locals with a good living, the practice has been outlawed by European health and safety regulations. Shrimps are now picked and packed mechanically in a new, state-of-the-art processing plant.

If you want to eat brown shrimps, the ones to buy are those taken from offshore trawl fisheries that use 'veils' (bycatch reduction devices) on their nets. Or you can support the traditional tractor shrimp fisheries of Lancashire and

MCS RATING: 3

REC MINIMUM SIZE: 3cm

SEASON: N/A as spawning period is protracted, so hard to avoid

Norfolk, who sell their catch through local fishmongers. Potted shrimps freeze well, and many fishmongers keep frozen stock – often from one of the old family firms, such as Baxter's, still fishing and potting in Morecambe Bay today. They are also available by mail order (see the Directory, page 590).

Best of all, go and catch your own. Get yourself a proper shrimping net – with a solid wooden bar across the front to push through the wet sand and send the shrimps into the sweeping net that follows – and tap into local knowledge about their whereabouts. To deal with your self-caught shrimps it's best to boil them in seawater (or add 30g salt per litre of fresh tap water) for just 3 minutes, then drain well and leave to cool. You can then peel them and pot them in spicy butter (all the commercial recipes are secret, of course – but we're betting that cayenne pepper, a little crushed garlic and a pinch of mace will get you close). Or just eat them one by one – in which case peeling them is by no means compulsory. You can just remove the heads and crunch up bodies and tails, shell and all. Or don't remove the heads and eat the lot. Or mix and match – it's really up to you.

Prawn

Common *Palaemon serratus* **Deepwater** *Pandalus borealis*
Tiger *Penaeus monodon*

Do you remember tasting your first ever prawn? We both remember ours. The first Fearnley prawn came from a rocky beach on the Welsh coast near the seaside town of Aberdovy. It fell to the rock-pool net of the five-year-old Hugh. Boiled in seawater, peeled while still warm, it was like eating a fishy sweet (in a good way). The first Fisher prawn came in a warm, wet brown paper bag from a shellfish stall in Cromer. It was actually a substitute for brown shrimps, which they'd run out of. Prawns seemed huge, exotic and so much easier to peel!

Sadly, not many people have poignant prawn memories any more because, like so many things that were once a rare treat, the prawn has become just something else we take for granted – a bog-standard sandwich filler. In the UK alone, we eat £175 million-worth of prawn sandwiches every year.

The EU is the largest importer of prawns in the world, receiving around 400,000 tonnes annually. In the UK we import 78,000 tonnes of foreign trawled and farmed prawns – on top of the 2,500 tonnes that our own fishing fleets catch. A high proportion of those prawns carry distinctly dubious ecological credentials. The prawns we slather in mayo and pack into sarnies are either fished from the sea by trawlers or grown in shallow tropical prawn farms. Sadly, both means of production are desperately damaging to the environment.

Globally, three million tonnes of 'wild' prawns are caught by trawlers every year, at a variety of prawn grounds all over the world: Mozambique, Sri Lanka, the Philippines, Venezuela, Greenland. One big problem with prawn trawl nets is that the necessarily small mesh size used to catch pinky-sized prawns will trap all manner of other creatures and fish. These unwanted species, or bycatch, die in the process of being hauled on board and are then dumped back into the sea. Some bycatch ratios in tropical prawn grounds can be as high as 20:1 – which means that for every kilo of prawns taken, 20 kilos of bycatch have been dumped.

MCS RATINGS: deepwater 3; tiger 5 DON'T EAT! (except organic farmed); others not rated

REC MINIMUM SIZE: common, 6cm; deepwater, generally 8–12cm; farmed N/A

SEASON: common, avoid November–June (spawning); deepwater, avoid summer and autumn (spawning); release egg-carrying (berried) females at any time; farmed N/A

RECIPES: pages 236, 238, 257, 266–7, 267, 323

teenage years fishing. As a consequence, he developed a bottomless appetite for crab and a healthy respect for the local crab fishermen, whom he accompanied on numerous occasions to help them haul their pots.

In his *Guide To Cromer*, published in 1800, Edmond Burtell noted 'crabs in the finest perfection'. The reputation of Cromer crabs continued to grow, until by 1875 the marine scientist Frank Buckland decided to make a study of the fishery. The famous Cromer crab fishery was at that time in steep decline, with catches falling off rapidly. Buckland blamed the overfishing of immature crabs, known locally as 'toggs', which were caught, crushed and used for whelk bait. He calculated that up to three-quarters of a million undersized crabs were being removed from the fishery each month, with disastrous consequences. As a result of his findings, Parliament passed the 1876 Crab and Lobster Fisheries (Norfolk) Act, introducing a minimum size for crabs (4$\frac{1}{2}$ inches – about 11cm) and forbidding the sale of 'berried' (egg-laden) females. The next year this law was extended to the whole of England and Wales. It has stood the brown crab in fantastically good stead. With the exception of a few notable areas, there are no grave concerns about the future of our national crab fisheries.

Buckland had noted that the steep decline in crab stocks seemed to date from the introduction, some twelve years earlier, of a new type of crab pot – the 'ink well' – to the fishery. These were devastatingly effective, and rapidly replaced the labour-intensive, hand-fished hoop nets. The 'ink well' style of pot is still being used today. They are, in modern parlance, design classics. Originally made of hazel basketwork or hemp twine, now of heavy-duty nylon mesh, they are a simple, steep-sided chamber with a single funnel entrance in the top. Crabs, scenting bait inside, crawl over the pot, drop down through the entrance, and can't (usually) solve the conundrum of how to climb out again. A later modification, the 'parlour' pot, has since become more popular.

Parlour pots are slightly more complex than ink wells, because they consist of two 'rooms' – a bait room and a holding parlour. After feeding in the bait room, the crab climbs a mesh ramp, assuming it's the easy route out of the pot. But the ramp leads only to the parlour, from which there is no exit. Parlour pots are better at keeping crabs, which will eventually find their way out of the traditional ink well. If stormy weather prevents a crabber checking his or her pots for a few days, the ink wells will usually be stripped clean of bait and empty, whereas parlour pots will hold their catch more or less indefinitely.

Catching crabs in pots is, theoretically at least, one of the most fair-minded forms of fishing, because the creature is trapped alive and unharmed. So a crab in a pot is by no means doomed. Spend time on a professional crab boat and you might be surprised to see the vast number of crabs that are hauled from the deep, only to be eased carefully out of the parlour and then dropped back into the sea, unharmed. On some days, in the early summer especially, it's not unusual for a crab boat to return as much as 80 per cent of its 'catch'. Crabs may be returned to the sea alive for any of three reasons: if they're below the minimum landing size; if they're 'berried'; or if they're 'soft'. A 'soft' crab is one that has recently moulted – i.e. cast off its shell and started to grow a new one. These are also known as casters, white crabs, whitefoot crabs and glass crabs.

Soft crabs do *look* fantastic, with their pristine, shiny shells, but inside they're full of water, with deceptively little meat content. When a crab moults its shell, once or occasionally twice a year, to grow a bigger new one, its overall size increases by as much as 30 per cent. When the crab discards its old shell,

it pumps itself up with water to its new size, then waits until its soft skin gradually calcifies into new shell. Hardening takes up to two months, during which time the crab will hide in a secure place, owing to its vulnerable condition. So when the crab crawls back out into the big wide underwater world to show off its new shell, inside is just a lot of water and a very hungry, out-of-condition little crab. John Davies, a third-generation Cromer crab fisherman, puts it quite simply: 'The best crabs are the dirty ones,' he says. 'The ones covered in barnacles with old, battered shells – they're the ones you want to eat. They're the ones that have been feeding hard all year and are full of prime meat.'

John and his fellow crabbers are fiercely proud of the Cromer fishery and the informal code of conduct that helps it thrive. If you stand on Cromer prom at dawn and watch the crab boats preparing to launch, you'll see that the first thing to be loaded on board is baskets of empty crab shells and claws – leftovers from the crab-dressing workshops. These are dumped back into the sea around the crabbing grounds, to be picked clean by other crustaceans, including prawns and lobsters, who will use the extra calcium boost to help grow their own shells.

The second thing to be loaded on to the boat is the bait. With each boat regularly working up to 700 pots, in strings or 'shanks' of twenty-five, over a 20-mile radius, the Cromer fleet gets through an awful lot of bait. In the past, bait was caught locally, in the form of 'lesser' fish such as gurnard and scad. This no longer stacks up ecologically (it probably never did). These days, crab potters will buy in tonnes of frozen crab bait in the form of waste (heads and skeletons) from fish processing plants. This recycled fish makes a significant contribution to the diet of the local crabs. 'With the amount of bait we buy and put down day after day,' says John Davies, 'if you think about it, we're practically *farming* them. We don't mind rejecting as many as we do, because we know we'll get them again later, when they've grown bigger – on our bait!'

If you're choosing a crab at the fishmonger's, live or dead (and we'd say go for live every time), you may be offered the choice of a cock or a hen. One of each is the way to go! As a rule of thumb, cocks have slightly more white meat (mainly in their larger claws) and slightly stronger-flavoured brown meat; the hens, because of their bigger, more humped shell, normally contain a larger ration of brown meat. The one other consideration that should inform your choice is the season. The crab spawning cycle is complicated. Females move inshore to breed in late spring but they store the sperm after mating and don't fertilise the eggs until late winter, then carry them for about six weeks before hatching. So, all in all, this process takes up most of the year. Our advice is to avoid females between May and July, when they're preparing to breed, and to make sure you don't buy egg-carrying females – which you're likely to find between January and March.

The sex of a crab can be determined by looking at its 'tail' – a little flap of shell curled up under its body. The female's is wide and somewhat rounded – and, when she is berried, clasps the cluster of eggs to her body. The male tail is narrower and pointier.

A few warning bells have been rung of late, as reduced crab catches are being reported in some areas, including off Cromer, where catches were the lowest on record recently. Some blame overfishing elsewhere off the east coast, while others say it's all down to climate change. No one is suggesting we stop eating crab but it is important to shop with care: never buy small crabs but go for mature specimens that have had a chance to reproduce. Minimum landing sizes vary regionally from around 12 to 14cm, measured across the carapace. But it's easy to find much bigger crabs than that, and they are the ones to go for. Crabs caught off the South Devon coast are a particularly good choice. Subject to a policy called the Inshore Potting Agreement, crab fishermen here operate with a large minimum size and there are many sensible conservation measures in place, including some completely protected areas where crabs can breed in peace.

Of all the crustaceans in all the world, Nick would contend that British brown crab is the tastiest, Hugh would say a spider crab, see page 557, is *even* better. This is partly because brown crab has not one uniform kind of meat but several, of varying flavour and texture. There's the rich, nutty, creamy brown meat that lurks deep inside the carapace. There's the strands of sweet, tangy white meat that can be dug out of the leg sockets and body. Then there's a rich seam of short-grained white meat from inside the claws. And there's also the compressed pâté-like meat, tinged with pink and brown and tipped with black, that curls right up inside the 'toe' of each claw.

A freshly boiled brown crab is a wonderful thing to behold and to eat – best of all when you have chosen a live one and boiled it yourself. Cracking and picking your way through a whole crab, with the appropriate (or approximate) tools, and a bowl of homemade mayonnaise to hand, is one of the greatest pleasures to be taken from the sea (for the uninitiated, full instructions are on pages 90–2). Even if you cheat – by getting your crab ready dressed from the fishmonger's or some seaside eatery – it's never less than a pleasure. And the crab sandwich is certainly not to be sniffed at.

But although crab served cold is never dull, it would be a shame not to explore the hotter possibilities, in the sense of both temperature and spice. The sweet, robustly flavoured meat of crab can take a lot of strong flavours and still shine through. A curried crab soup (pages 266–7) and a piquant crab tart (pages 242–3) show the versatility of this armour-plated kitchen trouper. And, theologically controversial as it may sound, devilled crab (page 234) is sheer heaven.

Blue velvet swimmer crab *Necora puber*

Once, while fishing off the coast of Northern Ireland, we met a man who worked for Guinness Breweries as a draught beer pump fitter. He travelled around the province keeping the dark, velvety stout flowing. For many men, this would be a dream job, yet he was about to jack it all in and spend his savings on a boat, a winch and a collection of crab pots. His plan was to become a blue velvet swimmer crab fisherman. Needless to say, most of his friends thought he was insane.

Like many people in the British Isles, they'd never seen or heard of a blue velvet swimmer crab. Yet crab fishermen are plagued by them, particularly in the summer months. Commercial lobster and brown crab potters generally dislike blue velvet swimmers because they eat the bait intended for the other crabs, and have no commercial value in the UK.

In this country, it seems we like our crabs big. A blue velvet swimmer crab is tiny in comparison to the crabs we favour. The minimum landing size for a brown crab is 12–14cm across the carapace, yet your average velvet swimmer is no more than 8cm. They may be small in size but they're big on personality. Pay them some attention and they can become quite beguiling.

MCS RATING: not rated

REC MINIMUM SIZE: 6.5cm across the carapace

SEASON: avoid late winter and early spring (spawning); avoid egg-carrying (berried) females at any time

RECIPES: pages 234, 266–7, 327

The blue velvet swimmer gets its name from the covering of soft, thick hairs across its blue shell – and of course the fact that, for a crab, it's a surprisingly adept swimmer. Most crabs barely swim at all. They rely on crawling to get from A to B, and trust in their shell to provide protection in the case of an attack. But the two back legs of the velvet swimmer have evolved into distinct flat paddles. These allow it to travel at far greater speeds along and just above the sea floor, in a sort of swim-jump-crawl motion. So when faced with a hungry predator, the blue velvet swimmers don't just hunker down and hope their shell is a deterrent. They can scarper, and elude their tormentors with an impressive turn of speed.

Not that they're afraid to stand their ground. The velvet swimmer may be small, but it knows no fear. It will attack anything, of any size, and fight until the bitter end. A nip from one of these little crustaceans is no laughing matter. It hurts. The blue velvet swimmer crab is also known as the devil crab, or witch crab – names inspired by its wicked temper and fiery bright red eyes. They are devilish hunters, too. Their speed in the water makes them more efficient killers than other crabs – they can chase down prawns and ambush small fish, making them less reliant on carrion.

But the blue velvet swimmer – for all its attitude – has a tender side. When two velvet swimmers mate, the female needs to be in a soft-shell state in order for her to be receptive to a male's advances. It seems that a clash of hard shells simply wouldn't get a result. Having mated, the soft-shelled female remains vulnerable, so the male will clasp himself to her body and act as her shield and protector until her new shell has hardened sufficiently. During this phase, she will carry thousands of orange-coloured eggs (known as 'berries') under her body, until they hatch into tiny, shrimp-like larvae in the early spring.

Given their size, there's not a huge amount of meat in a velvet swimmer, but what you do get is very sweet and tasty. Of course, here in the UK we don't know that. But the Spanish do. They love our blue velvet swimmers, which they call *nécoras*, and they'll happily pay good money for them. Consequently there are now many crab potters who target velvet swimmers for export to Spain. All the crabs are transported live in seawater tanks. The trade seems to be booming, though it's hard to put figures on it. Currently, velvets simply get lumped together with all the other crab exports, including spiders and brown crabs. But according to the Spanish Fisheries Office, by far the greatest number of velvet swimmer crabs imported by Spain is coming from the UK.

In Spanish restaurants blue velvets are most often eaten in soupy stews. The crabs are served up whole, or halved, in the liquor, to be pulled apart with much cracking, sucking and licking of lips. A Galician favourite is *nécoras rellenas* – stuffed blue velvets. Meat is picked from the shell and claws of a few crabs and mixed with a seasoned béchamel sauce, then stuffed back into the upturned shell, topped with breadcrumbs and baked until golden brown. We have our own version of this – for which you can use any edible crab species – on page 234.

So why don't we eat blue velvet swimmer crabs? Why is it that something we deem a worthless nuisance sells for a pretty penny in Spain? Why is it impossible to buy velvets in this country, even though our crab fishermen are catching gazillions of them? Is it because they are too small? Too fiddly? Too scary? Too blue? We can't answer these questions, but we can encourage you to buck the trend. You'll need a little determination to track some down. You may even have to accost a fisherman, harbourside, and brandish some ready cash at him.

If you can organise some casual holiday potting, you may well catch a number of blue velvets. Even without a boat or pots, they can be caught off piers and breakwaters, with a simple drop net and a chunk of mackerel for bait. Summer and early autumn are most productive. After killing them with a spike (see page 89), boil for just 5 minutes in well-salted water. Let cool, then get cracking, with a bowl of mayonnaise to hand. You'll soon see what you've been missing... and why our Irish friend has turned his attention from Black Velvet to Blue.

Spider crab *Maia squinado*

There is something undeniably alien about spider crabs. With their mechanical legs and spiky, armoured bodies they look like *War of the Worlds* invaders. Their sheer redness adds to their 'Martian' aura – most shellfish only look that way *after* they've been cooked.

Every year they make further inroads, in numbers and range. Fifty years ago their northern expeditionary force, heading from their mothership in the Mediterranean, had only reached the Channel Islands and the tip of Cornwall. Now they've colonised crabbing grounds as far north as Anglesey. The odd one even turns up off Scotland. No one's exactly sure why they are doing so well, though global warming is an obvious possible explanation. They may be the beneficiaries of the same subtle rise in water temperatures that is encouraging red mullet, gilt-head bream and even trigger fish to establish breeding populations around our shores.

MCS RATING: 3 (2–3)

REC MINIMUM SIZE: 12cm across the carapace

SEASON: avoid April–July (spawning); avoid egg-carrying (berried) females at any time

RECIPES: pages 234, 239, 242–3, 327, 389

Their presence is becoming quite a zoological phenomenon. Every spring, in inshore waters from Sussex to Cornwall, there are huge migrations of *Maia squinado* tramping across the seabed. They appear as if from nowhere (though actually from further offshore) each May (hence *Maia*), tangling themselves up in fishermen's nets or clambering into crab pots where, according to more than one commercial potter, 'they scare the lobsters away'.

These migrations culminate in huge, orgiastic underwater mounds of crabs, appearing at intervals all along the submerged south coast. Divers and snorkellers regularly witness these heaving piles of spider crabs, yet marine biologists aren't really sure what the crabs are up to. One theory is that the males construct a castle of 'spiky shelled manhood' around the fecund females in order to protect their precious brood stock.

The sex life of the spider crab is certainly unusual. Most female crabs must moult from their shells, and so be in a soft state, in order to mate. Not so spiders. They'll mate with gusto even when both the male and female are hard-shelled and bristling with spikes. More astonishingly, the female spider crab can, if push comes to shove, dispense not only with the moulting but even with the male. In aquaria, female spider crabs that have been kept totally separated from males have been able to give birth to as many as five consecutive broods. This apparent gift for immaculate conception suggests that females can store sperm somewhere inside their bodies, if necessary for years, for use when good men are thin on the ground. (Or possibly even produce it themselves.) But no one has yet been able to locate their secret sperm stash. (Or gonads.)

It's no surprise that a creature as weird as a spider crab might want to take steps to camouflage itself. They may be big and spiky, but predators such as bull huss and big skate still think of them as lunch. To try to blend in, spider crabs have developed a technique that seems spookily intelligent (especially for a creature that, theoretically, is on the same intellectual plane as a woodlouse). They have been observed sticking seaweed 'cuttings' dipped in gummy saliva on top of their spiny shells. This kind of sub-aqua gardening-cum-hairdressing actually works. The more cutting-edge of these green-fingered crustaceans can be seen sporting growing fringes and comb-overs of self-planted seaweed, sometimes of several different species. (Apparently bladder wrack with sea lettuce highlights is very 'in' right now.)

Make no mistake – for all their other-worldliness, spider crabs are great eating (of which more shortly). Yet for years in the UK there was no recognition of their worth at all. (Is this sounding familiar?) Many potters, blaming them for the absence of other crustaceans, used to kill them as vermin. At best they'd be 'recycled' – smashed up and used for prawn pot-bait; at worst, simply thrown back into the sea, either dead or dying. What a waste.

This changed in the late 1980s, when British crab potters caught on to the lucrative continental market. Such is the Spanish love affair with the succulent *centolla* that they value it (and price it) even more highly than lobster. Nowadays, practically every spider crab landed in Britain is transported alive to Spain in specially designed lorries carrying oxygenated seawater tanks. No Spanish fish cook would ever contemplate buying a dead crab.

Thousands of tonnes of spider crabs are landed every year in Britain, many in nets but some, more sustainably, in pots. Pot-caught spider crab is on the MCS's 'Fish to Eat' list. However, actually buying one remains something of a challenge. You have to intercept the journey from Cornish crab pot to Catalan restaurant

somehow (preferably nearer to Cornwall than Catalonia). Unless you buy direct
from a boat in the harbour (we get them fairly regularly from the netsmen in
West Bay), or shop at wholesale fish markets such as Billingsgate and Brixham,
you'll find this hard to do. Meanwhile, in Spain even the supermarkets sell
spider crabs – most of which are no doubt caught in British waters.

It's madness. This is seriously fine eating – and there isn't even the excuse
that they are too fiddly to be worth bothering with. The Fearnley view is that
spider crab is better and sweeter than any brown crab. The Fisher perspective
(biased in favour of anything from Norfolk) puts it second only to a Cromer crab.

We both love eating it, whenever we can get it. The bigger the better. The
claws may look long and spindly, but they're deceptively meaty, and the body is
loaded with sweet white meat. You can prepare it as for any brown crab recipe
– including cold and dressed with good mayonnaise and lettuce. However, we
reckon that spiced, stuffed back in the shell, crumbed and baked in a hot oven,
it is unforgettably good.

At last, here in the West Country, there is some recognition of its true class.
Several local restaurants, such as the Riverside in West Bay, are serving spider
crab in season (late summer and autumn) and we hear rumours of others in
Cornwall doing the same. A few London chefs are catching on, too, and the
National Trust has just started taking them from Welsh fishermen to use in their
restaurants around the UK. We think we might just be on the cusp of a spider
crab breakthrough.

You could help this happen. Keep nagging your fishmonger; enquire at your
supermarket fish counter (at least then they'll have heard of it); and be ready
to board any crab boats you see pulling up to a quay near you, with cash at the
ready. Then serve up the spiders, evangelically, to your friends. Let's embrace
these charming aliens and make them our own.

would consider any deviation heretical. But we think it would be a mistake to imagine there is no room for improvement.

To get the best from whelks, buy them alive and cook them yourself at home. Scrub them well, then immerse them in a pan of cold water perked up with a splash of wine, a few twists of pepper, and maybe a sprinkling of fennel seeds. Bring them from cold to boiling on the hob. This helps to keep them tender, whereas plunging them straight into hot water toughens the meat. Simmer for about 10 minutes (a bit longer for really big ones, but don't overdo it or they'll toughen up), then serve them warm with garlic mayonnaise (page 332), or homemade tartare sauce (page 324). Or, if you want to mess only mildly with tradition, upgrade the vinegar to cider or red wine, to which you can add some finely chopped onions or shallots, and try paprika instead of white pepper.

However you're planning to enjoy them, first you need to get them out of the shell – a prod and a twist with a small fork will do it (pins are strictly for winkles). Opinion is divided as to how much of the contents you should eat. The big, curled, rubbery 'foot' is clearly the main meal – and the toenail-like trapdoor, or operculum, must be discarded. After the foot, from deep inside the shell, comes a trail of grey-brown innards. Many people discard these, but they actually taste quite sweet – liverish, rather like the brown meat of the crab. They can get a bit rich though, so we tend to eat a few and chuck a few.

Don't despair if you can only buy whelks pre-boiled and shelled (or even frozen – whelks freeze well, and are actually more tender, though a mite less juicy, when defrosted). It's still possible to transform the workaday whelk into something special. The exotic salsa on page 364 will whisk you straight from the drizzly seafront of a northern resort town to a palm-fringed hideaway. And should paradise ever become mundane, you can always reach for the malt vinegar and head home to Blighty.

Bivalves

Mussel *Mytilus edulis*

'Location, location, location' is the mussel's maxim. Get it right and life will be sweet. Get it wrong and the mussel will either starve, get munched by a fish, or cling forlornly to a rock near the low tide mark, wondering where its next meal is coming from.

Not that it's got much choice where it fetches up, buffeted as it is in its planktonic infancy by tides and currents way beyond its control. But if it, and a few thousand of its friends, should get lucky, and seed and settle themselves on a firm foundation in a moderate tidal current well stocked with nutrients, then they can hang out for a few years. They'll be going nowhere, just holding fast to see what the tide will bring to their doors. Their single-hinged, double-sided, hermetically sealed doors.

Mussels suck. All day long. A 5cm mussel will suck its way through 50 litres of seawater in a single day, extracting microscopic nutrition by using its flesh as a filter. Successful filter feeders need to live in water that is swirling with nutrients and deep enough to keep them wet, and feeding, most of the time. Some mussels spend their whole lives submerged, many metres beneath the surface of the sea. For others, life's a beach, as they end up living between the high and low tide marks.

Estuaries and shallow, muddy bays strewn with rocks and weed are good for mussels because they're normally silty, due to soil run-off brought down by the river and/or sediment stirred up by the tides. The only downside of living in the tidal zone is that you're left high and dry twice a day as the tide goes out. No water means no food. It also means exposure to hungry birds and mammals, who recognise the contents of a mussel shell to be an excellent feed. In the end it's a trade-off between good feeding opportunities and the risks of becoming someone else's dinner.

Whether a mussel is gripping the seabed, living in a rock pool, hanging from a mooring rope or clinging to a breakwater, it anchors itself with its 'beard', or byssal threads. If you've ever cooked mussels, you'll have first ripped out the cluster of fibres that protrude from the join between the two halves of the shell. Made from iron deposits that the mussel extracts from seawater, this 'beard' is remarkable stuff. Byssal threads collected from large mussels and other bivalves used to be dried and spun into cloth known as 'sea silk'. The resulting fabric was so light, so strong and so fine that a pair of gloves would fit into a walnut shell and a pair of stockings into a snuffbox. King Tutankhamen and many Roman emperors wore cloaks made of sea silk.

Mussels have been eaten for centuries all around the coastal regions of Europe and other parts of the world. But they fell out of favour in Britain in the second half of the nineteenth century, due to increasing industrial pollution. Being a bivalve filter feeder makes mussels prone to taking toxins on board. Like oysters,

MCS RATING: **2 (1–2) EAT MORE!**
REC MINIMUM SIZE: **5cm**
SEASON: **avoid May–August (spawning)**
RECIPES: **pages 202, 232, 238, 262, 264, 267, 272, 275, 276, 386**

they are at their most vulnerable during the breeding season: not only are their immune systems weaker as they lose condition but the seas are warmer, and bio-toxins more likely to thrive and multiply. This is why mussels and oysters are traditionally shunned when there isn't an 'r' in the month – from May to August. By the turn of the century, trust in the safety of the mussel supply was on the wane; food writers of the time devote very little space to mussel recipes.

Most of the mussels we now eat are farmed, their location chosen for them not by the vagaries of tides but by human planning. Of all forms of aquaculture, mussel farming is perhaps the most benign, and the least environmentally disruptive (see page 37). This is largely because the business of feeding – so fraught with the potential for irresponsible choices – is taken out of human hands and left to nature. In fact, the word 'farming' implies a higher level of intervention than is generally required to cultivate mussels. Choose a location where wild mussels are already thriving and all you need to do is provide some

suitable structures, easy to harvest from, for the future generations to grow on. The wild 'spat' – tiny, free-floating planktonic seed mussels – will find the structures, fix themselves to them and start to grow. No feed, no fertilisers and no chemicals required.

The first farmed mussels were grown on poles, especially in France, where the technique of erecting wooden *bouchots* – poles driven into the estuary mud – has been credited to a shipwrecked Irishman called Patrick Walton. According to French gastronomic legend, Walton found himself washed up in the Bay of Aiguillon in the early thirteenth century. The story goes that he erected crude nets between wooden poles hammered into the mud flats to catch migrating seabirds. He soon observed that tiny seed mussels were gathering on the poles. They fattened up beautifully, and so more and more poles were erected, as mussel cultivation took over from seabird trapping. *Bouchots* are still widely used, especially on the vast tidal mudflats of the Charente-Maritime.

However, most of today's farmed mussels are grown on lengths of heavy rope, studded with plastic spikes to increase the surface area available to the clustering bivalves. Suspended beneath huge floating rafts, the ropes are situated where mussels abound, currents are gentle and the seawater is full of nutrients. The mussels usually reach market size (5–7cm in length) within three years. They may have been 'farmed', but to all intents and purposes they are wild – a fact reflected in their quality and flavour. Farmed mussels, and the waters they come from, are regularly bug-tested, and those destined for supermarkets and the catering trade are often routinely treated with ultraviolet light in order to neutralise harmful bacteria. This does no harm to the mussel or its meat.

The suspended rope technique was a Spanish invention, and the rocky inlets around Galicia are still home to hundreds of mussel farms. Most British mussel farms are situated in the sheltered sea lochs of Scotland and Ireland, but bays, estuaries and harbours all around the coast have been tried with varying degrees of success. We get lovely local rope-grown mussels from Portland Harbour. (The huge, green-lipped mussels from New Zealand that you come across in supermarkets are not a patch on the best home-grown mussels.)

Unlike most other forms of aquaculture, a mussel farm can actually boost local biodiversity. The network of mussel-clad ropes attracts seaweeds, anemones and the like, providing a haven and nursery for various species of fish and marine invertebrates. So, what's the environmental downside? Well, the only serious accusation that has been levelled at mussel farms – usually by tourists – is their visual impact on a wild coastal landscape. And it's true that the floating rafts do not exactly adorn the remote sea lochs where they are often situated. But locals we have spoken to, in Skye and other Hebridean islands, are very supportive of their local mussel farms, which boost the islands' economies at little cost to the environment. A visitor's most constructive contribution is to order a big plate of these delicious mussels in one of the islands' many hostelries.

Mussels grow wild all around our coastline and can easily be collected at low tide. Given that you're unlikely to have an ultraviolet mussel zapping kit at home, how wary should you be about the safety of foraged shellfish? Well, we have gathered them regularly for years in the far north of Scotland, on the breakwaters of north Norfolk, and in and among the rock pools of Cornwall. Touch wood, neither of us has ever been caught out with a dose of poisoning.

We usually purge the wild mussels we collect, though, leaving them for at least eight hours in plenty of clear seawater laced with a little oatmeal. But this is not about making them safer, only nicer to eat. It encourages them to lose any sand or grit. Our own view is that paranoia about the safety of gathered wild shellfish is largely unjustified. However, you should always take local advice – and steer clear, for obvious reasons, of shellfish growing near sewage outlets.

In the end, the most important safety advice is simply this: only cook with live mussels. So, whether you've collected or bought mussels, reject any that don't close when you're cleaning them – they're dead, or as good as. Once they're cooked, reject any that have not opened in the pan.

Fresh, live mussels will keep for three or four days in the fridge and should take no more than 3 or 4 minutes to cook. As soon as they are open they are done, and should be removed from the pan. Cooked for just 2 minutes too long, they'll shrivel up and halve in size. This caveat aside, mussels are a doddle to prepare, perfect for those who yearn for some quick, intense sea flesh.

There are really only two ways we ever cook mussels, though the first, our default setting, has infinite variations on the theme. This is the classic *moules marinière*: the mussels are simply steamed open in a liquor of wine, butter and garlic, then perhaps finished with a dash of cream and a handful of chopped parsley. But wine can become cider, beer, a little fish stock or plain water. And aromatics can go in all kinds of directions: sake, soy, chilli and ginger; saffron; lemongrass and coriander, with or without coconut milk; Thai green curry paste.

Large mussels (like the lovely fat, wild ones we gathered on the Isle of Mull, shown on page 568) can also be barbecued in their shells until they pop open and then eaten as they are, or with a dab of butter or a few drops of olive oil and a squeeze of lemon juice. If you have complete confidence in the quality of the water from which they were taken, they can be eaten raw, like oysters. You may even prefer them this way – they are less substantial, but sweeter by far.

Oyster

Native *Ostrea edulis*   **Pacific** *Crassostrea gigas*   **Rock** *Crassostrea angulata*

To most people, oysters are the seafood that has come to stand for luxury and wealth. But it hasn't always been the case. In the mid-nineteenth century, Dickens wrote that 'poverty and oysters always seem to go together. The poorer the place, the greater the call there is.' So the status of this hefty bivalve has fluctuated over the centuries.

The Ancient Britons regarded most shellfish as subsistence food, to be scavenged when meat or fish wasn't available. But the invading Romans loved their oysters, and ours, and made prodigious efforts to cultivate and nurture them. They corralled the young seed oysters and grew them on in readily accessible beds in estuaries and sheltered bays. The most famous of these were clustered around Camulodunum (Colchester).

Once collected, the oysters were transported alive, in barrels of wet seaweed, to be enjoyed by wealthy Romans living far from the sea. In one 'shell midden' excavated at Silchester, Berkshire, more than a million oyster shells were found. British native oysters were deemed of such quality that they were even exported back to Rome.

MCS RATINGS: wild native 3–4; farmed 1

REC MINIMUM SIZE: wild native 5cm; farmed oysters should be harvested at appropriate size

SEASON: wild native, avoid May–August (spawning); farmed oysters N/A

RECIPES: pages 202, 268

colonies need all the help they can get. But certainly sample a few, as the fine flavour of these lovely natives sets a benchmark, we think, for oyster excellence.

When you want an oyster feast, however, it's to the cultivated stock you should turn. Unlike so much modern aquaculture, oyster farming is to be encouraged, even celebrated. Well managed, it needn't negatively affect the environment at all. Oyster farms don't produce tons of waste material and don't require tons of processed wild fish as fodder. All an oyster needs is enough good clean seawater to suck and it'll grow fat and happy.

If you're buying oysters alive to eat at home, the only hurdle between you and your pleasure is the sharp, tightly sealed shell. Getting into it takes some skill – or, at least, a knack. In our experience, most relationships have a designated oyster-opener, even if both parties are enthusiastic consumers. One of us, as it happens, doesn't shuck oysters at all. He's ashamed to admit it, and the other has agreed to cover for him. The shucker tells you how to do it on page 104.

Raw may seem the connoisseur's choice but there's no shame in cooking an oyster. Not everyone likes them raw. And those who think they don't like oysters at all may well turn out to enjoy them cooked. We like them barbecued in their shells, round side down, bubbling in their own juices until they pop open. Or you can achieve the same effect by placing them in the embers of a fire. And then there's our much-loved Leek, celeriac and oyster broth (page 268).

We'll always come back to raw, though. And we'll always buy them by the dozen, not the measly half-dozen, per person. The full set of condiments allows you and your friends to ring the changes through the feast: half a lemon, a bottle of Tabasco, black pepper and, if time has allowed, some homemade shallot vinegar. Nick's an out-and-out Tabasco fiend. And the one who can't open them is a shallot merchant.

Scallop *Pecten maximus*

If all the bivalves held a bodybuilding competition (not that likely, we admit), the scallop would win the Mr Universe title every time. To work the hinges on their big, heavy shells they have evolved a meaty portion of pure muscle – the white adductor – and when we eat a scallop, it is this we consume. For all its strength, it is amazingly tender and sweet.

The great or king scallop, which is the species native to our shores, is one of the mightiest and meatiest of them all. Even in Latin – *Pecten maximus* – it sounds like a gladiator with a six-pack. Yet the scallop shell is an ancient icon of femininity. In Botticelli's *The Birth of Venus*, the newly born goddess of love is imagined rising up from beneath the waves, gently cradled in a giant scallop shell. The scallop shape has early Christian connotations, too, and is often incorporated into the baptismal font of medieval churches as a symbol of fertility and birth.

Whichever side you lean on, biologically speaking all scallops are both masculine and feminine: they're true hermaphrodites. Nestling up to the muscly white adductor is the pinkish-orange and cream, tongue-like coral. This is the scallop's impressive genital paraphernalia. The orange segment contains the eggs – up to 100 million of them – and the creamy-coloured tip contains the

MCS RATING: 2 (1–3) EAT MORE diver-caught scallops!

REC MINIMUM SIZE: 10cm across the shell

SEASON: avoid May–August (spawning)

RECIPES: pages 141, 202, 267, 270, 313, 397

sperm. Spawning normally takes place between May and August, when the scallop will release sperm and eggs into the sea – at different times and in different places, to avoid fertilising its own emissions. So, depending on the time of year and the point in the scallop's breeding cycle, the coral will be either plump and swollen or shrivelled and insubstantial.

Like all bivalves, scallops are filter feeders that suck in and squirt out water all day long, removing nutrients in the process. They like to lodge themselves into ledges and crevices. Once parked, they will then lie flat side up, covered with a thin layer of sand to camouflage their shell. But unlike their cousins, the oyster and the mussel, scallops don't need to anchor themselves on to rocks, reefs or piers. They prefer mobility, and can be surprisingly fast, using their adductor muscle to open and close their shell rapidly, squirting out water to produce a jet-propulsion effect. They're really not bad swimmers, and may change locations several times in a day, depending on tides or current. If you're a scuba diver, you'll never forget the first time you see a 'flock' of scallops taking off from the seabed.

There are two main methods of fishing for wild scallops and one of them is, indeed, scuba diving. The scallops are hand-picked from the seabed and collected in a simple rope bag. The amount that can be taken by an individual is regulated by his or her skill at spotting and picking the scallops, and the rules of safe diving. Size restrictions are easily observed – any scallops that are under the minimum landing size (currently 10–11cm across the widest part, depending on local laws) are simply left where they are.

The other method of fishing is by dragging several tons of steel link and chain along the seabed. The scallops are either prised out by a row of steel teeth or are spooked into swimming up off the bottom and into the trawl net that follows behind the dredge. Scallop dredging is about as thoughtful as strip mining or forest burning. It can inflict vast amounts of damage on the seabed, and on the populations of fish and crustaceans that rely on reefs and ledges for food and shelter. The longer it is allowed to continue in inshore waters, the longer the seabed will take to recover.

In our view, what makes scallop dredging so heinous – apart from the incalculable damage it causes – is the sheer obviousness of the less damaging alternative. As fishing methods go, scallop diving could hardly be more low impact. Diving is to dredging what hand-picking apples is to grubbing up the whole orchard with a JCB. We always avoid dredged scallops, and we would only ever buy or cook diver-caught scallops. And sometimes, just to remind ourselves what a special and sensitive habitat it is down there, we actually dive for them ourselves. Incidentally, restaurants that serve only diver-caught scallops are usually proud to say so on the menu.

A great scallop can live for over twenty years, but most are harvested at between three and five years old. This growth rate means that farming or 'ranching' scallops is a viable option. Like mussel farming, it need not impact heavily on the local ecosystem – mainly because the shellfish feed naturally in a largely unmolested habitat. The first stage of scallop life is difficult to replicate in the aquarium and so the spat (seeds) are collected from naturally breeding wild scallops. The spat is grown on in fine mesh net 'pockets' until they are around two years old and an inch or so wide. In European farms, they are then released to roam the seabed and feed and fend for themselves (in some other countries, the scallops are left in the nets until they are ready for harvesting). They won't go far – particularly if conditions in the chosen bay or fjord are favourable – and are easy to collect by diving when they reach market size. There are a few successful scallop farms, or 'ranches', around the British Isles and Scandinavia – and, of different scallop species, around the world.

Because ranched scallops are gathered by divers, they may simply be called 'hand-dived' or 'diver-caught' and you will have no way of knowing if they're wild or not. But in a way, this doesn't really matter. In sustainability terms, a ranched, diver-caught scallop from a well-managed fishery is awfully similar to a wild one.

British diver-caught scallops are a great product, in high demand in Europe and the Far East, but still good value in this country – especially if you buy direct from a commercial diver. If you can, spoil yourself and buy loads. They will be cheaper to buy alive, in the shell, than shelled and cleaned. Preparing them yourself is easy, and more than a little satisfying (see pages 105–7). It also gives you the benefit of keeping the trimmings, which make a delicious, sweet addition to any fish stock. Otherwise they can be saved and frozen – they are deadly bait for bream (see page 484).

When it comes to cooking scallops, keep it simple, and keep it fast. Simplest of all is raw – and they are quite sweet enough to enjoy without so much as a squeeze of lemon. Though if you have it handy, a smear of wasabi or mustard, and a dash of soy, is pretty damn good. If they're big ones, though, you might want to slice them horizontally into three or four thin discs. We also love to include scallops in our Ceviche (page 141), where they're 'cooked' in lime juice and spiked with a little chilli.

For *actually* cooking scallops (in the sense of applying heat to them), the frying pan is the tool of choice (the barbecue a more labour-intensive, but delightful, option). You can 'sear' scallops by dry-heating the pan (or barbecue, or ridged griddle), then very lightly oiling each surface of the muscle with your fingertips. Season them with a tiny pinch of salt and pepper and give each side a scant minute – just enough to caramelise the surface with speckles of brown. (It's fine – desirable, some would say – for them to be raw in the middle.) You can also fry scallops more conventionally in an oiled pan, in which case you should give some thought to a few supporting flavours – garlic is a must. You could also add chilli, fennel seeds and ginger – one, two or all three of them. A favourite trick of ours is to fry up some slices of our homemade chorizo, then throw scallops into the pan to take on the flavours of the highly spiced oil (see page 313).

Some cooks don't use the coral at all, and serve only the white scallop muscle. This is madness – except when the coral is withered. Plump and orange and in rude health, the coral is delicious – in fact, with its lightly granular, roe-like texture, it is complementary to the white muscle meat. The two should be cooked together, still attached, if possible – though on really big scallops it may be a good idea to separate them, otherwise the coral can 'hang' from the middle of the muscle without ever quite making contact with the pan.

There's certainly no need to think of scallops, as some seem to, as restaurant fodder. If chefs love them, it's for the same reasons you should: they are blissfully easy to cook, and even easier to eat, with no bones, skin or cartilage – nothing to hamper your pleasure. The only thing you could possibly do wrong is to overcook one – which isn't hard to do. So, whenever you cook them, just keep reminding yourself how great they taste raw, and aim to serve them at least rare. Three minutes is the most you will ever need to cook a scallop – and about three seconds to eat it.

Cockle *Cerastoderma edule*

If you've ever wondered what the difference is between a clam and a cockle, the answer is, not much. Both are bivalve molluscs that live in muddy sand and feed by sucking seawater from which they filter minute planktonic organisms. Both clams and cockles belong to the same genus, and both are found in similar habitats, often living side by side. The only clear difference between them is the shape, size and direction of the ridges on their shells – i.e. from side to side on most species of clam but from edges to hinge on the cockle.

However, once you take them away from the beach and into the kitchen, a gulf opens between them – and it's largely social. Clams are posh. Cockles are common. Clams are used in classy continental dishes such as *spaghetti alle vongole* (Italy) or *palourdes à la commodore* (France). Meanwhile, here in Blighty, cockles get hard-boiled, drowned in industrial-strength vinegar and sold on the pier in polystyrene cups. Why? Hard to say really, except for the force of history and habit – neither of which is entirely to be trusted when it comes to assessing our native seafood.

You could play up the class distinction by arguing that a posh clam such as a palourde is a shade more tender and a touch sweeter than its close cousin, the cockle – but in most countries other than Britain you'd be wasting your breath. Everything you can do with a fancy clam you can do just as well with the humble cockle. Yet we continue to pay top whack for clams that have been imported from abroad (and often farmed) while our native, fresh, wild, hand-picked cockles (at least those we haven't pickled to death) are sent in the other direction – to the discerning seafood markets of France, Spain and Holland. Here they are deployed in all sorts of tasty dishes – the kind for which British chefs would generally insist on palourdes and other clams. It's all back to front.

MCS RATING: **2 EAT MORE!**

REC MINIMUM SIZE: **2cm**

SEASON: avoid May–August (spawning)

RECIPES: pages 202, 232, 262, 264, 267, 272, 275, 276, 278, 384, 386

Make no mistake, to foreign seafood buyers British cockles are known to be the best in the world. Amongst the most highly prized specimens are those from the famous cockle beds of Stiffkey (pronounced 'stookey') in Norfolk, known as Stiffkey Blues because of their blue-tinged shells – a result of the unique anaerobic mud they inhabit. In Wales, the Burry Inlet cockle fishery near Swansea has been renowned for the quality of its harvest ever since the Romans first discovered it.

The entire British cockle harvest is currently worth around £20 million a year, making it one of the UK's most valuable fisheries, but over three-quarters of that harvest is being exported. Much of the business is now in the hands of Dutch, German and Spanish companies who bought up many British cockle firms in the 1970s and 1980s. European companies now effectively control the market for UK cockles, including those exported to Spain and France. Sadly, most of our cockles are no longer ours.

There are two main methods of harvesting cockles: a modern industrial one and an old-fashioned labour-intensive one. Cockles in the Wash and the Thames Estuary are dredged or vacuumed up by large, fuel-guzzling vessels, while cockles in the Burry Inlet and Morecambe Bay are still raked by hand using converted gardening equipment, then hand-riddled or graded to ensure the immature seed cockles – or spat, as they are called – are returned safely to the mud and left to grow on. Dredging is obviously cheaper than hand-picking, but its impact on the cockle population is much greater. Dredged cockles sell for less than hand-picked ones because the final quality isn't as good – they often get cracked in the machinery. But the real downside of dredging is that it disturbs and even displaces entire cockle beds, and can damage or destroy the all-important spat.

Dredging has never been allowed in the Burry Inlet and methods haven't changed much since the 1800s, when harvesting was done by women with donkeys in attendance to carry the load. Throughout the entire history of the fishery, only hand-raking has been allowed, although donkeys and carts have been replaced by tractors (and women largely by men). Licences to pick are strictly controlled and there is a daily maximum quota of 250 kilos per picker. No night collection or Sunday picking is allowed.

As a result of this commitment to low-impact methods, the Burry Inlet cockle fishery has been awarded Marine Stewardship Council certification – the only British cockle fishery to be so distinguished. Even though the fishery restrictions are devised with conservation in mind, it still manages to yield well over 7,000 tonnes of top-quality, market-leading cockles every year.

It seems a great shame that these world-renowned cockles are being gleefully appreciated on the Continent – but not at home. So we think it's about time for a Great British Cockle Revolution. We'd like to get the misunderstood mollusc out of the vinegar vat and in amongst the garlic, cream and parsley. With that in mind, we've a couple of fine cockle recipes for you (pages 384 and 386). But we'd also urge you not to be shy of using them in recipes where palourdes or other clams are called for. And if you've got a favourite mussel recipe, try it with cockles for a change – it won't be the same, but it will be delicious.

To join the Cockle Resistance, press your local fishmonger for cockles that are fresh (i.e. alive, in their shells) rather than pickled, and if they can be sourced from a well-managed fishery, such as the certified Burry Inlet one (see the Directory, page 590), then so much the better.

Or, of course, you could have a go at collecting some of your own. Sandy mudflats at a low spring tide are where you'll find them – and it's always worth seeking out a little local knowledge. A garden rake, a bucket and bare feet are all the kit you'll need. The cockles live a couple of inches beneath the muddy sand. Rinse them off in a bucket of clean seawater as you find them. They should then be purged in a fresh bucket of seawater (or salted cold tap water) to which you've added a handful of oatmeal or breadcrumbs, and left for at least a few hours, or overnight.

After that, all they will need is a quick scrub under the cold tap and they're ready for cooking. If you've only ever had them pickled in vinegar before, you're in for a serious treat. We recommend you simply sweat a little garlic in a lot of butter and, just before it starts to brown, add a small glass of wine and another of water. When this liquor comes to the boil, tumble in the cockles, put a lid on the pan and give them a couple of minutes to pop open. It may be years before you cook them any other way again, and a lifetime before you even think about having them in vinegar.

Palourde (or carpet shell clam)

Tapes decussatus / Venerupis decussata

The carpet shell clam is one of your posher bivalves. Francophile chefs – almost all chefs, come to think of it – like to give them their French name, *palourdes*. We are rather charmed by the carpet shell tag – but somehow have got caught up in the whole palourde thing (one of us, at least, has the excuse of being married to a shellfish-loving Frenchwoman).

We have made a case for ranking the cockle alongside the palourde (see page 578). For those who've never tasted palourdes it is, we can see, a rather pointless comparison. But should you happen to be familiar with both, we're sure you'll understand that our position on this stems from our sense that the cockle is underappreciated – and not that the palourde is overrated. Let's be clear: palourdes really are delicious. They're a bit bigger than cockles and their meat is exceptionally plump and sweet. They are held in huge esteem in France, Spain, Portugal and Italy, where they're eaten raw in the half shell, like oysters, or cooked in all sorts of delicious ways, almost invariably including garlic.

Unfamiliar as they are to many, palourdes are native to Britain. They like more or less the same kind of rich, organic, silty, muddy sand as cockles, with a preference for the more gravelly end of the spectrum. When the two species are found together, cockles tend to dominate, and clams will be in the minority. But when you find a colony of palourdes on their own, they can be thick on the ground – or, more accurately, just under it. Compared to cockles and mussels, however, clams barely seem to have registered with the British shellfish forager. Apart from a few canny commercial clam collectors, most people don't have the foggiest idea what they are or where to find them.

They haven't always been so neglected. In his 1884 masterpiece *The Edible Mollusca of Great Britain and Ireland, with Recipes for Cooking Them*, the Victorian naturalist M. S. Lovell wrote admiringly of the palourde, noting that a popular term for it along the Solent, where it was gathered eagerly by locals

MCS RATING: **1 EAT MORE!**

REC MINIMUM SIZE: 4cm

SEASON: avoid April–June (main spawning period)

RECIPES: pages 232, 264, 272, 275, 276, 278, 279, 384, 386

(and still thrives) was 'butter fish'. This term has been applied to different fish and shellfish by various cultures (the Gambians use it for a type of puffer fish, the Sri Lankans for pompano). It's always intended as a compliment, of course, implying a rich sweetness and melt-in-the-mouth texture. Lovell also stated that connoisseurs preferred the palourde to the more humble cockle. Personally we're reluctant to concede clam superiority, but it's interesting to note that this whole 'clams are better than cockles' malarkey has been around for a while.

Palourdes appear inconsistently on the fishmonger's slab. They may be home grown and gathered but are also quite likely to be imported from the Continent – mainly France (the coast of Brittany and the Charente-Maritime region around La Rochelle are productive). If ever you see them, be ready to pounce. But before you part with your cash (of which you'll need quite a bit), you should really find out how they were caught. Those that have been dredged are best avoided; this method causes unnecessary damage to many other forms of marine life and may fill these tasty morsels with sand (see page 579 for information on cockle dredging). Hand-gathered palourdes are the ones to buy.

Near us in Dorset, there are a few commercial fishermen who turn their attention to palourde collecting in the early spring, hunting for them at low tide, digging and raking them out from beneath the sand, mud and gravel. These currently fetch around £6–8 a kilo wholesale (expect to pay at least double that at the fishmonger's). One of our fishermen, Kelvin (a regular guest host of our River Cottage foraging days), has been collecting local palourdes for the Spanish market for over twenty years. He admits that he hardly ever gets to taste one: 'They're much too valuable. At that price, we can't afford to eat them. Or rather, we can't afford not to sell them.'

As palourdes are always hard to come by in British fishmongers, and always pricy when you do, collecting them yourself can be an exciting experience – like panning for gold. If ever, on family holidays or fishing adventures, we find we are in striking distance of muddy, gravelly tidal flats, we'll try to check them out. If we don't find palourdes, we may well turn up cockles, or even razor clams. Should you be tempted to do likewise, set out at low water with rakes, spoons, boots (or bare feet) and buckets (maybe take some salt too, in the case of razor clams – see page 584). The palourde's giveaway sign is two air holes, side by side in the wet mud (cockles leave only one). Dig, rake and scavenge around the low-water mark or any 'tracks' you find, and you could get lucky.

Scrub the palourdes well, in clean seawater or fresh water. They don't usually need purging, and you may want to sample a few of them raw, right there on the beach. If you get a decent haul and take some back to the kitchen, the simplest *marinière* treatment serves them well (see page 272). But if you want an even bigger hit of garlic and butter, then steam them open in just a little water, drain them well, remove one half of the shell and arrange the flesh-filled other halves on a plate. Trickle a little hot garlic and parsley butter (or, realistically, a lot) over each clam and into the half shell. Slurp away.

We have also included a rather lovely recipe, Palourdes with chanterelles (page 278), which was devised as the culmination of a particularly gratifying day's foraging last October. To recreate it, you'll probably have to do some foraging yourself, or at least prostrate yourself before your bank manager. It'll be either one of the most luxurious free meals you've ever had or one of the most extravagant you've ever shopped for.

Razor clam *Ensis ensis*

MCS RATING: 2 EAT MORE!
REC MINIMUM SIZE: 10cm
SEASON: avoid May–September (spawning)
RECIPES: pages 262, 264, 278, 279

Collecting wild shellfish is always fun, but normally it's a rather one-sided affair. You might have to do a spot of digging or mud raking to expose cockles, or scramble over a few rocks to find a sprinkling of mussels, winkles or limpets. Once located, however, most molluscs haven't got much to offer in the way of fight or flight. A forager of native shellfish is therefore generally very much a 'gatherer'. Not so the razor clam collector, who is most definitely a 'hunter'.

The razor clam is a bivalve that, like most of its kin, sucks sandy, silty seawater for a living, extracting the minute creatures that are its food. To do this efficiently, it has to keep its water-sucking siphon above the sea floor, while its tasty body is enclosed within its shell, deep in the wet sand and out of danger. Most of the time, the razor clam's patch of sand is covered by the sea, beneath shallow inshore waves. Only on certain big spring low tides, particularly around the two equinoxes, will this habitat be exposed. And when it is, the razor clam must stay hidden beneath the sand, biding its time until the tide rolls back in. This is the window of opportunity in the razor clam hunter's diary.

He or she will walk these rarely exposed expanses of sand, searching for clues. But they are not obvious. Least subtle, but rarest, is a little spout of water, ejaculated from the siphon as the clam either dives from, or climbs to, the sand's surface. The eagle-eyed may also detect figure-of-eight 'prints' in the wet sand. These curious marks are caused by razor clams that have been caught out by the rapidly receding tide and left lying stranded on the sand. They don't stay there for long – and you hardly ever see them like this. They'll rapidly right themselves from horizontal to vertical before burrowing downwards, leaving these shallow scrapes in the sand. But the merest ripple of water will wash them away. Finally, there's the little pinprick of a breathing hole. Look closely and you'll see it isn't quite round, but elongated like the eye of a needle. (Fail to look closely, and you probably won't see it at all.)

Razor clams have excellent 'hearing', detecting vibrations above ground. They will dive at the merest footstep, even if it's several yards away. With the streamlined design of its shell and powerful thrust of its muscular 'foot', the razor clam can propel itself down through wet sand like a rocket launching in

reverse. The speed of its retreat is remarkable; it can easily plunge through the sand quicker than someone with a spade can dig after it. This makes gathering these shellfish one of the great free-food challenges for the amateur enthusiast.

Clever hunters make no attempt to beat the clam at the digging game but instead endeavour to persuade it that danger has passed and the tide is coming back in. They achieve this deception by putting neat salt or, better still, a strong saltwater solution, down the clam's escape hole, to imitate the approach of the incoming tide. The clam will pop its siphon up out of the sand at the taste of a new tide, and it's this moment the hunter must seize. You need to pinch the shell or siphon firmly between your fingers and apply an even, upward pressure. Don't try to lift them straight out or pull hard on the siphon; it's like a lizard's tail – designed to break off and re-grow – and works as a defence to stop birds hauling them out. The trick is to pull steadily and gently, then loosen a little and then pull again. Vary your rhythm and at some point, as the clam flexes its foot muscle, you'll feel it give, and it should slip out of its hole easily enough.

Razor clams can be found on tidal flats all around the British coast but the biggest and fattest are generally collected in Scotland. In Orkney, razor clams are called 'spoots' (we imagine that's 'spouts' with a Scottish accent) and spoot hunting is a favourite local sport. It can be a surprisingly tense and exciting activity – if somewhat bemusing to behold. George Henry Lewes captured it very nicely in his *Seaside Studies* of 1856:

There is something irresistibly ludicrous in grave men stooping over a hole, their coat tails pendant in the water, their breath suspended, one hand holding salt, the other alert to clutch the victims – watching the perturbations of the sand, like hungry cats beside the holes of mice…

A modest restaurant market for razor clams at home and, more vigorously, on the Continent, has spawned a few small commercial fisheries in Britain. In Scotland, divers wear scuba gear so they can collect the clams in shallow water at any state of the tide. In Ireland there are fisheries that use hydraulic dredgers to extract the clams; these tend to be of an inferior quality, with a high proportion of cracked and broken shells. As with the dredging of scallops, cockles and palourdes, hydraulic dredging of clams also causes damage to a sensitive habitat that supports a very complex food chain. We recommend you avoid them.

Commercially collected razor clams are sold live, usually in bunches of ten or twelve, depending on their size. Most razor clams collected in Britain are exported to Europe, and the Spanish, who call them *navajas*, and the French, to whom they are *couteaux courbes*, love them. Only a few are sold in the UK, mostly to enthusiastic restaurateurs. There's absolutely no reason, though, why a decent fishmonger should not be able to order some for you. Or you can always cut out the middleman and buy some direct from a fish wholesaler (see the Directory, pages 590–1). You'll be expected to order a decent quantity – but they're not that pricy. So why not have a spoot party?

The best way to cook razor clams is briefly, or not at all. Overcooked, they'll quickly develop the texture of a garden hose. If you've never tried them before, have a couple raw first – with a sprinkling of shallot vinegar, or sashimi-style with soy and wasabi. For shellfish sweetness, they're up there with scallops. Steam the rest open with garlic, butter and wine as for *moules marinière*, or grill them on a barbecue – adding a dash of lemon and olive oil as you serve them. They may well leave you marvelling at what you've been missing, and at the sheer madness of allowing so many of them to leave our shores.

Cephalopods

Cuttlefish *Sepia officinalis*

Most of us meet our first cuttlefish in the pet shop rather than the fishmonger's. Poking out between the bars of any well-kept budgie's cage is a rigid, white, ovoid disc of cuttlefish 'bone'. Though hard, it has the weight, look and feel of a piece of polystyrene. The budgies gnaw at it to keep their curved beaks from in-growing. How do they know to do that? In the wild, you don't see many budgies scouring the beach or dive-bombing the deep in search of cuttlefish.

Escaped budgies – or whoever collects these things for pet shops – should come to Dorset. Walking along Chesil Beach in the spring or early summer, you'll find hundreds of these buoyant 'bones' peppered across the shingle. They're not bones really, but the dried-out cartilage that gives rigidity to the cuttle's otherwise soft, fleshy body. These are the remains of female cuttlefish who have recently reproduced – an act that, as it creates new life, brings about their own death.

A seabed littered with dead female cuttlefish might seem like a grisly cephalopodic tragedy but to the rest of the locals it's a bonanza – and in some cases a vital part of their life cycle. Black bream, wasted from their own breeding exertions, restore themselves by feeding greedily on dead cuttles. Once a carcass has been picked clean by crabs, prawns and lobsters, its buoyant endoskeleton floats to the surface, where it bobs around, a plaything for curious young seagulls, until it washes up on the beach, ready for the pet-shop boys.

So, all we generally see of our Channel cuttlefish is either an odd piece of white jetsam (or is it flotsam?) on the beach, or a clean white cone of thick flesh on the

MCS RATING: 4

REC MINIMUM SIZE: 17cm

SEASON: avoid spring and early summer (spawning)

RECIPES: pages 260–1, 270, 284, 285, 396

fishmonger's slab. What we *don't* see, though, is truly amazing. For example, a cuttlefish has three hearts with which it pumps different types of blood around its veins in different directions. It moves about, often at some considerable speed, courtesy of two water-siphoning jet-propulsion systems. It has binocular vision and it also possesses the largest of all cephalopod brains, making it more intelligent than any other fish, and possibly even as smart as a rat.

To top it all, a cuttlefish can change colour faster than a chameleon. It's a true master of camouflage, and even at birth an infant cuttlefish has a repertoire of thirteen different disguises. If this doesn't work, a cuttlefish can protect itself by creating a 'smokescreen' with its ink. Even the ink itself is thought to be 'smart ink'. Apart from obscuring the direction in which the cuttle fled, it contains a scent-decoying element that interferes with the predator's sense of smell, giving the cuttle more time to escape. That it has evolved such an array of defences is quite understandable, given how thick, tender and delicious its soft flesh is.

But cuttlefish are themselves predators, and highly effective ones. We get mugged by them often, or at least our lines do, when we're fishing for bass with sand eels for bait. We know the cuttles are about when our sand eels come back to the boat bitten clean off just behind the head. More grisly still, some eels that first appear to be intact prove on inspection to have a mysterious semicircular crater in the flesh of their necks, as if clipped out by a cigar cutter. This macabre insignia of death is the mark of the cuttle's razor-sharp beak. It likes to begin by disabling its prey with a vertebra-severing bite behind the head. In the case of our baits, we can only imagine that, having performed its ruthless despatch, the cuttle detects the hook, mistrusts the meal, and moves on. Sometimes, it's not so smart and hangs on to the bait, or gets a tentacle caught on the hook, and we can reel it in, scoop it with a landing net, and get excited about sashimi for supper.

Besides these accidental catches by anglers, there is also a modest commercial fishery for cuttlefish around the south coast. A couple of boats that fish from our local harbours, West Bay and Lyme Regis, target them in April, May and early June when they come inshore to breed. These mature adults are, at up to a couple of kilos, impressive slabs of seafood.

The problem with this tactic, of course, is that there's a danger the cuttlefish will be scooped up before they've had a chance to spawn. Another risk is that they will actually lay their eggs on the traps and the eggs will then be destroyed as the traps are hauled in. There's some evidence to suggest that our cuttlefish populations are currently in trouble and we do need to be careful. Our advice would be to eat cuttlefish, if possible, outside their early-summer spawning season. We'd also love to see some innovations in the cuttlefish-catching techniques used in our waters – like the very clever traps devised by fishermen in Brittany. These have a removable outer layer so any eggs found on them can be returned to the sea.

Almost all of the British cuttlefish catch is currently exported direct to Spain. There's barely a viable market in Britain. Why not? We eat squid, for heaven's sake. Britain imports thousands of tonnes of frozen squid every year, yet a fresh cuttlefish knocks a frozen squid into a cocked hat any day of the week.

The cuttlefish traps that local fishermen use are like giant circular crab pots. Instead of being baited with food, these are fitted with an imitation cuttlefish, which lures more cuttlefish into the trap. Spawning time is a frantic period when the males are busy wooing the females, or trying to fight off other males. So it's hard to be sure, when a cuttlefish is enticed into the trap by the lure, whether

it actually wants to fuck it or fight it. And, since the decoy cuttlefish is nothing more stimulating than a plain piece of white plastic, about the size of an office envelope, flapping limply in the current, we can only conclude that the average cuttlefish is either extremely aggressive, extremely horny, or both.

Just like a squid, the cuttle uses its ink as a last line of defence, and being dropped on the deck of a boat is by no means too late to deploy it. We both have stains on our favourite fishing jackets that testify to this. A cuttle generally has a lot more ink than a squid, and a good dose usually remains, even if several shots of it have been fired. (Ink extracted from cuttlefish was used in early sepia print photographic processes – hence its Latin name, *Sepia officinalis*.) These days the ink is more likely to be saved for the kitchen than the darkroom (see page 102). It lends sweetness and a deep, seaweedy flavour, as well as a thickening texture, to a pasta sauce, fish stew or risotto.

Cuttlefish flesh is very similar to squid, a little sweeter and a little thicker, with a bit more bite to it. And, like squid, it needs to be cooked very quickly (in a wok or on a grill or barbecue, for just a couple of minutes) or very slowly (stewed long and gently, ideally with tomatoes and garlic, plus that ink if you've managed to save it, for a good hour). In the case of a very fresh specimen, zero minutes is also effective: cuttlefish makes excellent sushi, sashimi and ceviche.

As stocks of prime fish in our waters dwindle, it makes sense to explore some less obvious alternatives. And they don't come less obvious than the triple-hearted, ink-squirting marine chameleon.

Squid *Loligo forbesi*

If the squid didn't exist, Hollywood would have had to invent him. He is the Ethan Hunt of the sea, tooled up with gadgets, gizmos and secret weapons. He is capable of clever disguise, deceit and jet propulsion. He can swim backwards or forwards, in deep or shallow water. He has night vision, an armoury of hydraulic, sucker-covered arms, and a hidden, parrot-like beak that can slice right through a fat prawn like a laser. He is so well equipped that his mission – to eat, grow and reproduce – is far from impossible. And our mission is to eat him as often as we possibly can.

Like its close relative, the cuttlefish, the squid has a short and frenetic life. It is sexually mature within a year, and dead within three. The female squid spawns in her second year and dies soon after she has laid her eggs. Because squid live fast and die young, a squid fishery can fluctuate wildly from year to year, as numbers depend largely on the success or failure of each individual breeding season.

We're lucky to have a reliable seasonal opportunity to catch squid ourselves on rod and line. It's a winter-afternoon affair, kick-started by the drop in water temperature and shortening days some time around mid-November. This is when the squid migrate close inshore, around Weymouth and Portland harbours, in search of easy food. We often catch them in no more than 4–6 metres of water, just as the day fades and the night sucks up the light. In the encroaching darkness, the squid become bolder. They are less worried by predators, and their huge, bulbous eyes give them a strong advantage over their prey of small fish, prawns and crabs.

The hunting squid uses its enhanced night vision to locate prey, then grabs them with two extra-long extendable tentacles that shoot out like a Rocky Balboa jab. Once the victim's suckered, it's dragged into a lethal embrace, and the squid will start chewing its ear.

But it isn't hard to turn the tables on such a hungry and relentless predator. To catch squid, we use prawn-shaped lures called squid jigs, which have a cluster of tiny, barbless hooks around their tails, like a bizarre but deadly upturned grass skirt. The jigs, fished from a rod and line, are raised and lowered within the bottom metre or so of the seabed. The squid wrap their hunting tentacles around a jig, becoming entangled with the hook skirt. A smooth, steady retrieve is required to get them to the surface, where they can be scooped up with a small-meshed landing net.

In the absence of jigs, or sometimes as an extra enticement, we often use a small dead pouting as bait. No hooks are needed. The squid simply grabs the fish, holding on until you get it to the top. But if you fluff it with the landing net, beware, because a squid can open up its water-jet propulsion valve and rocket back and down at an impressive speed.

If you do manage to net it, a squid has one last secret weapon in the briefcase: its ink. Of course, once it's on board, the ink is hardly going to save it from capture. But it can give the squid the last laugh. An angry spray of fresh squid ink is practically impossible to wash out of clothes, and leaves the deck black, sticky and, a few days later, pretty stinky too.

Back in the squid's underwater world, the ink is used to evade predators, of which, as a soft-fleshed, protein-rich cephalopod, it has many. And so, if a hungry tope or marauding bass is closing in on it, it'll use its opaque ink ejaculation

MCS RATING: 3

REC MINIMUM SIZE: 15cm (body length, from tip of nose to end of body)

SEASON: avoid December–May (spawning)

RECIPES: pages 204–5, 267, 270, 284, 285, 332, 396

system as a smokescreen, to blind the enemy temporarily. The ink cloud of the squid (and cuttlefish) works on a number of levels. For a start, it is thought to contain a substance that will dull the predator's sense of smell. There are also theories that the squid's ink spurt isn't merely a random cloud but a rough and ready replication of its body shape. It's a squid silhouette, in other words, squirted to deceive the predator and leave it attacking a ghostly shape while the real squid beats a retreat. (It's a device uncannily like Arnie's handy hologram in *Total Recall*.)

If you ever have an opportunity to go squid jigging, grab it. It doesn't have to be a complicated boat trip. Many exceptional squid and cuttlefish are caught from piers and harbour walls using exactly the same basic methods. Even if you don't intend to kill and cook your catch, it is a revelation just to see one of these creatures alive. Angry at being caught, it will have shimmering ripples of light and colour pulsing over its body like a high-speed chameleon. It's really quite a show.

Around Britain, most squid are caught incidentally as bycatch in trawl nets, but they are also pursued intentionally by hand-fished jigs and baits. This locally caught squid is most likely to turn up on the fishmonger's slab in the autumn and winter months. However, the majority of squid sold in the UK comes from the Pacific coasts of North America and the Asiatic seas. It's fished by commercial jiggers that use banks of fluorescent deck lights to attract the squid to hundreds of automated jig-lines. The big ships working out of the Far East are capable of landing up to 50 tonnes of squid a night, processing and freezing them all on board.

Given that these squid occupy an important position at the base of the marine food chain, and few of the females will have yet reproduced, it would be questionable to apply the word 'sustainable' to this kind of fishing. Some well-managed squid fisheries (such as that around the Falkland Islands) take into account their effect on the ecosystem and limit catches accordingly. However, it's still better to buy British squid if you can, as it is the product of far less intensive fishing and hasn't travelled thousands of miles to end up on your plate.

Most imported squid is sold deep frozen, or previously frozen and defrosted, (which means that it shouldn't really be frozen again). It can vary in size from tiny whole squid no bigger than your little finger ('Japonica' squid), via hand-sized all-rounders, to a monster squid the size and shape of an ironing board, which will be cut and packed in 1cm-thick strips. Frozen squid makes reasonable eating but it never quite has the bite, tenderness or sweetness of fresh locally caught squid.

When you get some of that, the simplest cooking methods are the most rewarding. The skill (and a certain amount of fun) is all in the preparation (see pages 97–100). Larger squid make excellent fried squid rings (page 332) or portions for butterflying, marinating and barbecuing (pages 204–5). The really tiny ones can be stir-fried whole in less time than it takes to boil a kettle. In fact, never cook fresh squid for more than a few minutes – unless you are going to simmer it gently (in a rich tomatoey stew, for example) for around an hour and a half, until it is meltingly tender.

Cooked in any of these ways, super-fresh squid is a sheer delight. So don't just order it in restaurants, tackle it at home. Or, if you want the freshest possible squid, and the thrill of the hunt, try to catch some yourself. It's an experience you'll never forget.

Index

Bibliography

Bagenal, T. B.:
The Observer's Book of Sea Fishes
(Frederick Warne and Co, London, 1972)

Bareham, Lindsey:
The Fish Store
(Michael Joseph, London, 2006)

Buckland, Frank:
Natural History of British Fishes
(SPCK, London, 1880)

Clark, Duncan:
The Rough Guide to Ethical Living
(Rough Guides, London, 2006)

Clover, Charles:
The End of the Line
(Ebury Press, London, 2004)

Cutting, Charles L.:
*Fish Saving: A History of Fish Processing
from Ancient to Modern Times*
(Leonard Hill Books, London, 1955)

David, Elizabeth:
Elizabeth David Classics
(Grub Street, London, 1999)

Davidson, Alan:
North Atlantic Seafood
(Macmillan, London, 1979)
Mediterranean Seafood
(Penguin Books, London, 1972)
The Oxford Companion to Food
(Oxford University Press, Oxford, 1999)

Downes, Stephen and Knowelden, Martin:
The New Compleat Angler
(Orbis, London, 1983)

Erlandson, Keith:
Home Smoking and Curing
(Ebury Press, London, 2003)

Fearnley-Whittingstall, Hugh:
A Cook on the Wild Side
(Boxtree, London, 1997)
The River Cottage Cookbook
(HarperCollins, London, 2001)
The River Cottage Year
(Hodder and Stoughton, London, 2003)

Floyd, Keith:
Floyd on Fish
(BBC Books, London, 1985)

Gibbons, Euell:
Stalking the Blue-eyed Scallop
(David McKay, New York, 1964)

Grigson, Jane:
Jane Grigson's Fish Book
(Penguin Books, London, 1993)

Hartley, Dorothy:
Food in England
(Macdonald, London, 1954; republished
Little, Brown, London, 1999)

Hix, Mark:
British Regional Food
(Quadrille Publishing, London, 2006)

Houghton, the Rev. W.:
British Fresh-water Fishes
(William McKenzie, London, 1879;
republished Webb and Bower, Exeter,
1981)

Jackson, C. J. and Waldegrave, Caroline:
Leiths Fish Bible
(Bloomsbury Publishing, London, 2005)

Jenkins, J. Travis:
The Fishes of the British Isles
(Frederick Warne and Co, London, 1925)

Kurlansky, Mark:
*Cod: A Biography of the Fish that Changed
the World*
(Walker and Company, New York, 1997)

Mabey, Richard:
Food for Free
(Collins, London, 1972)

Mason, Laura and Brown, Catherine:
The Taste of Britain
(Harper Press, London, 2006)

Montagné, Prosper, and Gottschalk, Dr:
*Larousse Gastronomique: The Encyclopedia
of Food, Wine and Cooking*
(Hamlyn, London, 1961)

Naylor, Paul:
Great British Marine Animals
(Sound Diving Publications, Devon, 2003)

Paston-Williams, Sara:
The National Trust Book of Fish Cookery
(National Trust, London, 1988)

Stein, Rick:
Best of British Fish
(in Association with the Royal National
Mission for Deep Sea Fishermen) (Mitchell
Beazley, London, 2005)
English Seafood Cookery
(Penguin Books, London, 1988)

Yeatman, Marwood:
The Last Food of England (Ebury Press,
London, 2007)

PICTURE CREDITS

Acknowledgements

In researching and writing this book we have benefited from a phenomenal amount of help and encouragement, which has been offered in all cases with staggering enthusiasm.

For guiding us through the tangled mesh of conservation issues we are immeasurably grateful to Dr Bryce Beukers-Stewart of the Marine Conservation Society. In particular, we would like to thank Bryce and his colleagues for their permission to use the MCS sustainability rating system. For his patient response to countless ecological queries, many thanks to Dr Tom Pickerell, Fisheries Policy Officer at WWF. For reading our Fish as food chapter and advising us on nutritional issues, we are most grateful to nutritionist Natalie Savona. For reading and commenting most incisively on our salmonid and fish-farming text (and not least for steering HF-W to at least half the salmon he has ever caught), special thanks to Andrew Wallace.

Many other conservationists and marine experts have fielded specific queries, and we are grateful for their time and for the inevitable effect of passing their expertise off as our own. They include: Chris Davis of Natural England; Jeremy Langley, specialist fish buyer at Waitrose; Professor John Walton at Leeds Metropolitan University; Dr Cat Dorey of Greenpeace UK; David Palmer of the Centre for Environment, Fisheries and Aquaculture Science; Peter Tinsley of the Dorset Wildlife Trust; Professor Steve Hawkins of the Marine Biological Association; Dr Clive Askew of the Shellfish Association of Great Britain; Jim Portus of the South Western Fish Producer Organisation; Gordon Goldsworthy of Loch Fyne Seafarms; writer Jon Beer; Dr Euan Dunn of the RSPB; and Bob Kennard of Graig Farm Organics.

For providing us with the very best fish to cook, photograph and (without fail) eat, thanks to all of the following: Geoff Davies at Ocean Fish; Howell Davies at Aquascot; Simon Bennett of the Wet Fish Shop in Lyme Regis; John Gilbertson of Isle of Skye Seafood; Fowey Fish of Cornwall; Falfish, also of Cornwall; Dermot Sanders of Fishmongers in Honiton; Samways of Bridport; Tony Free of Purely Organic; the team at Hooke Springs Trout Farm; Paul and Andrea Crocker for their crayfish; Jimmie and Penny Hepburn of Upper Hayne Organic Carp Farm; Bos Lawson, Janine Gould and Kelvin Moore for some wonderful Weymouth fish and shellfish; everyone at Weyfish; John Patten for supplying us with zander; Rik Nicholls for his deck and angling skills; and Matthew Warr for his Billy Winters and other capital crustaceans.

For sourcing and caring for so much of this outstanding fish, a special thanks to 'Big' Tim Graveson; another to Matt Toms, our skipper on *Dawn Mist*, and his wife Sharon, who are always a pleasure to fish with. For keeping us afloat on our Arvor boat, a big thanks to Nick Barke and all the team at Essexboatyards.com.

Thanks also, for the less fishy elements of the cookery, to our local producers and suppliers, including Bothen Hill Produce; Bridget's Market greengrocers; Brig's Farm Vegetables; Five Penny Farm; Ganesha Wholefoods; Millers Farm Shop; Pat Foxwell of Ourganics; Riverford Organic Vegetables; the Town Mill Bakery; and Washingpool Farm Shop.

For the stunning photography we have to massively thank Simon Wheeler, whose feel for the 'natural moment' has characterised every River Cottage book to date. He has proved to be equally at home on boats and among the fishes as on land among livestock and people.

Huge thanks to Paul Quagliana, whose additional photography has captured the character of many beloved species – a testament to his skills as an angler and photographer. Many lovely images have also come from Marie Derôme (Hugh's wife). She has recorded moments at sea, on the beach and in the kitchen that capture the very essence of a good family relationship with fish. And thanks, of course, for supporting Hugh inexorably throughout the project. Thanks also to Helen Fisher and family for the frequent use of their kitchen, and indeed their bodies, in much of the photography.

And thanks to various angler-photographers who have allowed us to use their pictures: Jon Beer; Richard Brigham; Pat Carlin; Richard Fishbourne; Charles Rangeley-Wilson; Mike Thrussell; and John Tickner. Thanks to Greenpeace and WWF for permission to use their photographs of tuna.

For the televisual incarnation of this book, *River Cottage: Gone Fishing*, hearty thanks are due to the versatile team at Keo, especially Katherine Perry, Larissa Hickey, Freddie Foff-Smith, Belle Borgeaud, Richard Hill and Bryan Johnson. Extra thanks to directors Ben Roy and Tom Beard, editor Simon Beeley, and to Andrew Palmer for executing the project and welcoming us all on Raasay. And thanks to all the fisherfolk of the Channel Islands, Hebrides and Southwest for their hospitality and time.

Collectively, the River Cottage team have been brilliant. Recipes have been honed by our chefs Gill Meller and Daniel Stevens. Photo shoots have been co-ordinated with great resourcefulness by Pip Corbin. The invasion of Park Farm has been effortlessly negotiated by Jessica Harris and Steven Lamb. Hugh has been kept (almost) sane by his incredibly wonderful PA, Jess Upton. The whole team has been buoyed throughout by the leadership of Rob Love.

But two members of the River Cottage team need to be singled out as genuine 'without whoms' for this project: Helen Stiles has researched many aspects of the book, overseeing the logistics of photography, fish and fishermen with equal alacrity and good humour. Nikki Duffy, the River Cottage Food Editor, has supported us from start to finish with her fantastically well-targeted research. She has calmly collated our raw prose, kept a weather eye on the drifting shape of the book, and brought it all together into one sturdy, watertight vessel. Without Helen and Nikki we would all have fallen apart.

A trio of freelancers has also earned a prostrate debt of gratitude. Our editorial guru on the latter stages of the project, Janet Illsley, has quietly set about solving and sorting all the problems and niggles that inevitably accumulate on such a wide-ranging and long-running publishing saga. She's been brilliant.

Our fantastic copy editor and recipe tester Jane Middleton has been as vigilant and constructive as ever. She should have a medal (or several) for her patience, skill and dedication to our cause over the years – so we are delighted that she won a Glenfiddich award for her own writing earlier this year.

Lawrence Morton, our designer, has been a great pleasure to work with, brimming as he is with elegant, eloquent solutions to the knotty problems of designing such a multi-layered monster of a book. And he's done it all with the good cheer and breezy enthusiasm of a man walking on the beach.

At Bloomsbury, the entire team has responded brilliantly to the challenge of producing such a complex tome in what became, in the final months, an increasingly insane schedule: Penny Edwards, Sarah Beal, Colin Midson, Natalie Hunt and Erica Jarnes have all made us feel that this project mattered to them *almost* as much as to us.

On the other hand our editor, Richard Atkinson, really did live, breathe, eat and sleep this book for most of the last year (and we can only hope his wife Sue will forgive us for that). He has worked phenomenally hard to make sure every aspect of it meets his own extraordinarily exacting standards. His proper, old-fashioned editing skills are present, if invisible, on every page.

And a particular thank you to our agent, Antony Topping, at Greene and Heaton. He may have other clients, but he gives a remarkably good impression of caring only about us.

Finally, we would like to thank one man whose contribution to this book is deeper and more valued than he can possibly know. Pat Carlin has taken us on many unforgettable fishing trips and helped us catch many unforgettable fish. But more importantly, throughout all of these deeply enjoyable forays he has imparted his remarkable knowledge about fish, fishing, the sea, wrecks, tides and weather in a truly selfless and always entertaining manner. We admire him immensely and thank him for helping to give us the confidence to write this book.

Hugh and Nick, September 2007

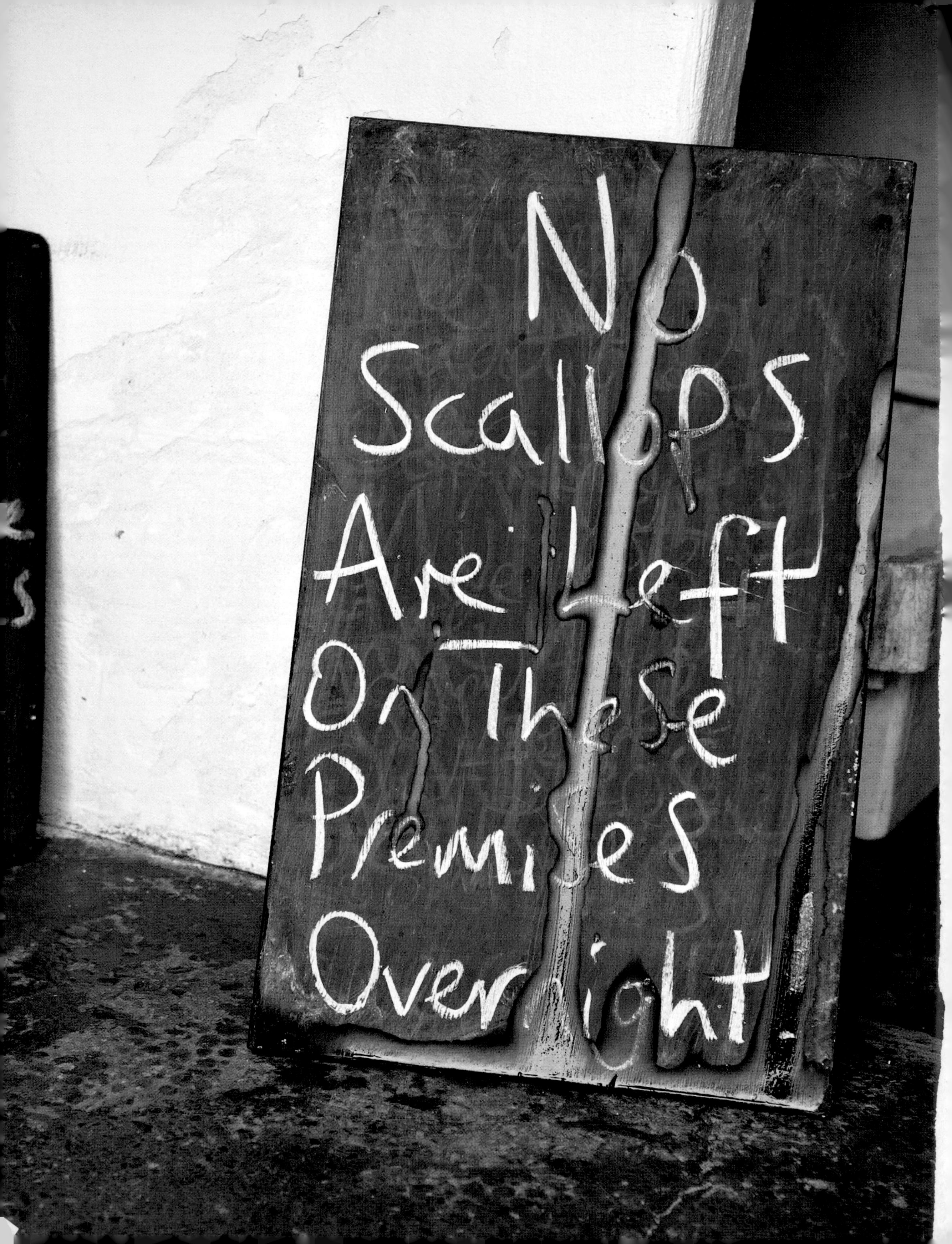
No
Scallops
Are Left
On These
Premises
Overnight!